YO-CLX-605

GREATEST SHOW ON EARTH

By the same author

CLOWN. A Novel
CLOWNS AND PANTOMIMES
CHAMPAGNE AND WINKLES
THE COWELLS IN AMERICA (edited)

YOUNG ASTLEY AT VERSAILLES
From a Coloured Engraving in the Collection of Mr. Sydney Bernstein
by whose kind permission it is reproduced here

GREATEST SHOW ON EARTH

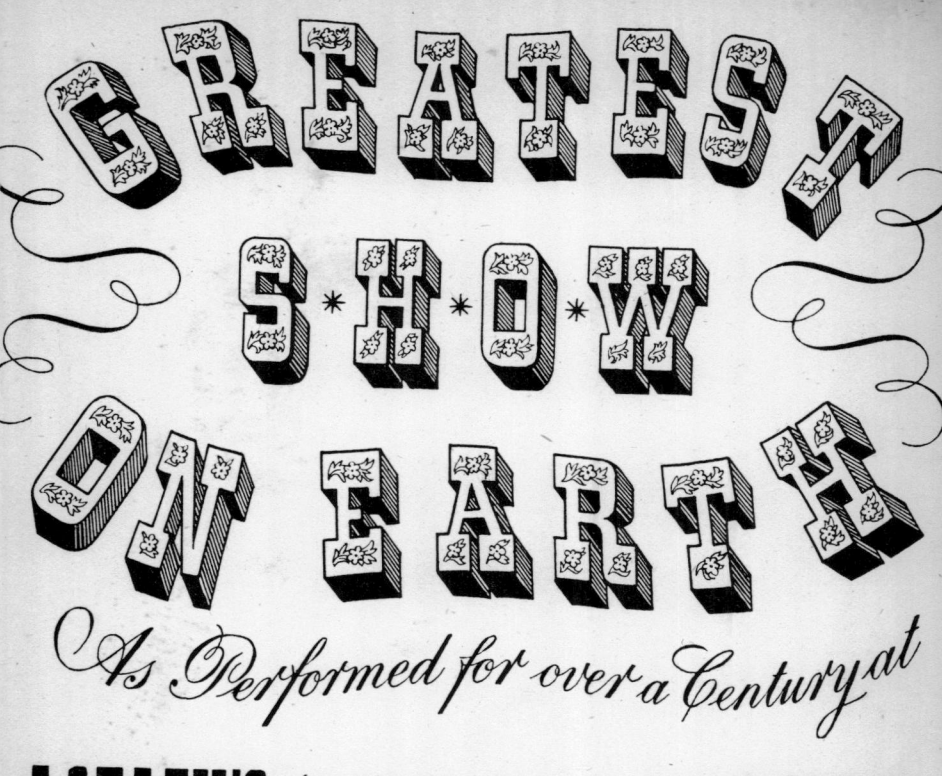

As Performed for over a Century at

ASTLEY'S (AFTERWARDS SANGER'S) ROYAL AMPHITHEATRE OF ARTS, WESTMINSTER BRIDGE ROAD.

Recorded with Illustrations from Contemporary Sources by

M. WILLSON DISHER

With an Introduction by

D. L. MURRAY

*

G. BELL AND SONS LTD, PUBLISHERS, LONDON

First published 1937

Printed in Great Britain by the Camelot Press Limited
London and Southampton

TO
MR. and MRS. T. J. DISHER

THANKS ARE HEREWITH TENDERED

to Mr. D. L. Murray for his performances on a model stage of *The Battle Of Waterloo*, *Timour The Tartar*, *The Crimean War*, and *Baron Munchausen*, all formerly played at Astley's Amphitheatre;

also to Mr. W. S. Meadmore and Mr. Ray Stott, Editors of *The Sawdust Ring*; Mr. John Parker, President of *The Critics' Circle*; Mrs. Gabrielle Enthoven and her theatrical records at the Victoria and Albert Museum; for their assistance in compiling and illustrating this history;

to Mr. Charles B. Cochran, for the loan of unique records, Dr. J. M. Bulloch and Mr. George Slater, for notes, Miss Florence Sanger Reeve, for arranging meetings with old friends of her grandfather, and Mr. Richard M. Tatham, for preparing sheets for the press;

to the Editors of *The Quarterly Review*, *The Edinburgh Review*, *The Nineteenth Century And After*, *The Listener*, *Britannia And Eve*, *The Evening News*, and *The Billboard*, for permission to incorporate here the substance of articles contributed by the author to their pages;

and to Mr. Benjamin Pollock, of the Toy Theatre Shop in Hoxton, for kindly allowing sheets from his justly celebrated *Penny Plain, Twopence Coloured* Plays to be reproduced.

August 3, 1937

Introducing M. Willson Disher and Astley's
BY D. L. MURRAY

THIS is a fascinating book; it is a book that all London lovers, circus-enthusiasts, and Dickensians have long needed; and it is the work of a man who, though he may condescend to be a drama critic and to give his spare time in the evening to considering the propositions of Shaw, Ibsen, Chekhov, Galsworthy, Noel Coward, not to omit Mr. —— and Miss ——, is nevertheless before everything else a lover of the show-booth and the most electric of circus fans. His *Clowns And Pantomimes* is the classic for lovers of the art of Grimaldi and of Grock, and *Greatest Show* should become a classic for lovers of the sawdust. I can remember disputing a little with Disher about this book.

'Why Astley's?' I said. 'It was only one circus (and only partly a circus at that) and you could, if you liked, give us the whole history of the circus as no one else could. Why not go from the universal to the particular?' Disher was unconvinced, and I now see that he was right. To write about the circus in general is to make your initial appeal, at least, only to the circus fan. To write about Astley's . . . well, it is to write slices of English life at its stoutest and merriest; it is to floodlight whole chapters of English literature; it is to resuscitate romance that may have been buried but can never die.

There is no need for the barker to go on shouting a long while – unless the show is a bad one. Only consider a few of the glamorous figures and thrilling scenes that Mr. Disher is going to show 'on the inside.' There is Philip Astley, who ran away from the cabinet-maker's bench in Newcastle-under-Lyme to become a cavalryman and fight the French at Emsdorf in the cause of our ally King Frederick the Great of Prussia. He came home to found a new style of entertainment by exhibiting 'feats of activity on horseback' in a turf circle at Lambeth – you call that form of entertainment 'the circus' to-day; and Astley is its real founder whatever Roman gladiators or medieval jousters may have done; do not believe Disher himself if he tells you anything different. Astley, who built the amphitheatre on the south side of Westminster Bridge that carried his name on down to the end of the nineteenth century, and another one across the river that became famous afterwards as the Olympic Theatre; who conquered Paris as well as London with his horsemanship – where could you find a more romantic first 'act' or one more full of the sap and savour of eighteenth-century England?

Then on the programme must come Ducrow, who took Drury Lane itself by equestrian assault, and enriched the language by an observation on the relative value of 'cackle' or 'dialect' and ''osses' – we might say to-day 'gas' and ''osses.' He invented the Courier of St. Petersburg, with which the ladies steal our hearts in this more athletic age, and married the prototype of all the equestrian *ballerine* that circus audiences have since adored, Louisa Woolford, about whom the cockney laureate, Bon Gaultier, made ballads, while Dickens described the thrill of her and Dicky Doyle drew her large eyes to illustrate Thackeray's *Newcomes*. Mr. Disher must tell us about Widdicomb, ancestor of ring-masters – beg pardon, 'equestrian directors,' horrid phrase ! – 'Napoleon' Gomersal, Dion Boucicault, and E. T. Smith, and work up to a grand equestrian, dramatic, emotional, and pathetic climax with the life story of 'Mazeppa' Menken ('the classical style of whose dress does *not* much trouble the sewing-machine,' as the song of the sixties put it). For Epilogue he must give the last splendid feudal days of Lord George Sanger, most popular of England's peers before the Demon L.C.C. waved over the old house the same malignant wand that has buried Waterloo Bridge in the waves. If he neglects any of these items (but he won't) demand your money back – and go to him to correct all the unintentional errors of these notes of mine (circus fans live by correcting one another). I have done beating the big-drum, and the band is playing for the entrance of a stately gentleman, red-coated, jack-booted, and three-corner-hatted, on his charger Gibraltar. Not Dick Turpin this time, but – ladies and gentlemen, the only original and real Mackay – Philip Astley !

CONTENTS

INTRODUCING M. WILLSON DISHER AND ASTLEY'S. By D. L. Murray . . ix

I. 'SMELL OF HORSES, SUGGESTIVE OF COMING WONDERS.' – *Old Curiosity Shop*
1. Romance Scented With Oranges . . 3
2. Samson And Delilah Of Islington . . 10

II. THE VERY FIRST CIRCUS OF ALL
1. Sergeant-Major Astley 19
2. Royal Circus Rivalry 29
3. Twice Burned Down 52
4. Horses As Actors 73

III. 'DEAR, DEAR, WHAT A PLACE IT LOOKED, THAT ASTLEY'S.' – *Old Curiosity Shop*
1. Andrew Ducrow 91
2. Mazeppa, And The Wild Horse . . 103
3. Queen Victoria Rides In The Ring . . 126
4. Again Burned Down 144

IV. THE ASTLEY'S OF PARIS
1. Antoine Franconi 163
2. Napoleon's Circus Wars 175

V. EQUESTRIAN DRAMA
1. The Terrible Fitzball 191
2. Shakespeare On Horseback . . . 207
3. The Female Mazeppa 225

VI. LORD GEORGE SANGER
    1. Zoological Pantomimes 249
    2. Battles In Tents 273

VII. EPILOGUE IN PARIS
    Heroines Of The Haute École . . . 291

INDEX 303

ILLUSTRATIONS

I. Plates

YOUNG ASTLEY AT VERSAILLES	Frontispiece
SILHOUETTE OF PHILIP ASTLEY	facing page 40
ASTLEY'S ROYAL AMPHITHEATRE OF ARTS	40
ASTLEY'S ADVERTISING CART	41
THE ROYAL CIRCUS	41
MONSIEUR NICOLET	56
BILL OF PARIS PERFORMANCE	56
ARENA OF ASTLEY'S AMPHITHEATRE	57
MRS. WYBROW, THE CELEBRATED SWORDSWOMAN	74
DELPINI 'SHOOTING AT THE SPANIARDS'	75
CHARACTERS IN *Timour The Tartar*	92
CHARACTERS IN *The Battle Of Waterloo*	93
JOHN DUCROW'S TEA AND SUPPER PARTY	116
ANDREW DUCROW AND HIS HORSE, PEGASUS	116
ANDREW DUCROW AS THE GOD OF FAME	117
ANDREW DUCROW AS THE HUNTER	138
The Vicissitudes of A Tar	139
ASTLEY'S AS REBUILT IN 1843	139

ILLUSTRATIONS

LORD GEORGE SANGER . . . . . *page* 282
DICK TURPIN IN SANGER'S TENT 283

II. In the Text

MAP SHOWING HALFPENNY HATCH	24
BILL OF OPEN-AIR PERFORMANCE	37
ASTLEY'S ACROBATS IN PARIS	60
COLONEL NEWCOME'S BOX AT ASTLEY'S	104
PLAYBILL HEADING FOR *Mazeppa*	122
DUCROW AS THE YORKSHIRE FOX HUNTER	134
KIT IN THE GALLERY AT ASTLEY'S	158
A PIECE OF ASTLEY CHINA	196
DRAWING FROM *Punch* in 1851	202
DRAWINGS FROM *Punch* IN 1851	203
DRAWINGS FROM *Punch* IN 1851	205
DRAWINGS FROM *Punch* IN 1851	213
BEHIND THE SCENES AT ASTLEY'S	237
ADAH ISAACS MENKEN	239
WILD WOLVES IN LONDON	267
BILL OF SANGER'S CIRCUS	275

I

'SMELL OF HORSES SUGGESTIVE OF COMING WONDERS'

– Old Curiosity Shop

I

Romance Scented With Oranges

CAN you remember the day when, clambering up a chair to look out of the window, you gave a shriek (loud enough to alarm the whole household) because you had seen another horse? At that time of wonder about all sorts of amazing phenomena, from the buzzing of a blue-bottle on the pane to the throbbing lid of a kettle on the boil, you saw your first circus. That you took, in solemn silence, for granted; and you have taken it as much for granted ever since as the wind and the stars. Circuses, in a life properly conducted, go days farther back than memory. While the cornucopia of a grocer's shop is encountered at an age when we are old enough to be astonished, the elephant in a clown's hat seems to have been there from the beginning. Pictures in the fire should be a more recent puzzle to us than the perilous slant of Columbine on her fat white horse.

There was the circus of the seaside and there was the circus of the town. One was in a tent. The other was in a building over the bridge from the Houses of Parliament, at the end of a long journey so tiring that you had to be borne there in parent's arms. Before you could settle down to watch and listen to the chandelier, other sights and sounds were clamouring for grave consideration – people crowding into hard seats at the back, urged by the shouts of a man in uniform; bandsmen down below making fiddles groan and trumpets squeak; men in aprons, pushing into the already crowded space with huge baskets full of bread and bottles (chained to prevent their being used as missiles), and chanting over and over again:

'Saveloys, Banburys,
Lemonade or stout.'

And then there was that smell. Stables were in it with a whiff of ammonia exuded by lions; and many oranges. All the sights and sounds together were not as exciting as that smell.

. . . .

There are long, long minutes to wait, but not time enough to observe all the strangeness of the place. The people are sitting down in rows that form a huge horseshoe. Their faces are bent towards a circle of earth, where men are sowing sawdust. Music bursts out. People clap. Little Sandy runs in and shouts, 'Here we are again!' The gentleman conscious of personal grandeur follows in evening dress, with a whip. Little Sandy cheeks him, and jumps, at once, into the air to dodge a slash from its long, writhing thong. A poetically trouserless person is now climbing towards the string stretched across the ring; he stands on a little platform, strokes the string with the side of his foot, carefully lays his sole upon it, as though to grip it between his big toe and second toe, waves a Japanese umbrella tautly in the air – and walks mincing across. While he is still bowing himself out backwards a lady with a wasp waist, top hat, and flowing skirts makes her horse dance; and another, in short fluffy skirts, leaps from the ground upon a horse and back again, while Little Sandy falls over. That done, knights in armour in great numbers fight a battle which ends in a combat between two who hurl the names of 'R-R-Richard' and 'R-R-Richmond' at each other as though they were insults.

Then there is peace for a while. Attendants rush into the ring, turn off the lights, and unscrew pipes, while escaping gas adds to the already heavy burden of the atmosphere. So much tobacco is burning, and so much alcohol is being puffed out through moustaches, that the puzzle is why the whole building does not go off bang like one large bomb. But it survives, while half the ring is being covered with chairs that are occupied before their legs touch the sawdust. Down upon the other half of the ring descends a large flap to serve as stage, and when a curtain falls upon it we are no longer in a circus, but a theatre. Parents read from the programmes, *Harlequin Cinderella And The Little Glass Slipper; or, The Kitchen Maid That Was Made A Princess.*' Pantomimes we have seen before, but never another like this. We have been prepared by past experiences for the 'Great Kitchen of Bombast Castle' and the 'Grand Ball-room of the Prince's Palace,' but not for the 'Grand Congress Hall of the Golden Palms in the Silver Fernery,' for here the Monarchs of the World assemble on horses, camels, dromedaries, and elephants, attended by zebras, horned horses, and giraffes, lions and Britannia. The stage becomes desperately overcrowded. An unnerved zebra kicks out, and the chorus girls, vainly attempting to fly, push against the monarchs. The pageant degenerates into a riot. Into its midst steps a swarthy, slightly bearded, determined figure in evening dress. 'Lord George Sanger,' whispers are saying. He uses his whip vigorously upon horned horses, fleshings, zebras, fairy-tale folk, dromedaries, and those monarchs. He clears them all off the stage to make room for the 'Grand Defiance Ballet Delineating The Afghanistan Campaign.' Dashing Indian warriors are represented by Miss Tessie Gunniss and the Sisters Flora. 'It's getting late.' We fear we shall be taken home.

'Must wait for the Harlequinade.' We are reassured. Little Sandy joins the Army. Pantaloon is rejected. The Union Jack is waved. There is a lot of shouting. It grows dimmer and ever dimmer. We nestle where we have always nestled. Sights and sounds fade. We wake up hearing the jolting of wheels. We look out of the windows of the growler at the moon gleaming in the heavens more gloriously even than the chandelier in the dome of 'Sanger's, late Astley's.' We watch it. As we go along it goes along as well. We watch it in wonder until the comfort of encircling arms grows dearer by far than the desire to be as gods, knowing both the good and evil of circuses and celestial bodies.

But in our waking thoughts for ever after curiosity about Astley's will grow, for from the beginning to the end of its eccentric career – one of the longest in the history of public entertainment – the spirit that possessed it no word will describe. At first you are inclined to say that clowning and romance are there inextricably mixed, until you find that what seems absurd one moment and moving the next is, like *The Dong with The Luminous Nose*, of unaltered woof. That spirit was not confined to Astley's; it spread to the Surrey close by, and thence to Covent Garden, declaring itself in the year 1797 by the birth of melodrama, to say nothing of how it expressed itself through Christmas pantomime. Thus never named, and having influence in life over an uncharted sphere, it haunted the nineteenth century from the beginning, brought the endeavours of even the most major of poets to naught when they tried their hands at tragedy, and raddled, so to speak, the noses of the great.

Call it Astleian and let it take shape, agile-limbed, fleet-footed, stern of brow, somewhat blue of chin, draped in fustian, god-like till it opens its mouth – the spirit of romance that tumbles and smells strongly of oranges. Its behaviour at Astley's for more than a century is strangely consistent: all that happens there can be neither wholly mocked nor taken altogether seriously. Turn to Astley's Continental cousin, Franconi's, and you will see that this same spirit has power to overthrow Governments, raise ephemeral empires, and change the destinies of nations.

Why it should have manifested itself in one spot more than another can only be explained in a manner like its own. Astley's, to use a language intended neither to be mocked nor taken seriously, was her temple. She chose it for herself. That much is plain when you watch the building Philip Astley designed for a lordly, or at least genteel, riding-school, becoming what may be called, by understatement, the birthplace of the circus, before a turmoil caused by the fight for the freedom of the stage, and joyful excitement over the fall of the Bastille, forced it to serve the dramatic needs of democracy. What he had created becomes fully apparent only on the arrival of the man who matched the place, that radiant genius of tinsel, Andrew Ducrow, who conquered Covent Garden and Drury Lane for Astley's spirit, and turned the stage version of Byron's *Mazeppa* into the world's most popular play (without inducing critics of the drama to lift a pen). Though little known to-day, when his 'Cut the dialect and come to the 'osses' (Surtees, in *Handley Cross*, changed 'dialect' to 'cackle') is constantly quoted, he scrawled his mark over the novels of Dickens and Thackeray, the *Bon Gautier Ballads*, the *Ingoldsby Legends*, the *Noctes Ambrosianæ*, and half a century of *Punch*.

Neither that nor the succeeding epoch, when other showmen of peculiar gifts stepped into his shoes, are hard to understand. But unless we firmly believe that Astley's was *possessed*, how can we account for what followed? Adah Isaacs Menken, beckoned from America, was the spirit of the place – if we retract 'blue of chin' – incarnate. Clowning and romance are so mixed in her that you cannot distinguish one from the other. Those who revere her are as misguided as those who mock her. She was Astleian. So were all who answered Astley's call. Disraeli, always inclined that way with what had been termed his glitter, takes on the same hue when he comes within range of its Bengal lights (as playwright or spectator), and Queen

Victoria wields her imperial power to make, as her smallest subjects wanted to make, a circus parade pass by her twice. Its last ruler is an Astleian Lord (of his own creation), and its overthrow with the Ecclesiastical Commissioners profiting by the uncharitable misdeeds of bureaucracy, is Astleian too.

Both Dickens and Thackeray, like all who write about Astley's, assume that the Astleians are of a renown too great for any word of guidance concerning their identity to be needed. It is needed now. Their fame must be restored, and that is what I have attempted in this account of the spot where they shone. Though the walls were pulled down over forty years ago, one part of its site still bears no burden of bricks. Cross Westminster Bridge from the Houses of Parliament, make for the corner site jutting out from behind the hospital, and walk along its pavement for a few yards towards the side street. The block of dwellings there is named Hercules Buildings, after Hercules Hall, the house of Philip Astley, and behind that building is a garden where a yard known as The Ride used to be in Lord George Sanger's time. And as what we call the ring and he called the circle, was what Astley called the ride – the ring was then what we call the fence – this garden may be part of the original arena where the spirit we are observing found a local habitation and a name.

2

Samson And Delilah Of Islington

BEFORE Philip Astley himself comes on the scene there must be a prologue about the showmen in north London who taught him the tricks of his trade. Round about the Angel nowadays trams and buses come and go in a great stir of traffic; there is a clamour in Islington's busy High Street to deaden the noisiest clatter of tongues; but wish yourself back rather more than a hundred and fifty years and you will be quiet enough in this spot, London's playground, to heed how one trick-rider was ruined by another's treachery.

Steep streets were then little green hills with the poplar-lined New River flowing among them. Hugh Myddelton, whose statue you may see against a background of cloistral trees on Islington Green, was knighted for bringing London this water supply, a great engineering feat in the early seventeenth century; its long ghost of grass still stretches along Colebrooke Row to Charles Lamb's cottage and Bleak House (alleged). The Angel, now a tea-shop in tavern's clothing, was a balconied hostelry, welcoming the Liverpool stage-coach with open yard, and at Sadler's

Wells Musick House, set among gardens, there was on a wire no thicker than a sewing thread, so Winifred Jenkins says in *Humphry Clinker*, firing of pistols in the air, and blowing of trumpets, and swinging and rolling of wheel-barrows (all of which is borne out by prints of Duncan Macdonald, of the shire of Caithness, Gent., the Scottish Equilibrist).

Haunts of health and happiness abounded there. Ever since Sadler gave his name to wells of iron-impregnated water, rival establishments had been advertising chalybeate springs to the world of politics and fashion. Princesses had stepped out of their coaches at Islington Spa, on the opposite bank of the New River, to a salute of guns. Very fine ladies and gentlemen made a habit of taking the waters at Bagnigge Wells,[1] a few minutes' walk away to the west, and gallants knew what might be planned over a dish of tea in the Great Room there. Card-sharpers lay in wait throughout the district by day, and footpads by night. Apprentices went there to make holiday, and many a daring maid who ventured there came back with cause to rue her evening's entertainment.

Mid-way through the eighteenth century Islington took a sudden fancy for trick-riding. This was highly significant of the social history of the times. Fully to understand why, you must consider the decline of the tourneys of the middle-ages after royal combatants had received fatal injuries in the lists. Jousts changed into *carrousels* in the seventeenth century with tilting at the quintain amid pageantry that cost vast sums. When a

[1] Ye Olde Bagnigge Wells tavern, opposite the scene of Arnold Bennett's *Riceyman's Steps*, marks the site.

curb was put on the spending powers of kings, these gave place before the eighteenth century to riding-schools, built by the nobility for the exercise of horsemanship and arms. These, in turn, suffered from the pinch of economy and riding-masters had to turn showmen. Jacob Bates, the first of note, made the Continent ring with his praises. His example was followed by many, including Johnson, the Irish Tartar, who rode three horses together at Islington. There is evidence of their royal descent in *entrée*, a term used at the capture of cities, in tourneys, *carrousels*, riding-school, and the circus, before it dwindled into *entrée of clowns* on the circus programmes of to-day.

The beginning of the story is an advertisement, dated 1766, that 'Mr. Price will exhibit Horsemanship, this and every afternoon, if the Weather permits, in a field adjoining to The Three Hats, at Islington: Where Gentlemen and Ladies may be accommodated with Coffee and Tea, Hot Loaves, and Sullybubs,[1] the Loaves to be ready at Half an Hour after Four O'Clock every afternoon, by your humble servant, Joseph Dingley.' As Garrick was causing a great stir at Stratford-on-Avon and Drury Lane with his Shakespeare Jubilees, Dingley had scenes from Shakespeare painted on the boxes round his arena, which were soon filled with spectators. Among these was a horsewoman, who came regularly and at length asked for lessons, a request Price misunderstood. Another newspaper advertisement read, 'Mr.

---

[1] Syllabubs, sometimes a drink, sometimes a dish, were made under the cow in large bowls containing wine or brandy and cider to curdle the warm milk. They were a familiar part of English country fare for four centuries though almost forgotten now.

Price begs leave to return his sincere and hearty thanks to those Ladies and Gentlemen who have been so kind in honouring him with their Appearance at Islington, and hopes to deserve a continuance of their Favours; but Tomorrow he is engaged (by Desire) to ride at a particular Place for that Day only.'

Out in the solitude of verdant Barnsbury there was no conquest as Price had planned. From that day onwards he had fits of temperament at the hour fixed for his performance. Joseph Dingley read in the *Daily Courier* of feats of horsemanship exhibited at Mile End by 'Mr. Sampson, lately discharged from Lord Ancram's Light Dragoons,' at the Weaver's Arms, Mile End – 'Admission one shilling' – and Sampson came to the Jubilee Gardens of the Three Hats. From his first appearance, standing in the saddle on one leg, while putting his horse to the gallop, he kept the tea-parties in a state of constant surprise. He rode at full speed, hanging so low that his hand swept the ground; he dismounted at full speed, discharged a pistol, and remounted in an instant; he rode two horses at once, besides putting them to a jump; he rode at a gallop, head on the saddle and feet in the air.

Both at work and in love, the light dragoon triumphed. His boyish delight in the freedom of civilian life, his reckless joy in flinging away the guineas he found so easy to earn, won the horsewoman's heart. They married, and Dingley advertised the 'First Equestrienne,' who proved that 'The fair sex were by no means inferior to the male, either in Courage or Ability.' The world of fashion, including the Duke of York, brother to the King, kept the Jubilee boxes full.

Price plotted revenge at the neighbouring tea-gardens, named Dobney's after a widow who once had them. While the new owner was transforming his bowling-green into a ride, Price lured Sampson to Bagnigge Wells. Past a fish-pond, where Cupid rode a swan which spouted water to a great height, they mingled in the crowd which grew denser as they approached the doors of the Great Room. The waiter said there was a house by the waterside at the far end of the grounds for those who wished to drink the coarser beverages or to smoke: so wine was brought. Sampson, accustomed neither to such liquor nor to such surroundings, grew dazed, and it was then that a Delilah in hooped skirt and full powdered wig came sweeping by. After urging a rendezvous elsewhere, she did at last consent to walk in the grounds, where Price became parted from them and was lost. Delilah stayed close to Sampson's side till he was stirred by the rustle of her silk skirts. In the darkness of the grotto, she stumbled against him and drew his arm around her.

At dawn, when Islington's first equestrienne was peering from her window down the country road, he was in a drunken slumber half a mile away. Hours later, when she was making anxious inquiry at the Three Hats, he gazed at an unfamiliar ceiling until brought to his senses by the demand of a drab, barely recognisable as the beauty in full sail of the night before, whether 'this' was all the money he had. She held his breeches, and told him, before locking the door, that he could have them when he had sent to Dingley for fifty guineas. That was how Mrs. Sampson at last heard, through Dingley, that her husband had not been strangled by footpads. She left him. The holiday-makers went to Dobney's.

Dingley held on to Sampson's horses until their owner was ready to submit. Then a Mr. Coningham, who would vault over two horses as they jumped the bar, or play a march on a flute as he stood on their backs, became the hero of the Jubilee Gardens with the fallen favourite for servant. So Sampson's wife found him when she returned; and Mr. and Mrs. Sampson were Coningham's assistants until the debt was paid off. While Price retired on a fortune 'Old Sampson' went to Southwark, where he enjoyed great popularity at a shabby little ale-house called the Dog and Duck after the duck-hunting round about. The owner of Vauxhall Gardens used his power as a magistrate for the county to take away the inn's licence, and Old Sampson had to move on. Though he announced 'the grandest feats of horsemanship that were ever attempted' at his riding-school in Tottenham Court Road, he had to close down and offer himself for hire to any showman that would have him.

Dobney's was changed by a parson into a boarding-school, which failed, and the old enthusiasm was rekindled for a spell when Daniel Wildman gave a display, in 1772, of trick-riding and bee-keeping at the same time. While balancing himself with one foot in the saddle and the other on the horse's neck, he let the swarm cover his head and face; he would also stand on the saddle with the bridle in his mouth and fire a pistol as the signal for one part of the bees to march over a table and the other part to swarm in the air before returning to their hive. He went from Islington to

Lambeth, where this tale must travel too, dragging with it a nervous chronicler, still fumbling for words to fit jerry-built wonders that appear indescribable because while looking at them no one may know whether to scoff or be amazed.

Anyhow one thing is plain. Astley's, not Barnum's, was the GREATEST SHOW ON EARTH.

II

THE VERY FIRST CIRCUS OF ALL

I

Sergeant-Major Astley

Hot temper began it. When Edward Astley, the cabinet-maker, told his son to stick to his bench, Philip would refuse. Thus they had lived at loggerheads in Newcastle-under-Lyme, practically ever since the boy was born on January 8th, 1742. It was a thriving town of low thatched cottages and many inns that lined a broad thoroughfare where the notes of stage-coach bugles were ever preluding the clatter of hoofs over cobbles. Whenever Philip heard these sounds he stopped work. Shavings and sawdust would be sent flying as he flung the workshop's door wide open, and ran, heedless of oaths and orders, down the street to the gates of the inn, while the sweating team wheeled from highway to yard. Maids and porters came running down from the dark galleries, the host hurried out to hear news, and a crowd of boys clamoured to ride the horses to the stables. Philip Astley, the quickest to pick up a knowledge of harnessing and grooming, was a horseman very early in his teens.

Old Astley would be waiting with a strap when he

returned to veneer cutting, but the boy grew too big to be laid across a knee. At seventeen he did credit to a name borne by many a horseman, swordsman, and soldier, members of the ancient family whose seat was at Potshull, not far distant. Having wasted his time in riding, swimming, and fighting, he was strong enough to wrestle with a father who stuck to his job. One night there was no thrashing; the strap was wrested from Edward in spite of his towering rage. Philip, regretting nothing but to part from a tender-hearted sister, left.

There was no difficulty in getting a mount for the first stage of the journey south, since Coventry was holding its great November horse-fair. Philip sat one of the yearlings from Staffs when yeomen from several counties came riding down eight converging roads to jostle in the narrow streets of overhanging buildings. There was an added stir at this fair of 1759. Beribboned sergeants were holding passers-by at street corners with tales of military glory. One who caught Philip Astley's eye was shouting, 'Here's Colonel Eliott, aide-de-camp to His Majesty King George, come here to enlist you in his new regiment, the 15th Dragoons. Let powdered hair, drums and colours, speak for themselves; and if you have a mind to whet your whistles with His Majesty's double beer, follow me.' Philip followed him, and was put in charge of the new mounts. When he had broken them in, he was given the pay of 'rough-rider, teacher, and breaker,' with the rank of corporal.

Very soon he became expert in other branches of horsemanship. Domenico Angelo was instructing picked men from the cavalry in his new method of riding, with the hope of making the Government adopt it. As one of the most active men of 'the well-known crack regiment, Eliott's light horse,' Astley was brought to Lord Pembroke's place at Wilton. His agility and mastery over his horse, says the younger Angelo,

> so astonished the common people in the neighbourhood of Wilton that they thought Corporal Astley was the devil in disguise. They might naturally feel surprised at seeing a man ride full speed standing upon his horse, and then leap off, and mount again without slackening his pace; but they stared with astonishment when one day his horse cantered round a circle, with Astley upon his back, standing upon his head, with his heels in the air.

Pomp now ruled his bearing. His speech rolled with the magnificence of the manage, hampered by misplaced aspirates and sentences too involved for grammar. He was nineteen years of age when the regiment embarked at Tilbury to serve with the armies of King Frederick of Prussia. The troopships anchored off Hamburg, where Astley had to superintend the landing of horses. One reared with fright, fell from the boat, and swam away from shore with the tide. Astley swam in pursuit, seized its bridle, and brought it back. That gained him another stripe and the chance to develop his 'perfectly stentorian' voice.

Eliott encountered the enemy at Emsdorf, where the 15th 'broke through the line, composed of several thousand French, in the most gallant style.' Astley seized an enemy standard, was surrounded by a party of French infantry, and had his horse shot under him.

They wounded him as he rose, but he remounted and galloped off, still grasping the standard. Before the engagement at Warburg, he commanded an advance guard which chanced upon a skirmish between French and Prussian horse. The Duke of Brunswick fell in the enemy lines. With only four dragoons at his back, Astley charged the enemy hussars and brought him away under heavy fire. The regiment was recalled shortly afterwards for the expedition against Havannah. When they paraded in Hyde Park to become 'The King's,' wearing black-steel helmets with silver-tasselled scarlet 'turbans,' Sergeant-Major Astley laid the Emsdorf standard at the feet of aged George II in his tent.

At twenty-four Astley had enough military glory. What he aspired to was a riding-school where he would instruct the young nobility in the pure *art d'equitation*, and he discovered how funds for this could be raised. While in billets at Derby he heard that the landlord who had just bought the big inn had made his money by trick-riding: he used to ride, standing upright on horseback, in a field, and then go round with the hat. Being assured that London was still much given to such amusements, Astley went straightway to Lieut.-Col. Sir William Erskine, who commanded the troop at Derby, and sought his discharge. It was granted as a reward for his 'general proper demeanour,' on June 21st, 1766. With a certificate of service in the pocket of his uniform, he went south again, this time astride the white charger given to him by his commanding officer. In Islington, the playground of the town, he thought of hiring a field for a display, but there was much to learn. He found employment not as a performer but as a breaker. He packed his regimentals away, settled himself in London, took a horsewoman for wife, and invested five pounds at Smithfield in a little horse which was good-tempered and well put together.

'This here animal,' he told his bride, 'has eyes, bright, lively, resolute and himpudent, that will look at an hobject with a kind of disdain.' He bought another horse for five pounds, but the little one, Billy, was his favourite when he found it could do all the tricks that Zucker's Learned Little Horse performed at the Belvidere Tea Gardens, Pentonville.

Early in the spring of 1768, Astley set up his show in Lambeth, mid-way between the bridges of Blackfriars and Westminster. Along the south side of what he advertised as his riding-school, was the short cut from one to the other, and tolls were collected at its eastern end through a window which gave to his field the name of Halfpenny Hatch. It was enclosed partly by sheds and partly by rough palings, and in its centre was a pigeon-house that became the bandstand when a boy sat upon it while beating a drum. Earlier in the day, Astley himself, in full uniform, rode his white charger on the highway and handed out bills.

'That there is the riding-school,' he shouted, and with drawn sword suggested that the whole countryside was his manage. In the afternoon he stood at his gate, charging a shilling for a seat, and sixpence for a place to stand, before making speeches in his best word-of-command voice about the activities he would perform. After riding round to excite expectancy he stood on the saddles of two horses and put them to the jump.

'Now I will hold by one arm and leg with my toe in

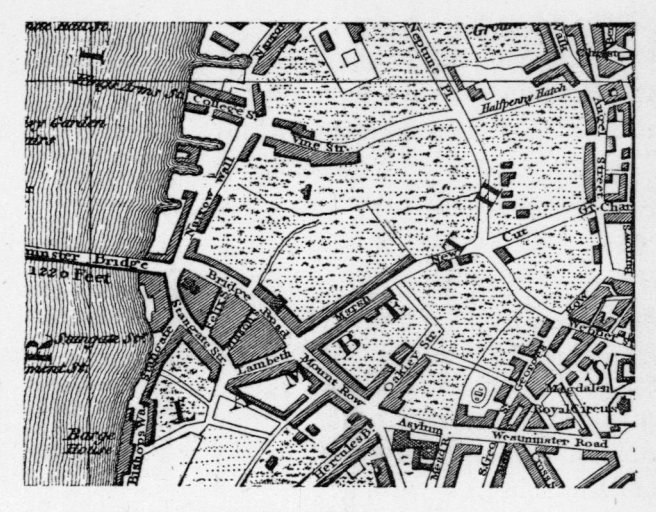

MAP SHOWING HALFPENNY HATCH
(top right hand corner)
Astley's (junction of Stangate Street and Bridge Road), and Royal Circus (bottom right hand corner)
From *The Picture Of London For 1809*

my mouth' – that done, he said the Little Military Learned Horse would, 'in a manner very extraordinary,' appear as if dead, and spoke a prologue for 'this here deception':

> My Horse lies Dead, apparent at your sight,
> But I'm the Man can set the thing to right,
> Speak when you please, I'm ready to obey
> My faithful Horse, knows what I want to say,
> But first pray give me leave to move his foot;
> That he is dead is quite beyond dispute.
>   (*The Horse appears quite dead*)
> This shews how brutes by heaven were design'd
> To be in full subjection to mankind.
> Rise, young Bill, and be a little handy,

To serve that warlike Hero, Granby.
              (*The Horse of his own accord rises*)
When you have seen, all my bills exprest,
My wife, to conclude, performs the rest.

In wet weather he charged two shillings for 'seats in a room' which was a barn. Receipts rose to forty guineas a day. But before the summer was over his season had to close because Mrs. Astley was presenting him with a son. They called him John.

Meanwhile Astley exhibited at the New Spring Gardens, Chelsea, a pretty spot with bowling-greens and shrubberies, and fountains playing at the head of the canal. In the autumn he travelled north, adding to his fortunes, although at Carlisle he was flooded out by the River Eden. When looking for the site of a permanent riding-school on the south side of Westminster Bridge where timber yards lined the banks of the Thames, he profited by the lesson. Land by the water's edge was not to his fancy; he desired the second frontage on the western side of Westminster Bridge Road. It was a corner site, owned by an old man who had a preserve of pheasants there; it had brought him no profits, and he badly needed £200 to get out of the country. Astley had the property secured to him by a mortgage in 1769. While crossing Westminster Bridge on this business, he found a diamond ring, worth £60, whose loss was never advertised. Its price bought deal boards for a fence.

Before the performance Mrs. Astley, accompanied by two pipes, beat a drum, while Astley invited idlers to walk up at sixpence a head. Many paid: so many more did not that the road was blocked by crowds outside every gap between the boards. 'Act 1' began with the sham death of the Little Military Learned Horse. Mrs. Astley went round the ride 'standing upright on the saddle of two horses,' and discharged a pistol while balancing between them. Next Astley explained that they would each ride two horses at the same time. 'And yet,' he said with emphasis, 'we have only these here two to ride on.' In other words they would ride together until Mrs. Astley chose to alight 'on full speed from these here two horses, with elegance and ease.' After that the Little Military Learned Horse marked the name of Astley, letter by letter, in the earth; was aided in thought-reading by a nodding figure called the Little Turk; told gold from silver and ladies from gentlemen; took a handkerchief in his mouth and indicated the owner; struck the hour of the day and day of the month with his hoof; fell lame, shammed a pain in the head, imitated sickness, and lay down as if dead when told he must fight for the Spaniards, a feat which caused him to be known as the Spanish Horse. He rose and fired a pistol on being ordered to go to Germany with his master and Eliott's Dragoons.

Out of his profits, Astley built a house over the entrance and stands with a pent-house roof. He showed, besides horsemanship, Fortunelly, the clown, on the slack rope, Signor Colpi's feats of strength with his children,[1] lofty and ground tumbling, and 'Egyptian

---

[1] Signor Colpi balanced boys on the soles of his feet after the fashion of the Risley Act, named after Professor Risley who came from America with a rather different act in the eighteen-forties. That such children used to be cruelly trained seems evident in the old circus rhyme:
> The poor Risley kids and the slanging buffers
> Nobody knows what they got to suffer.

Slanging is performing, and a buffer is a dog.

Pyramids; or, La Force D'Hercule,' men standing on each other's shoulders,[1] which he advertised in a painting on his walls. Another part of the entertainment was 'The Little Military Horse Turn'd Conjuror; or, The Magical Mechanical Sympathetic Clock, The Magical Table And Several Magnetical Experiments, Operations, etc.'

Before the open-air performance began at six, 'Automaton Figures' in the Great Room over the entrance, played the German flute and a kind of harpsichord in a manner 'beyond conception.' Outraged informers declared that Astley had dealings with the

[1] This feat, still called 'the Pyramids,' is regarded by acrobats now as mere gymnastics unless embellished. In the past it had distinguished spectators. In *Remarks On Several Parts Of Italy* (1701–3), Addison describes how at Venice a set of artisans, by the help of poles which they laid across each other's shoulders, built themselves up into 'a kind of pyramid' with four or five rows of men rising one above the other and a boy at the apex. To show that the Venetians were not the inventors of the trick, he quotes Claudian:

> Men, pil'd on men, with active leaps arise,
> And build the breathing fabric to the skies;
> A sprightly youth above the topmost row
> Points the tall pyramid, and crowns the show.

Next Goethe, when Wilhelm Meister meets Mignon at what we should regard nowadays as a horseless circus, makes men and women form 'the Hercules' Strength' (as Carlyle translates it); that the child on top should be dressed as a ball and weather vane is probably a touch of fiction. The public joy when the chief acrobats are brought home through the streets in litters to have silks and nosegays flung upon them, prompts a surmise whether Goethe saw the very troupe which at length came to Lambeth and had their likeness (using the poles which have long since been discarded) placed outside the Amphitheatre. Their mark is left on the district to-day in the name of Hercules Road.

How the feat had changed by Dickens' day is evident in *Hard Times*, where the father of one circus family often makes a pyramid of two other fathers 'with Master Kidderminster for the apex, and himself for the base.' Cossack troupes, returning to London in 1937, performed the pyramids on horseback at speed.

Devil. With all his servants, horse and foot, he set out on a semi-royal progress to Bridewell when required to answer the trumped up charge, and there he was admitted to bail until the general Assizes at Kingston. When he surrendered to take his trial, the mere mention of the Little Horse, the Little Turk, and the Magical or Mechanical Table, threw the whole court into great good humour. The truth then came out; he had borrowed the idea from the figures of the clock at St. Dunstan's, Fleet Street.

2

Royal Circus Rivalry

WHATEVER the shape or temper of that sprite which brooded over the south bridgehead of Westminster there can be no mistaking its feeling towards Astley. How he came by the land proves that, for the old man he had it from behaved like the sprite itself in disguise, even before you ask why the diamond ring Astley found there should have had no owner. Further evidence of supernatural aid manifested itself one day in 1771, when George III was riding over the bridge. What else should happen than that his horse should take fright at the cheering and rear, at the very spot where Astley was at hand to pacify it like the master he was? The King asked his name.

'Sergeant-Major Astley, sire,' was the answer in his own peculiar style of oratory, 'late of your Majesty's 15th Light Dragoons. The honour you was pleased to confer by commanding me to lay the standard which while serving under General Eliott in Germany I had taken from the French at Emsdorf, and now I am the proprietor of this here place for the exhibition of feats of activity on horseback.'

Before the King passed on, the order had been given for a command performance, and one summer morning Astley rode with his wife to Richmond Gardens at the head of his company. There was respect in every face but that of Charles Hughes, Astley's best horseman, a dark, envious man, strong enough to carry an ox on his shoulders; favoured by nature with a handsome face and figure, and by art with a peculiar felicity of manner, although he had neither breeding nor education. Astley demonstrated all his powers that day (except his authority over Hughes, who won too loud a murmur of approval), and was invited to France by the French Ambassador.

Masts and crosstrees were frightening to Mrs. Astley. When they arrived at Greenwich in the early spring of 1772, he left her to her fears in the cabin, brought his horses aboard, saw them lowered into the hold, walked round with a lamp while rats darted between his legs, and gave the Little Military Learned Horse an apple as they waited in the darkness for the midnight tide. The trials of the voyage were rewarded when he rode before Louis le Bien Aimé in the midst of the Great Camp at Fontainebleau, and aroused the interest of a court of horsemen.

In the May of 1772 his showground opened as the British Riding School. At the same time Hughes leased a field due south of Blackfriars Bridge, fenced in a ride similar to Astley's, and called it Hughes's Riding School. The hot temper Astley had inherited from his father drove him to expose 'these here pretenders to horsemanship.' He dressed himself in his old blue uniform and rode his white charger into Westminster, at the head of a procession of two trumpeters, two riders in costume, and a coach where the Little Military Learned Horse sat, helping the clown to bestow handbills. Here and there they would halt for Astley to announce feats 'too tedious to mention' which could be performed only by himself and 'this here company etcetera, being in number upwards of fifty all different.' He accused his rivals of using his bills; he expected the new ones would share the same fate, and he offered any person two hundred guineas to equal his achievements.

Crowds went to see 'these here pretenders.' Hughes vaulted backwards and forwards over three horses, and then over a single horse forty times without stopping; stood backwards in the saddle while his horse jumped a bar; balanced head downwards on a broad-bottomed bottle in the saddle while the horse galloped; rode with one foot on its head, then with one foot in the saddle and left toe in his mouth. His company included Mrs. Hughes, who fired a pistol while taking a flying leap, the celebrated Sobieska Clementina, who rode standing upright in the saddle at full speed, and a 'Young Lady eight years old,' who did the same. To rival Astley's Little Military Learned Horse, Hughes had a Horse of Knowledge, who fired a cannon and pistol, and was advertised as 'the only Horse at present in this Kingdom that will fetch and carry.' The performance finished with 'the droll position of the Taylor.' Between the 'Diversion of the Riding School' at six o'clock and the horsemanship at eight, there was an exhibition of conjuring, 'particularly on watches,' at seven.

Astley at once turned conjurer – without forgoing his right to denounce imitation of his own ideas. He uttered his severest rebukes while demonstrating 'the different cuts and guards as in real action, or an imitation of a general engagement, sword in hand, with the different postures of offence, for the safety of man and horse, and what is really made use of at the word *charge*, by all the light-troops in Europe – Eliott's, the Prussian and the Hessian Hussars.' Here he cleared his throat, struck an attitude of severe indignation, and shouted in his best word-of-command voice, 'This here piece of activity which ought, for the honour of the British Troops in general, to be displayed with the greatest warlike appearance, but I am sorry to say it is generally imposed on by some *modern* pretender – to that noble hart.' After describing his own claims to know the noble art, he forthwith showed the audience 'the manner of Eliott's charging of the French troops in Germany in the year 1760 when it was said the regiment were all tailors.' There were five 'Acts' of varied entertainment before the final burlesque of a tailor on horseback.

In addition to running his riding-school Astley built a large bathing-machine in the Thames at Vauxhall. Though he advertised it by swimming from Westminster Bridge to Blackfriars, holding a flag erect in each hand, for a heavy wager, it was a failure. And as Hughes was drawing people from his shows, Astley became dispirited. While determined 'to make the performance this season the completest in Europe,' he would exhibit no longer than that summer. In September he closed down, leaving his rival to exult in handbills:

Hughes humbly thanks the Nobility etc. for the Honour of their Support, and also acquaints them his

Antagonist has catched a bad cold so near to Westminster Bridge, and for his recovery is gone to a warmer Climate, which is Bath in Somersetshire. He boasts, poor Fellow, no more of activity, and is now turned Conjurer, in the character of 'Sieur the Great.' Therefore Hughes is unrivalled.

Five years had passed since Astley had lent £200 on his site and secured the mortgage, and he was now expecting the landlord to return. But that elusive old man, whose behaviour throughout places him under suspicion of being fey, had disappeared. Astley foreclosed, thus obtaining a lease of the land until 1839. Once again he had faith in his star, and in the spring of 1774, boldly opposed the British Horse Academy of his rival. In the July the magistrates informed both that their performances did not conform to the licences granted for music and dancing. They were forced to shut up shop. Hughes, disheartened, went to perform before crowned heads abroad – the kings of France, Sardinia, Naples, Spain, and Portugal; the Emperor of Germany and his royal brother; the Sultan of Morocco at his summer residence, Mequinez.

Astley, with more at stake now that he was a landlord, begged his influential friends to influence the magistrates, and while awaiting the result wrote, *The Modern Riding Master; or, A Key To The Knowledge Of The Horse And Horsemanship*, printed for and sold by the author at his Riding School. It was dedicated to the King in Astleian prose:

> As your Majesty gives great Encouragement to the Breeding and Training of Horses and Horsemanship,

DE

and well knowing your Majesty's great Perfection in the Knowledge of that noble and manly Art, made me ambitious of wishing this small Production might appear under your Noble Patronage: not only to add to its lustre, but what an old Soldier values most, the Sanction of his Royal Master.

He also published a book on conjuring called *Natural Magic*. It bore a close resemblance – word for word on many pages – to *The Conjurer Unmasked*, a translation of *La Magie Blanche Dévoilée* by Decremps.

Permission to continue his performances was given. In 1775 he reopened his show more ambitiously, and found the craze for horsemanship still at its height. Freed from serious rivalry, he made his name a household word. Garrick engaged him to ride with Mrs. Astley at Drury Lane in the revival of *Shakespeare's Jubilee*. Dr. Johnson paid him the compliment of, 'Were Astley to preach a sermon standing on a horse's back, he would collect a multitude to hear him.' What less could he do, while basking in such fame, than become magnanimous even to his father? He sent for Edward Astley, patronised him with open arms, and once more delighted in his sister's admiration. When she became Mrs. Gill he was sure of his right to hold forth at her fireside.

The riding-school was no longer grand enough; it needed a roof for entertainments all the year round. Timber was dear, but there was to be a royal funeral and an election, and planks might be saved from the burning. Astley made himself known to those who guarded the hustings. If they would save the wood from 'the deprecating hands of a licentious populace' at the close of procession or poll, he would reward them for whatever they should bring to his doors. The bonfires of time-honoured custom were cheated.

Astley began to roof his establishment during the winter of 1778-9. While this was being done he hired a room at 22 Piccadilly, for 'Fire-Side Amusements,' consisting of *Ombres Chinoises* (moving shadows of Chinese figures on a screen), Signor Rossignol's imitations of birds, the Little Military Learned Horse, and learned dogs. In January the programmes stated :

> The Amphitheatre Riding-House, Westminster Bridge, the most complete building of its kind in Europe, will be opened in a few days, for completing Gentlemen and Ladies in the polite art of riding of horseback with ease and safety, as also for breaking horses for the Army, Road, Field, Draft, Shooting, Storking, etc.

The roof changed his entertainments. With his usual readiness to borrow ideas, he set himself up as the rival of Sadler's Wells. He also bestowed upon himself the right, which they had not, to open all the year round. In the November of 1780, he advertised 'Winter Evening's Amusements' (by candlelight), which combined *Ombres Chinoises* with horsemanship, the pyramids, vaulting, balancing, and all manner of feats on ladders, slackrope, and springboard or 'trampoline,' which was his way of spelling *tremplin*.[1] Master Astley, who was about ten years old, although he was described

[1] *Tremplin* still means 'springboard,' but 'trampoline,' although it has not found its way into the dictionaries, has long been the name of that peculiar spring-mattress bounced upon by acrobats.

as 'aged five' on the handbills, now entered the arena as 'the greatest performer that ever appeared in any age, and as a horseman, stands unparalleled by all nations.' In a 'most amazing equilibrium, whilst the horse is on a gallop,' he danced and vaulted, played on the violin, and displayed a flag in attitudes which had 'never been exhibited, or even thought of by any horseman in Europe.'

So fine a showman had Astley become that he no longer paraded the town; he published the information that he 'never more intended that abominable practice.' Yet he saw fit to walk, bearing candles along the ride, behind freaks while holding forth on 'these here' exhibits in a manner which delighted the gallery and provoked many a rude mimic. In his inspired moments he would refer to the 'krockudile wat stopped Halexander's harmy, and when cut hopen, had a man in harmour in its hintellects,' and, in confidential mood, he declared he would be a ruined man for 'these here horses eat most vociferously.' His pet subject was his wife's flaxen hair, which lay several feet on the ground when she paraded with Astley and his candles in attendance. One night the flames were held too near. There was a little damage and a great deal of abuse; and Mrs. Astley determined evermore to hide her tresses in a wig. She tucked her immense quantity of hair in a vast caxon, so that her head was as out of proportion to the rest of her figure as a whale's. Another Lady With Long Hair had to walk round with the Man In Miniature and the Grimacer, and a clown now did the talking. Astley was very critical. 'The Clown to interpret and articulate better,' he wrote on the Prompter's Plot.

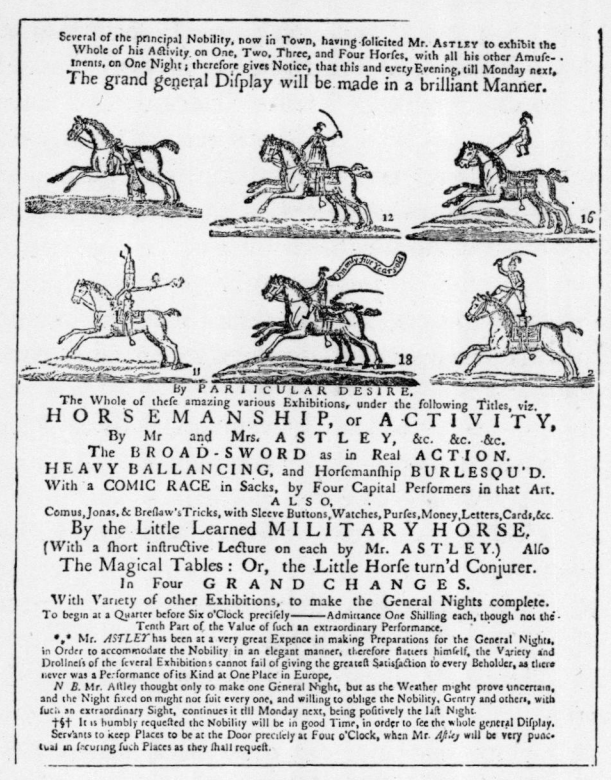

> Several of the principal Nobility, now in Town, having solicited Mr. Astley to exhibit the Whole of his Activity, on One, Two, Three, and Four Horses, with all his other Amusements, on One Night; therefore gives Notice, that this and every Evening, till Monday next, The grand general Display will be made in a brilliant Manner.
>
> By PARTICULAR DESIRE.
> The Whole of these amazing various Exhibitions, under the following Titles, viz.
> HORSEMANSHIP, or ACTIVITY,
> By Mr and Mrs. ASTLEY, &c. &c. &c.
> The BROAD-SWORD as in Real ACTION.
> HEAVY BALLANCING, and Horsemanship BURLESQU'D.
> With a COMIC RACE in Sacks, by Four Capital Performers in that Art.
> ALSO,
> Comus, Jonas, & Breslaw's Tricks, with Sleeve Buttons, Watches, Purses, Money, Letters, Cards, &c.
> By the Little Learned MILITARY HORSE,
> (With a short instructive Lecture on each by Mr. ASTLEY.) Also
> The Magical Tables: Or, the Little Horse turn'd Conjurer.
> In Four GRAND CHANGES.
> With Variety of other Exhibitions, to make the General Nights complete.
> To begin at a Quarter before Six o'Clock precisely——— Admittance One Shilling each, though not the Tenth Part of the Value of such an extraordinary Performance.
> *** Mr. ASTLEY has been at a very great Expence in making Preparations for the General Nights, in Order to accommodate the Nobility in an elegant manner, therefore flatters himself, the Variety and Drollness of the several Exhibitions cannot fail of giving the greatest Satisfaction to every Beholder, as there never was a Performance of its Kind at One Place in Europe.
> N.B. Mr. Astley thought only to make one General Night, but as the Weather might prove uncertain, and the Night fixed on might not suit every one, and willing to oblige the Nobility, Gentry and others, with such an extraordinary Sight, continues it till Monday next, being positively the last Night.
> ††† It is humbly requested the Nobility will be in good Time, in order to see the whole general Display. Servants to keep Places to be at the Door precisely at Four o'Clock, when Mr. *Astley* will be very punctual in securing such Places as they shall request.

BILL OF OPEN-AIR PERFORMANCE

showing Young Astley on horseback by the recumbent form of his father, uttering the words, 'I'm only five years old'

Those conversations in the ring between riding-master and clown, which became a circus tradition of the nineteenth century, grew out of these superior feelings towards Mr. Merryman. What the dialogue was like when Astley himself spoke the ring-master's part, is evident in this passage from Henry Angelo's *Reminiscences*:

One evening I was very much entertained at Astley's Theatre, at the time he amused the public with his dialogue with Master Merryman. Having a pencil in my pocket I could not refrain from writing it down. He seemed so confident and pleased with every word he uttered, bawled so loud, smiling at his own wit, and the superiority which he *must* convince the audience his eloquence displayed over the clown's. He excited my curiosity to retain it in my memory. Those that have seen him, cannot forget what Astley's erudition was.

Astley – Alto – Mister Merryman, Mister Merryman, where are you, Mr. Merryman?

M. I be coming directly, master.

A. Coming directly, Mister Merryman, so is Christmas.

M. I am glad to hear that, master.

A. Why, Mister Merryman?

M. Because I likes plum-pudding and roast beef, dearly.

A. Plum-pudding and roast beef, dearly! that's very good stuff, Mister Merryman; but come, Sir, get up upon the top of that there horse, and let the ladies see as how you used to ride before the Emperor of Tuscany, and the Grand Duke of Switzerland. Mister Merryman, ladies and gentlemen, has had the honour to attend me in my different excursions out of the kingdom, and has been much admired for his wit and his activity. Come, Sir, mind as how you sit upright on that there horse, Sir. What are you about?

M. Why, master, I am only combing his wig.

A. Combing his wig, Sir; did you ever hear of a horse wearing a wig?

M. Yes, master; and an ass too.

A. Vastly well, indeed, Mister Merryman. Ladies and gentlemen, Mister Merryman has a great deal of wit.

M. Yes, master; I should like to be a poet laureate.

A. Poet Laureate, Mister Merryman? What! I suppose as how you would write manuscript on horseback, like the Roman Arabs in the time of Pontius *Pirate* – you would never want a bridle or saddle.

M. No, master; I would write a book about the French war.

A. About the French war, Mister Merryman? Why, you know nothing about it. You must leave it to Mr. Parnassus, and people of high breeding and learning[1]; but come, Sir, let us see you off.

M. I go, Sir.

A. I go, Sir! but you have got your face the wrong way.

M. Never mind, master; it will be right if I go to fight the French.

A. How so, Mister Merryman?

M. Why, master, if my horse was to take fright and run away, I should not like to have it said I turned my back on Mounseer.

A. Vastly well, indeed, Mister Merryman; but as

---

[1] Astley wrote *A Description And Historical Account Of The Places Now The Theatre Of War In The Low Countries,* compiled from some bulky *Universal History,* although announced as having been 'chiefly written in camp,' and *Remarks On The Duty And Profession Of A Soldier.*

our brave countrymen will prevent the French from coming to eat up all our roast beef and pudding, you had better turn about; so off you go.

Though further visits to France were prevented by the war of 1778-83, Astley did not give up the idea of Continental conquests. Whereas he had striven at the start of his career to make himself 'conspicuous and known' wherever he went in England, his present aim was to make himself conspicuous and known to all the crowned heads of Europe. In his travels, 'taking Brussels, Vienna, etc., in my road to Belgrade in 1782,' he says, 'Sir Robert Murray Keith, then minister plenipotentiary at the court of Vienna, did me the honour of introducing me to the Emperor.' Astley was invited to show his skill in the famous Viennese riding-school. With overpowering modesty, he begged for an old horse saying that as he was a young horseman, 'two who are both inexperienced might not afford his Majesty much pleasure.' He found fault with the adjustment of saddle and bridle, and being told that he had no occasion for fear, very politely uncovered, and said there was 'more merit in preventing an accident than curing one.' After his demonstration of *passage*, *terre-à-terre*, *pirouette*, and *piaffe*, he thanked the Emperor for condescending to honour him with approbation, wiped the horse's face with a handkerchief and rewarded it with an apple. 'His Imperial Majesty smiled and requested me to walk into the palace.'

On his return to England, he found that his success had once again aroused jealousy. Noting how 'very much admired' horsemanship was, Charles Dibdin had

SILHOUETTE OF PHILIP ASTLEY
From Astley's *System Of Equestrian Education*, 1801

ASTLEY'S ROYAL AMPHITHEATRE OF ARTS
From *The Microcosm Of London*

ASTLEY'S ADVERTISING CART
From a water-colour in the Print Room of the British Museum

THE ROYAL CIRCUS
From *The Microcosm Of London*

entered into partnership with Hughes to build a Royal Circus and Equestrian Philharmonic Academy near where the British Horse Academy had stood. The site bought for their project by a Colonel West was in Great Surrey Street (Blackfriars Road), by the obelisk at the turnpike. Another thoroughfare which ended here was Westminster Bridge Road, so that the threat to Astley was not far from his door. In alarm he tried to hinder his rivals by patenting his 'agility on horseback,' and his methods of training horses 'to stand the noise of drums, trumpets, music, explosion of large ordnance.' There was also more than godly warmth in his support of the Rev. Rowland Hill's protest against the speed of the Circus's bricklayers, as compared with those who were building his Surrey Chapel. A passage in one of his sermons on the subject pleased Astley:

> There are two ships within sight of a spice island. One is manned by the elect of heaven, and freighted with good works – the other, directed by the devil's crew, and laden with sinfulness. The object of both these craft is to reach the spicy port as soon as possible; but the devil's ship, if not a better vessel, is more actively manned – for, to do Satan justice, he is always industrious. Let it only land, and the whole shore will become tainted – this fine aromatic flavour which invites you now, will become fetid – mephitic, as the scientific people call it – and you will be poisoned on the very pastures which ought to be yours.

Pegasus was mounted on the roof, and the Royal Circus was complete. Inside, 'very handsome, commodious and neat,' it was remarkable for possessing both circle (as the ring was called) and stage. Pit, boxes, and gallery formed an oval with the stage at one end, and the circle in the centre. 'Simple grandeur' was suggested by the straw-coloured walls, silver ornaments, and silver balustrades. Above the stage the roof opened so that fireworks could be let off without discomfort to nostrils. So far was public curiosity excited by reports of the novelty that on November 2nd, 1782, the day of the opening, 'an incredible number of persons' besieged the doors, and more than half had to be shut out. The fortunate ones inside saw the poet of the company enter a lottery and draw tickets for a tragic ballet and a pantomime. He asked for the horses, and was told that some had been sent abroad to mount our enemy's cavalry, and others engrossed by ladies for their cabrioles. Those that remained entered 'one, on his hind legs, another on his knees,' and all lay down to a dead march, until Hughes, on a managed horse richly caparisoned, came to review his troops. The prelude ended with a chorus by the Fairies, thanking Fortune for having placed them in a land of freedom. What remained consisted of the grand ballet of *Admetus And Alceste*, danced by children; a variety of feats of horsemanship by Mr. Hughes and his pupils, including a boy of eight and a girl of nine years of age; and a burlesque pantomime parody called *Mardarina: or, The Refusal Of Harlequin*, played by children.

As he noticed the combined use of stage and arena, Astley shook with jealousy, plainly enough for Hughes to see. There was an added bitterness in their rivalry now. It began with the charge that Astley had poisoned Hughes's horses. Another charge followed. Information had been laid against Hughes as a rogue and vagabond who had performed for his gain and reward at a place not licensed for stage entertainments, and Astley was accused of being the informer. He swore that he was innocent and totally unaware of the prosecution until ordered to stop his own performance on November 5th. Such annoyances were too much for his temper. He raged in his home, and found himself, once again, in conflict with his father. Old Edward left the house, and on December 24th swore on oath before the Lord Mayor that Philip Astley had frequently struck him; had turned him out of the house and 'used him with such unbecoming abuse and scurrilous language, that the Deponent cannot, without impropriety, state the same in a public paper.' He appealed for donations to be left at No. 3 Reeve's Mews, and Astley's Punch-house, Ludgate-hill. Philip's answer was that he cared for his father 'until he thought proper to engage as a doorkeeper to a place of public amusement.' Old Astley was henceforth, 'thro' charity,' employed by Hughes to distribute bills for half a guinea a week at the foot of Blackfriars Bridge. Afterwards he became Hughes's ostler.

In open defiance of the law, both houses resumed performances. One night three justices went to the Royal Circus, jumped from the pit into the ring, marched to the dressing-rooms, and ordered Hughes to an ale-house, where they asked by what right he dared to let a boy make speeches in a piece called *The Dumb Orators*. He was committed to Bridewell. Then they visited Astley's riding-house, and carried him off to Bridewell also. Fortunately, the daughters of Lord

Thurlow, the Lord Chancellor, were among his pupils, and through their good offices he was released until the Surrey Sessions in January, 1783. Then Hughes triumphed. His case, the first to be tried, took the better part of the day; by wrangling each point of the law he won the right to retain his musical performances. When Astley appeared, the hour was so late that he had to give an immediate undertaking (not to include music and dancing in his entertainments) to obtain his release. He tried fireworks instead, and employed that celebrated pyrotechnist Signor Hengler. In honour of General Eliott's defence of Gibraltar, he presented 'The Gibraltar Charger,' who remained undisturbed by a circle of fire while Astley on its back saluted the public with an olive branch of fireworks.

The Circus reopened on March 15th. It was now completely under Hughes's control, for he had obtained a licence in his own name. Ever since Colonel West had died through the reopening of an old wound while he was riding an unmanageable horse – warranted by Hughes to be a gentle, safe hack – this rascal had been at loggerheads with Lady West and the other proprietors. She ejected his brother-in-law from the Equestrian Coffee House, which formed one of the Royal Circus's wings. In retaliation, he now obtained a drink licence for the interior of the Circus and opened a bar at the back of the side boxes.

While they squabbled, Astley – as ready to borrow as he was slow to invent – adopted their plan of a combined arena and stage. But as he lacked understanding of music and dancing, his audience were still drawn away by the Circus, even after Dibdin had left because of a quarrel with the proprietors. Signor Giuseppe Grimaldi (saturnine father of the stage clown after whom circus clowns are named 'Joey') stepped into his shoes. He had charge of the children who played in the pantomimes and ballets. When they behaved badly, he placed them in a kind of stocks, but these were large enough for the prisoners to play at tops or marbles. To provide a more effective punishment, he pushed each offender into a cage which was drawn up to the flies. He came to grief when he arranged a dance called *Quakers*, which was too keen a satire on the Society of Friends for the magistrates to tolerate. Dibdin returned in 1784 as Hughes's ally against the proprietors, and would not engage performers who had remained while he was away. Among those who had was John Decastro,[1] a comic singer. Over a bowl of punch at Wheelwright's Tea Gardens, commonly known as the Gig shop, in Mount Row, Lambeth, he heard that the rival house would give any salary to burletta singers, and went at once with a friend to the attic where Astley, sitting on a bed for his ease as he was very tired after travelling from Paris, heard them sing a skating duet called, *This Snell And Frosty Morning*. His eyes sparkled, as he shouted to his housekeeper, 'Ah! ah! Mary, this will do; these are the men I want.' Pen, ink, and paper were brought, an engagement signed, and Decastro went back to more punch at the Gig Shop. Then they persuaded Mrs. Asker, a 'good breeches

[1] To whose *Analysis Of The Life Of Philip Astley, Esq.*, all succeeding circus writers, especially the present one, have been greatly indebted. Few authors are more artless than Decastro. His epitaph on the mother of a large family who outlived her husband by only a few months, is 'Frailty, thy name is woman.'

figure,' to desert with them. Later the tide turned and Astley had to write on the Prompter's Plot:

> All the Company, no excuse; nor will any of them be permitted in future to perform at the Circus; the Gentlemen Proprietors of that place ought to get Performers, or shut up their House – the Manager thinks they are bad neighbours for not doing the one or the other.

Horses had to be left to the grooms now singers had become important. It never entered Astley's head to find a musician to rival Dibdin or a ballet-master to rival Grimaldi. He himself turned impresario. Planking his chair on the front of the stage, he drilled his company at rehearsals as he would the awkward squad. *Sailors And Savages* was the title of a little piece he fancied. To make it livelier he called for 'Dr. Herring' – his real name was Heron.

'Doctor,' said Astley, 'I want you to compose me a tune for this here combat of two broadswords, to go re, tang, tang, tang.'

When he directed John Astley, in the part of a naval lieutenant, how to fight a savage, there was not enough noise.

'Johnny! Johnny! This won't do,' Astley bawled. 'We must have shields.'

Heron, thinking he was asking for music by Shields, collected his band parts, clambered on to the stage, and tore them to bits. Astley pacified him: he was used to dealing with the artistic temperament. There was Charles Dibdin's son, Thomas. Questioning Philip's right to name himself in the play-bills as the author of any piece he might pay for, the youth said that he sold his wares 'at so unassuming a price as fourteen pounds fourteen shillings for three burlettas and a pantomime,' in order to obtain some degree of professional credit. Philip the Great exclaimed, 'Credit? Oh! ah! More credit in fourteen guineas, eh? And not a light one among 'em? They can't fail; they'll go down, sir! They are jokes that everybody will take. Eh, won't they? And your pieces, if you *will* have them yours, Mr. What's-your-name, may be damned. Eh? What d'ye think?'

As Dibdin would argue, Philip pointed out that the owner of a shoe warehouse, though he had never made a shoe in his life, was certainly the owner of all the shoes he had for sale, and could reasonably claim that they were all his make.

'But he bought them, d'ye see? Paid for them in the lump, or perhaps in lots of fourteen guineas-worth, as I buy these here things of you, and devilish slim some of them are for the money, and then by that means they are his shoes, his make, and his all round the ring. Eh? Just as these thingumbobs are mine. D'ye see that? Oho!'

Young Dibdin gave way, as he was happy to see the fourteen guineas. Directly he had agreed, Philip changed his mind. 'Now I tell you what,' he said, 'you *shall* have your name to them, and for anything I know, it may do some good. People may think it's your father. Eh? What d'ye think?'

The Amphitheatre's stock poet was a drunken hack named Oakman, who supplied minor dramas for a guinea a piece. Astley, while charging him to keep sober, slashed his manuscript as he thought fit. As he was leaving, Oakman scribbled in chalk over the door, 'Mangling done here.'

Thus by a mixture of bullying and goodwill, he got things done, until, one unhappy night, he was made to feel how far he had been carried from his original path. There would have been no mistake had the rehearsal not been called for a Sunday, when all his performers were so respectably dressed there was no telling them from the nobility. Astley, ever on the watch for Hughes's spies, saw a stranger watching the rehearsals from the ring.

'Come here, Sir, I want you upon the stage!' he thundered. Johnny held his arm. 'Father, that's his Grace the Duke of Gordon you're speaking to.'

Astley had a sudden remembrance of two horses that he had been ordered to break for His Grace.

'By God, my Lord Duke,' he stammered, pulling off his hat very humbly, 'I beg your pardon, I took you for one of my performers.'

The Duke of Gordon smiled and they bowed to each other. As his Grace walked out, Astley considered that this was what came of mixing with singers. In that moment he saw how his ideal of himself as a master of the pure *art d'equitation* had been twisted askew by a mocking fate. He had been led astray by his rivals of the Royal Circus.

Even if left to themselves, they would have ensured their own destruction. Hughes would see to that. After falling out with Charles Dibdin over a plan for an Arne festival, Hughes dismissed the treasurer, and seized the money at the door. He refused to pay the bandsmen, and they struck. That evening, after apologising to the audience, Dibdin began to play the accompaniment to his burletta, *Clump And Cudden*, on the piano. Hughes at once led his *grand entrée* of horse into the ring, headed, as usual, by a noisy drum and fife. That was the end of Dibdin.

Yet this was a time of peril for minor theatres. Legally they had no right to exist. Their licences for songs and dances did not authorise the pantomimes and burlettas regularly exhibited by Astley's, the Circus, Sadler's Wells, and the Royalty (Whitechapel). When the patent theatres took action in 1788 against all these houses, the managers of the Wells brought in a Bill in the House of Lords to give them the exclusive right to give such performances as they had a prior claim. Astley, Hughes, and John Palmer prayed for relief at the hands of the Lords and Commons, Astley reinforcing his arguments with his certificate of service. Lord Thurlow, looking at the Bill presented by the Wells, said, 'Is it because they are the oldest offenders that they they should claim this? No – all or none !'

Thus the law-breakers had become law-makers. From mere showmen, barely tolerated by the authorities, Astley and his fellows had turned themselves into theatrical managers. The Amphitheatre acknowledged its own importance by having trees painted on its walls and ceiling and becoming known as the 'Royal Grove,' and later as the 'Royal Saloon and New Amphitheatre,' while Astley built for himself a dwelling called 'Hercules Hall,' after 'La Force D'Hercule.'

The Royal Circus, unworthy of the honour won, steadily degenerated. Quarrels between Hughes and

Lady West were the cause. She tried to turn him out of his home; he persuaded a wealthy friend to buy the lease, and defied her. Then he neglected the Circus in order to buy blood stallions and breeding mares at Newmarket for Count Orloff, favourite of Catherine the Great, who sent him to England in 1793 for this purpose. Hughes embarked with the stud, and also shipped his own company, with Edward Astley as ostler, for St. Petersburg. When he was presented to the Empress of all the Russias, his charm swayed her susceptible heart. She presented him with an Imperial Circus within the walls of her palace in St. Petersburg, and gave orders for another at Moscow. Directly the first had been built, the highest in the land were commanded to attend, and when the Court wanted to be taught the English style of riding, there was temptation enough to stay in Russia. Yet the news that Lady West had put an execution for ground rent into the Royal Circus made him burn to return to London. Catherine granted him leave of absence on condition that he should leave his horses and boys. He tactfully hinted that he was willing to sell, and they became crown property at a royal figure.

Despite the execution for ground rent, Hughes took charge of the Royal Circus and used both stables and arena as pens for mules, African sheep, and Sicilian goats left in his charge. When Lady West at last gained possession, he again outwitted her by inducing Benjamin Hardy to rent the building without disclosing that he would present 'Mr. Hughes and his troop, lately returned from Russia.' Their success was small. At length Hughes offended the magistrates and lost his licence, a blow said to be responsible for his death, at the age of fifty, in the December of 1797.

But his wraith has the best of the joke, since it was he who has christened Astley's child. 'Amphitheatre' being too awkward a word, it has answered to the name of 'circus' for no other reason than that this is easy to say. The ancient circus was a chariot-course, never circular, so that even the geometric figure of its plan bears no resemblance to the arena of trick-riders. There is even less evidence of a link between the circus of the Old World and the circus of the New, than there is between the *pantomimus* (who acted before, and found a rival in, Nero) and the English Christmas pantomime. 'Amphitheatre' dwindled into a name in London theatres for the frontal part of the gallery which used to form a horseshoe over the whole auditorium, boxes included.

3

Twice Burned Down

'WHILE these here horses are on full speed,' Philip Astley shouted, 'I will spring up with my feet on the saddle and stand on one leg, imitating Mercury flying.' He had displayed this feat of activity – 'without,' as he boasted, 'any happaratus whatsever from the saddle' – times without number. This night, however, he winced as he was landing from the spring, and could barely stand, let alone lift one leg behind in imitation of Mercury flying. That old wound received at Emsdorf was causing twinges of pain to shoot up and down his thigh. He staggered and almost fell. While the spectators stood up in the hope of seeing him break his neck, he beckoned an ostler to the horse, and Mercury painfully bent down to grasp a shoulder in order to dismount. He had to lay up for a week. After that he would only appear as the 'Taylor from Brentford' who rode facing the tail.

It was time to retire. His tricks while standing in the saddle, such as throwing his left foot on his right knee, and carrying his left foot in his right hand, were out of date. John on horseback danced minuet and hornpipe. In Paris, the Anglomania of the French Court, where English horsemanship was even more fashionable than English democracy, shed a glamour over his handsome figure and grace. London at that time of the year, Horace Walpole wrote in 1783, was

> as nauseous a drug as any in an apothecary's shop. I could find nothing at all to do, and so went to Astley's, which, indeed, was much beyond my expectation. I do not wonder any longer that Darius was chosen King by the instructions he gave to his horse; nor that Caligula made his Consul. Astley can make his dance minuets and hornpipes. But I shall not have even Astley now. Her Majesty the Queen of France, who has as much taste as Caligula, has sent for the whole of the *dramatis personæ* to Paris.

The Astleys were received at Versailles with a splendour which eclipsed Philip's memories of Richmond Gardens and Fontainebleau. When John danced a minuet on three horses, high white wigs nodded like tall lilies in a breeze as lovely lips spoke of the Apollo Belvidere. He was brought to the Queen. 'English Rose,' Marie Antoinette called him – the French Rose was Vestris, whose dancing was the rage of Paris – as she gave him a gold medal set with diamonds. Philip was not so deeply impressed that he could refrain from mentioning a suspicion which entered his head – 'That there King can't be the father of the Dolphin. Why, he's omnipotent.'

Theatres, opera, and ballet were deserted. Fashion went to the Faubourg du Temple to see the Astleys, who performed there in the open. Before they left in the spring, such assurance was given of royal patronage should they return, that Astley chose a site near his field for an 'Amphithéâtre Anglais,' with roof, stage musician's gallery, and thirty candelabra to shed light from twelve hundred jets of flame.

Each autumn as soon as their London amphitheatre closed, in obedience to the law protecting the patent theatres from rivalry in the winter, the Astleys installed themselves here for two or three months. While John created the lure of romance in an entertainment of acrobatics, fireworks, and horsemanship, Philip made speeches in chaotic French.

In the *Mémoires Secrets* attributed to De Bachaumont, there is a note dated November 3rd, 1783, mentioning how some of his horses danced the minuet, how one fetched and carried, another sat up like a dog, also how there was a fight between an English tailor and his mount which, though docile with any other rider, shied and reared on catching sight of the tailor,[1] rushed at him, tore his coat, seized his whip and carried it off between its teeth. Philip Astley's horsemanship was greatly admired, but his son aroused the envy of men and the love of women. Young Astley's success, indeed, was so great at the French Court that Walpole thought he 'expected to be Prime Minister, though he only ventured his neck by dancing a minuet on three horses at full gallop.' In that attitude he had 'as much grace as the Apollo Belvedere.'

[1] 'Le Tailleur' in French circuses came to mean the act of sitting in a chair on horseback. The Brentford tailor's habit of riding backwards was adopted by *le Paysan Alsacien* and was part of *les farces de Pierrot*.

They divided their establishment. While John remained at Lambeth, Philip 'exhibited with uncommon applause in several capital towns in England,' leaving an amphitheatre behind him wherever he went until he had earned the nickname of Amphi-Philip. Undaunted by the St. George's Channel, though many a player and acrobat lay there full fathom five, he shrewdly appraised an old bishop's mansion in Peter Street, Dublin. As it belonged to Sir Capel Molineux, who had influence at Court, he decided that a patent might await its purchaser, and he was right. Ireland's Amphitheatre Royal was speedily jerry-built,[1] and in gratitude Astley prepared a great display of fireworks on Stephen's Green to celebrate the convalescence of George III. Stationing a bombardier on the leads of a house to let off a signal rocket when it was time, he set off to the castle to wait upon the Viceroy. A wag who had overheard the arrangements, shouted in imitation of the showman's voice, 'Holloo, you 'tilleryman, let auf that there rocket !' Away went the rocket and off went the whole display so that not a squib was left by

---

[1] When Grimaldi and the greater part of the Sadler's Wells company were brought here by Thomas and Charles Dibdin (the younger) in the autumn of 1805, they discovered that the roof was not waterproof. In the *Memoirs of Grimaldi*, which Dickens edited, it is said:

At length, one night towards the end of December, a very heavy rain coming down during the performance, actually drove the audience out of the house. The water descended in torrents into the pit and boxes; some people who were greatly interested in the performances put up their umbrellas, and others put on great coats and shawls; but at length it came down so heavily upon the stage that the performers themselves were obliged to disappear. In a few minutes the stage was well covered, the scenery soaked through, the pit little better than a well, and the boxes and galleries streaming with water.

the time the *cortège* arrived from the Castle. Astley stamped and swore like a trooper before the delighted crowd and offered twenty guineas for the hoaxer's name. For many nights after, he had only to appear in the ring for the gallery to cry, 'Holloo, you 'tilleryman, let auf that there rocket!'

Philip's horsemen joined John's for a short London season before the combined troops went to Paris. There was no command to appear before the French Court now the affair of the Diamond Necklace was being talked about. Lacking royal protection, they were made to feel the jealousy of their rivals of the Faubourg du Temple (not yet famous as 'le Boulevard'), particularly Nicolet, whose father's booth had been styled 'Théâtre des Grands-Danseurs du Roi,' ever since his troupe had performed at Choisy before Louis XV and Madame Dubarry. The son now possessed the sole right to present entertainments of tumblers and wire-walkers, just as Astley had the monopoly of trick-riding. Consequently when the bills of the Amphithéâtre Anglais announced 'Le Sieur Sanders du Théâtre Royal de Londres, Célèbre Danseur le Fil-d'Archal,' Astley was warned. Possessing a spirit that would not yield to opposition, he still gave acrobatic exhibitions on his stage. Nicolet applied to Monseigneur le Lieutenant Général de Police, who forbade all performances not on horseback. The difficulty was overcome by harnessing horses together to bear a platform for the tumblers, so that they rode, though not in the saddle, while somersaulting.

But the days of triumph had passed and Paris seasons now meant drudgery, as Mrs. Astley felt when she

BILL OF PARIS PERFORMANCE

From the Collection of Mr. W. S. Meadmore by whose kind permission it is reproduced here

MONSIEUR NICOLET

From *Le Monde Dramatique*, Paris, 1837

ARENA OF ASTLEY'S AMPHITHEATRE, SURREY ROAD.

From Wilkinson's *Londina Illustrata*, 1815

wrote this letter, preserved in a scrapbook in the British Museum:

> According to promise in my last, I sitt down to write to my dear Mr. and Mrs. Pownall first I forgott to mention in my last concerning the monkey, if it has no tail, and tractable Mr. Astley would be glad you would purchase it for him, but if a tail he wont lern anything, we have lost another since we came to Pariss the little Blackfaced one dyed partly the same as the other, I think we are rather unlucky in that Spetia of Animells. Now for our Journey from Calais; I was taken very ill the first night there with a viloent pain in my heart shot throw to my shoulder coud not turn in my beed, scears breath without screeming continued so 2 or 3 days, but thank God now am quite well – Mr. Astley was so kind to accompany us in the carige, but I must not ask that favour anymore, for there is none in troop can be trusted to bring them to Pariss. Except John Taylor or Son he could not be spaird poor J Taylor I think he is a little cracked for he had not been in Paris a week but he packd up his alls and was going to London Kipd in his Room as if he was just come to Bedlam he sett of and lay one night at the place he was to take his carige from (which was a fish cart by the by) but the smell I suppose either turned his stomach or his reason returned so he came back I have told him what you wrote, we was much (but not agreeably) surprisd to find the nearer we came to Parys we found snow, it continued 9 days very cold indeed we could not keep our selves warm but now we can sitt without

Fire again thank God for fireing here is a dear article we burnd near 2 Guineas the first week Genl Jacio did not arrive before the 18th, and we opend the 19th it was lucky we saild when we did or we should have been weather bound many days as he was. the Strong Man is gone to Brussells for his children I dont know when he will arrive we had a poor house on Tuesday I hope our Pig will take as he performs very well. I fancy you are very busy about your little Boy – God send you boath your Healths to Enjoy it many years, pray does Mrs Smith remember to bring you some saleld as I begd of her, have you many Scholers, hope they will turn out better than they did in the Rodeing and years past.

I shall esteem it a favour you will write every opertunity you have as that will add much to my presant hapiness we go from here to Brussells in the time we wait for the park for we dont take but 14, 16 or 18 pounds a night only on the Sundays Mr. Nicolee has done all he can to hurt us he has got our tumbling taken away a way which makes it lay very hard on poor John as he does his Peasant and 2 Horses every night and his knee very bad wears him out, would to God we had to or 3 years bark taken care of our Cash and not run such lengths in Building as we might have enjoyd our selves in the Winter, but I doubt that grim looking Gentln Death will viset us before we have that comfort. Gods will be done.

Mr. Astley has made a stage to be supported by 8 Horses for them to tumble on but it is not finished yet, but we are in hopes we shall in spite of Nicoly obtain our old per mition; Mr. Hercule is not yet

arrived from Brussels. When he comes it will be a
little respite for Son expect him every day. I began
this letter the 23d bud in hopes of good news in the
schoole delayed sending it, but to no purpose so shall
conclude with all our respects
Most obedient humble Sert
at Command
P Astley
Paris Dec 4 1786

Direction
   Mr Pounell
     to be left at the
Royal Grove or Amphitheatre
   Riding House near
     West minster Bridge
        London.

The 'old per mition' was obtained and next year's bills advertised that the exercise would end with '*le Pont equestre,* sur lequel la TROUPE ROYALE fera plusieurs sauts.'

The fall of the Bastille was mirrored at Sadler's Wells and the Royal Circus in stage spectacles. To surpass these Astley went to Paris in order to buy exhibits from Dr. Curtius, whose waxworks were near the Amphitheatre. Thither, two nights before the Bastille fell, Camille Desmoulins had marched, by torchlight, with his green cockades, who had seized the busts of Necker and d'Orleans and borne them off, covered with crape, until charged by Prince Lambesc's dragoons. The doctor's niece – the future Mme. Tussaud – had had the head of de Launay, governor of the Bastille, brought to

ASTLEY'S ACROBATS IN PARIS
From *The Memoirs Of J. Decastro, Comedian*, 1824

her after it had paraded the streets on a pike; also the head of Provost Flesselles, which had been seized as a trophy after he had been shot dead on his way to trial. Astley bought the wax heads of de Launay and Flesselles she had moulded, as well as a few uniforms.

With these he hoped to challenge *The Triumph Of Liberty; or, The Destruction Of The Bastille*, at the Royal Circus, with *Paris In An Uproar; or, The Destruction Of The Bastile* [*sic*]. But while his rivals mounted their drama handsomely, with a popular actor[1] in the leading part and sentiments 'congenial to the lovers of liberty' for him to utter, Astley turned his Amphitheatre into a curiosity shop, with a Grand Model of Paris covering the whole of the stage, and a great to-do over 'The Uniform of the Governor, Major, Garde Criminelle and Garde Francoise; Emblems of Liberty, etc., taken on the spot.' When the assault came to be delivered in his arena, all that spectators had to feast their eyes upon was a scene-shifter carrying a finger-post inscribed, 'This is a draw-bridge.'

At the outbreak of war in 1792, Astley assisted in the embarkation of cavalry mounts at Deptford and Greenwich. Then, arranging to lease the Amphitheatre to his son for seven years, he rejoined the 15th[2] as a volunteer

[1] Henry Dubois, the hero, was played by John Palmer until he was sent to Bridewell for speaking prose on the stage, through information laid against him by Covent Garden and Drury Lane. Barratt, another Adonis, took his place, and was imprisoned too. The stage-manager stepped into their shoes unsuccessfully, for public emotions over the French Revolution had changed. When *Champs De Mars* was put on, houses began to thin, and legal pressure prevented further encroachment upon the rights of the Theatres Royal.

[2] It was in the 15th Light Dragoons that Coleridge enlisted as Silas Tomkyn Comberback, on December 4th, 1793.

in time for their charge at Ribecourt on August 7th, 1793. By a dexterous manœuvre he recovered a gun taken by the French. When presented by the Duke of York with the four horses that drew it, he put them up to auction, and with the purchase price bought wine for the troops.

The next year, he heard that Astley's had been burned to the ground. The Duke of York gave him leave of absence, as the escort of Prince Ernest to London, and a letter recommending him to the Queen's notice as a bold soldier. Astley fulfilled his commission, then hastened to Westminster Bridge, where only a charred desolation remained of all his glories. Within seven months, Astley's New Amphitheatre of Arts reopened on Easter Monday, 1795, which was just before the return of the Duke of York's expedition. To welcome his comrades, Astley placed rows of seats by the orchestra so that soldiers could see his *Siege of Valenciennes*, free of charge. When the King and the Duke of York were on their way back from witnessing the disembarkation of troops after the Peace of Amiens, he wore his uniform, sat his charger at the Amphitheatre's doors, and saluted in high military style.

'Who is that, Frederick?' the King asked the Duke, who answered, 'Mr. Astley, Sir, one of our good friends, a veteran of the German war.'

The King made a 'courteous assent' to Astley, which so flattered him that for a long time he would say to all he knew, 'My Sovereign did me the honour to bow to me; what d'you think of that, my dear boy?'

After a successful autumn, Astley went to Dublin. On the way home, he stopped at the Theatre Royal,

Liverpool, then owned by John Philip Kemble. When the accounts were made up, he found that deadheads entered by showing silver tickets.

'What, silver tickets, Adams?' he asked. 'My baker don't give me a loaf for nothing, nor my butcher a joint of meat for nothing. But don't stop 'em. Let 'em come in. I'll have 'em accounted for.'

The great Kemble called for his rent. Astley pretended not to know him until told his name. Then he made a show of professional equality and fraternity.

'Oh, brother! I suppose you want your money? Take a chair. You shall have it. Now, Mr. Adams, deduct the silver tickets, and now, brother, I suppose you have no objection to take a bill at sight for a week.'

Kemble majestically exclaimed, 'What? D'you think you are dealing with your horses?'

Astley was ready with an answer, 'Damn me, sir, and d'ye think you are playing Richard the Third with me?' He won the day.

There was another enemy to be confounded. Rees, a mimic at Sadler's Wells, promised a Learned Dissertation on 'This Here Little Horse, That There Great Man, Fiddles And Other Wind Instruments.' Young Astley threatened to use a horsewhip if his father were held up to ridicule, and took a box at the theatre that night as a warning. Rees, with apologies, omitted the 'Learned Dissertation.' As large numbers had attended for the express purpose of hearing it, there was a riot. In court the next day, Rees blamed young Astley, but had to be satisfied with a promise of the law's protection against a horsewhipping. Old Astley thanked the Wells' management for protecting what was 'as dear to him as to every description of Britons, namely, reputation and character.'

Now that it was not required by Astley, the Dublin Amphitheatre Royal was occupied by the combined companies of Benjamin Handy and William Davis. Towards the end of 1797 the company, including the wife and infant son of Davis, and Handy's daughter, the Child of Promise, left Liverpool in the *Viceroy* packet with twenty horses aboard. The old crazy vessel was gunnel deep when she got under way, and she was not heard of again; not a soul was saved, nor a vestige of the wreck discovered. Handy and Davis, joining forces with Crossman and Parker, formed another company. They bought a half share of the management of the Amphitheatre at Westminster Bridge. The other half was taken over by John Astley.

Thus relieved of the cares of management, Philip went to Paris and boldly asked compensation for the use his Amphitheatre had been put to. Napoleon's Ministers gave him possession of the building with the sum due as rent. Peace was short-lived. Napoleon suddenly laid an embargo on all ports and made Englishmen prisoners-of-war. Astley 'shammed Abraham,' bribed a doctor to certify that he needed to take the waters at Montpelier, obtained a passport, and set out on the journey with two of his nieces. Once there he contrived to remove to Piedmont. He took to driving in a chaise for his health. As soon as he was able to travel far from the town, he drew a brace of pistols and forced the postilion to make with all speed for the frontier. He escaped down the Main to the Rhine, and so to Holland. There he heard that his wife had died.

Also that his Amphitheatre had again been burned down.

On September 1st, 1803, sparks from fireworks had fallen on tow in the lamp room. Shortly before dawn the next morning the whole building was in flames. There was only time to save the horses. John Astley's old mother-in-law, once a stylish singer and now engaged at Hercules Hall in looking after the takings, came to a window but could not open it; neither could the first man to climb the ladder placed against the sill. While he slid down she made signs that she was going back into the house, perhaps to fetch the money. A thrust from the ladder's prongs shattered the glass and woodwork. Her face was seen, a patch of white amid blackness. That moment the floor fell in and she was lost in the hail of sparks and flame. The fire spread. About forty neighbouring houses, inhabited by poor people, were burned down and the Amphitheatre completely destroyed. It was two days later that Wordsworth, passing over Westminster Bridge, was inspired to write:

> This city now doth like a garment wear
> The beauty of the morning, silent, bare,
> Ships, towers, domes, theatres and temples lie
> Open unto the fields and to the sky,
> All bright and glittering in the smokeless air.

To Astley the only theatre that mattered lay only too open[1] to the sky, and his prospects had been rendered

---

[1] Wordsworth's oversight was made good by the authors of *Rejected Addresses* in their travesty of Fitzgerald:

> Base Bonaparte, fill'd with deadly ire,
> Sets, one by one, our playhouses on fire.
> Some years ago he pounced with deadly glee on
> The Opera House, then burnt down the Pantheon;

far from bright and glittering by his son's insuring a building worth £30,000 for £5,000. Yet he at once began to rebuild. Early or late, in rain, frost, or snow, he drilled the labourers as though training recruits for a winter's campaign, and crowds, including many people of note, came to applaud. When the new Amphitheatre opened on the Easter Monday of 1804, it was judged 'the handsomest pleasure haunt in London.' Though the front was unimposing – a wooden portico built over the pavement, sheltering doors which led to a passage into the pit and a plain staircase to the boxes – the interior was luxurious. At the top of the stairs was a lobby, sixty feet wide, with a 'large and handsome patent stove in the centre,' seats around the walls and a fruit room to stack crates of oranges behind. As the backs of the boxes were only five feet high, loungers could view the house, lit by a huge chandelier containing fifty patent lamps, a present from the Duke of York. Below was the ring of sawdust and tan, separated by the orchestra from the largest stage then known. Thus the spectator would consider himself to be in the finest theatre London could boast. Actually, it was a mere temple of showmanship, all outward seeming and very little inward worth. Ships' masts and spars had played far too large a part in the building. That handsome

---

> Nay, still unsated, in a coat of flames,
> Next at Millbank he cross'd the river Thames;
> Thy hatch, O Halfpenny! pass'd in a trice,
> Boil'd some black pitch, and burnt down Astley's twice;
> Then buzzing on through ether with a vile hum,
> Turn'd to the left hand, fronting the Asylum,
> And burnt the Royal Circus in a hurry –
> ('Twas call'd the Circus then, but now the Surrey).

ceiling was put together like a scaffold. Being merely canvas framed on fir poles, which were lashed together with ropes and tenpenny nails, the problem to every architect in London was why it did not fall. The memory of two fires did not make Old Astley over-concerned with the possibility of a third – and there was to be a third, though not in his lifetime.

By now his ambition could be dubbed vaulting in more senses than one. As his Lambeth headquarters were still compelled by law to close for the winter, he wanted an Amphitheatre across the river in Westminster, the Lord Chamberlain's domain. In Lambeth he could obtain only a magistrate's licence for summer performances; in Westminster a royal licence would allow winter performances. Using the Duke of York's letter, Astley appealed to Queen Charlotte, who directed the Lord Chamberlain to grant one. All he had to do now was build a theatre – a simple task to a man of his experience. The only snare lay in Astley's character. By this time he had developed a Napoleonic passion for tackling what to normal eyes seemed impossible.

'I am no man of straw, Sir!' he would say in an argument whether the statement applied or not, 'I have fought and bled for my country, and my King has rewarded me for it.'

And so, believing all things would yield to his command, he set about his new task in a spirit of defiance towards fate. The spot he chose, after a great deal of running over the town, was unshaped and unshapable, everything but square, round, or oval, a mangled star with points of almost every angle. The frontage was a gate in Wych Street where Hudson's House had stood, flanked by buildings which had to be propped together but the larger space was the site of Craven House, called the Queen of Bohemia's[1] Palace. Astley took a lease from Lord Craven for sixty-one years at a yearly rental of £100; he agreed to spend £2,500 in building, but reduced the sum by appointing himself his own designer and architect, and collecting his workmen from a tavern. The Olympic Pavilion was to be its name, because of its likeness to a tent. The roof was a conoid, covered with squares of block tin to 'cause a strong vibration of sound in the music.' The outside was canvased over, pitched, and tarred; inside the timbers, roof, and rafters showed.

The clearing of the ground began in the September of 1805. Day after day Astley sat in his one-horse curricle which had been constructed to fit his figure, now very corpulent, so closely that he looked like a prebendary in his stall. In February his funds gave out. On meeting the clerk of the works one Saturday night, he said, 'Let me ask you, Sir, this – if a man knocks at your front door and another at the back, at once and the same time, can you answer both at once?'

'No,' said the clerk.

'I thought not, Sir; no more can I,' said Astley. As he pulled out a little bag, and handed the clerk some tarnished guineas, tears welled into his eyes – the money

[1] For whose wedding festivities Shakespeare re-shaped *The Tempest* and from whom British Sovereigns are descended. The site is, roughly, that of the north portico of Bush House, Aldwych. 'Q' has told how Lord Craven, a Lord Mayor's son, 'having poured blood and money in her service, laid his last wealth at her feet to provide her a stately refuge and a home.'

was from a hoard so zealously guarded during former tribulations that he deemed it a sacrilegious offence to break into it now.

The Pavilion was opened on September 8th, 1806. Its seating arrangements took the public by surprise. To save space the orchestra sat in the stage-boxes, like one royal party fiddling the other, and the gallery, at the back of the pit, was a dungeon behind an iron grating, through which the crowd, like the untamed animals in Cross's menagerie at Exeter Change in the Strand, caught what they could, which was little enough. For equestrian displays part of the stage had to be included in the ride. There was no room for stables, and the horses had to enter by the stage-door. These preparations took a long time at each performance. Yet Astley's new venture was mildly successful for a year or two and he was able to foster horsemanship instead of trick-riding. He arranged, in particular, a country dance by eight horses. When 'strongly requested' to give some explanation of its utility, he sent a letter to the *Morning Chronicle*, explaining 'such noble exercises.' He conceived that 'the horseman may be greatly improved when in the act of reducing the horse to obedience on scientific principles ! ! ! and not otherwise,' and because a knowledge of the *appui* in horsemanship was highly desirable, he had expressly composed the various figures in the country dance for this desirable purpose, and called it *L'École De Mars*. The knell of 'such noble exercises' was rung in 1811 when Davis and others of the Amphitheatre Company went with their horses to perform in the equestrian version of *Blue Beard* at Covent Garden.

To check this fashion in mounted melodramas, Old

Astley planned to make his stage strong enough by means of massive uprights and joists, to bear 'a hundred horses if necessary.' Hearing that the *Ville de Paris* – Admiral Cornwallis's flagship at the blockade of Brest – was being broke in the yards, he bought her timbers and the 'Wheel de Parrey,' as he called her, raised the height of the Olympic so that the gallery could be where galleries are meant to be. In order to create a 'commodious pit,' he filled the arena with benches, and by an ingenious contrivance made the stage serve for a ring as well. Every time horsemanship was to be exhibited, sixteen large and heavy flaps had to be hoisted up by tackle in order to disclose the ride which was two feet lower. This not only caused prolonged 'stage waits,' but, even when the manœuvre had been completed, only one horse could enter at a time.

It was his first experience of failure; when he closed the Olympic Pavilion he had lost £10,000. But he had a theatre, and, what was still more valuable, a licence, and these he could sell. That hot-headed, impulsive actor, Elliston, swallowed the bait. The very morning he heard the news he was under the lintel of Hercules Hall. 'Father Philip,' with a great show of surprise, listened to the suitor's proposal. In the language of a fond parent, he replied that as he was certainly descending into the vale of years, he felt a natural anxiety to see his child well settled before he died, and should not be deaf to any honourable proposal which might be made for the hand of his little pet. 'For,' he said, 'it is verily my own flesh and blood.' By such eloquence Elliston was induced to pay Astley £2,800 and an annuity of twenty pounds contingent on the continuance of the licence. Elliston lost his licence a few weeks after he opened the 'Little Drury Lane Theatre' as a burletta-house in 1813.

That was the end of Astley's labours. He went to Paris and lived in his old home in the Rue du Temple. He wanted to be cured of a phlegmatic disorder, but he was now seventy-two, and his ailment increased. On the night of October 20th, 1814, he 'left this world as peaceful as a lamb.' They buried him in Père Lachaise, without much mourning. His nature was too crusty for the making of friends, or even the cherishing of his own kith and kin – among his papers they found doggerel verses expressing very unfriendly sentiments towards his wife and his son. Barely one of the many writers who mention him speak of him feelingly. Yet they reveal respect, all the more strongly because unwillingly or unconsciously, for him who was 'no man of straw.'

Should his achievements seem less than prodigious, compare his career with the failure of one who was bred to showmanship by a father who had exhibited feats of activity on horseback half-way through the eighteenth century. Abraham Saunders, born in 1748, was handsome of face and figure, and alert both as rider and *voltigeur*.[1] After his father's death he gave varied entertainments that included at one time 'Master Carey, the Pupil of Nature,' whose other name was Edmund Kean. By such means Saunders raised funds to buy a

[1] In the riding-schools *voltige* was the term for the more agile forms of horsemanship. In the ring *voltigeur* applies to trick-riders, tumblers, and funambulists who leap. But as English dictionaries give only its military sense, namely 'skirmishers,' the *voltigeur* seems to be losing his name as thoroughly as the *desultor*, the Roman rider who leapt from horse to horse and so supplied us with the word 'desultory.'

troop of horses, became rich, and installed his company at the Royalty, Whitechapel, until it was burned down. That was the first of a series of disasters. While his horses and men were crossing to Dublin, the ship foundered in a storm and all were lost. Saunders himself was transporting the Royal Hanoverian Creams[1] across the St. George's Channel for the visit of George IV to Ireland, and landed them safely.

During his heyday he was celebrated for his eccentric temper. If any member of his company displeased him at rehearsal, he would fling a handful of gold and silver at the offender, shouting, 'Damn you, take that.' He was proud of his daughter, gave her an education 'fit for a lady,' and would never let her perform: a girl so gently reared, he boasted, would make people walk up by merely standing in front of his booth. He recovered from one evil day only to be ruined again by bad speculations. His stud was sold by auction, and himself boxed in the Fleet. After his release he tried to earn a living in a penny-gaff, only to have it closed by the police; he opened a penny theatre at Haggerston, and was summoned to appear before a magistrate at Worship Street. The poor old man, now in his ninetieth year, was wearing a skin when he drove to the court in a little box on wheels, drawn by a shelty. He lived in Mill Street, Lambeth Walk, until his death, in 1839, at the age of ninety-one. After amusing the public for three-quarters of a century, he was unknown and a pauper.

[1] Hanoverian Creams drew the Royal Coach until replaced by British bays from the time of the Great War onwards. There are creams from the royal stud in Sanger's Circus.

4

Horses As Actors

I<small>N</small> between the exit of one great character and the entrance of another, interest in a play usually flags. That will not happen here once you are conscious of the dominance of an unseen spirit, for its manifestations become more fantastic and bizarre in the years when it is left to its own devices. And what devices these were ! Melodrama, which was conquering the legitimate theatres, took on fresh monstrosity of shapes south of Westminster Bridge, where it was born[1] at the Royal Circus, under the influence of gaudily jerry-built romance.

It is plainly the spirit of the place which is responsible now. If you look for any human guidance of its destiny, you will have difficulty in discerning it among those who attended the reading of Philip Astley's Will. Hannah, his daughter-in-law, with her sense of the stage and golden hair – there is a snippet of it in an

---

[1] The term 'melodrama' was imported a few years later from Paris, where the theatrical situation was strangely similar. The Boulevard du Temple was the French equivalent of Lambeth in its entertainments. The Amphithéâtre Anglais was there, and *mélo-drame* was born on the stage of one of its rivals.

Astley scrapbook at the British Museum – would have known how to take the centre of that tableau of grief. The Misses Gill, who had been his close companions, were plain girls, who sobbed in private and gave way to sorrow in the solicitor's presence with nothing more than a sniff. John Astley asserted himself even less than they did, and less than his partners, William Davis, with his two sons, and Parker, with his wife, who was to become famous as a veteran Columbine. Philip Astley, in leaving the whole of his interest in the Amphitheatre to his son, directed that should John die without issue, then Hannah Waldo Astley would inherit only a sixteenth, and the rest would become the property of the Gills. Hardly a spark of Philip Astley's fire could be kindled in his son. The English Rose might draw his life from the stables, but he was weary of the ordure and longed to grace the drawing-room. Hercules Hall, next door to the Amphitheatre, was not grand enough for the Astley of Astley's now. He had an estate in Surrey. There, while all his partners except Davis were amassing fortunes for their retirement, he piled up debts.

Venerating Astley and the things that were Astley's, Davis took particular care of the Little Learned Military Horse, now very advanced in years but none the worse for the ups and downs of his career. Having been lent, as an act of kindness, to Saunders just before that showman was seized for debt and boxed in the Fleet, Billy was included in the stud when it was sold in lots to the highest bidders. For three years he drew a cart for a tradesman, who called him Mountebank because he cut such odd capers. One day two of Astley's horsemen,

MRS. WYBROW, THE CELEBRATED SWORDSWOMAN
From a Print in the Author's Collection

DELPINI 'SHOOTING AT THE SPANIARDS'
From *Clowns And Pantomimes*, 1925

thinking they recognised him, clicked the nails of thumb and forefinger, which was his signal for counting pence or telling the time. As Billy pricked up his ears and curvetted, they paid for him and took him home. Even in his old age he would still 'ungirt his own saddle, wash his feet in a pail of water, fetch and carry a complete tea equipage, take a kettle of boiling water off a flaming fire, and act like a waiter at a tea gardens.' Occasionally, he was ridden by Davis when demonstrating the *piaffe*, to the tune of *Nancy Dawson*, while surrounded by blazing fireworks. In time Billy lost his teeth and had to be fed on soaked bread. When he died, at the age of forty-two, his hide was made into the thunderdrum on the prompt side at Astley's. Long before then others had been trained to dance the cotillion, walk on their knees, lay down, sit up, fetch and carry, tell the hour of the day, jump on a table, climb a ladder, and unsaddle themselves.

The only interest John took in horsemanship was forced upon him by his wife. She had some of her father-in-law's spirit – though vanity was the sole source of her energy. With her heart set upon acting, she enviously watched the career at the Royal Circus of Mrs. Wybrow, celebrated on the stage for cutting and slashing with the broadsword, and off the stage for her versatile love affairs, since she had, after ceasing to be kept by Lord Craven, taken four husbands. As a manager's wife, Hannah demanded scope to display her skill and graces on the stage in spectacles like those arranged at the Royal Circus by that ingenious clown Delpini. There the orchestra was bridged at both ends so that horses, leopards, tigers, and other beasts could draw the cars of Europe, Asia, Africa, and America from the stage to the ring and back again. When the Royal Circus turned its arena into a pit, and amazed the public with wordless but stirring melodramas, she coveted the apparatus of battles, sieges, burnings, sudden deaths, and last-minute rescues amid tempest, fire, and flood. Consequently, *The Fatal Pile; or, Virtue Revenged*, with the exact ceremony which takes place on the installation of a knight, and *The Siege And Storming Of Seringapatam; or, The Death Of Tippoo Sahib*, with elephants and camels, were seen at Astley's.

Stage spectacles at both houses during these years are important because in them can be traced the origin of that hybrid of circus and theatre, the equestrian drama. At first the sole aim was to dodge the monopoly of the patent theatres, Covent Garden and Drury Lane. While careful not to break the law that forbade any performance with spoken words not set to music, the Royal Circus presented performances in dumb-show, intermingled with songs and musical recitative. When declarations were necessary, one character would hold up a scroll. Thus, 'THE ENEMY IS BRITISH AND WILL DIE OR CONQUER' was shown to Blackbeard, the pirate, who cringed; to the audience, who cheered; to the captive princess, who refrained from precipitating herself into the sea; and again to Blackbeard, who, on second thoughts, became defiant. Or a more tender situation would be signalised by the display by a lover to his beloved of the statement, written with his blood, 'I SWEAR TO BE THINE.' The plot had to be wildly exciting in order to be clear to the meanest intelligence. That is why horses became actors.

During a grand tournament William Davis's Turk reared and tore down a streaming banner with his teeth. During a storm his Wonderful War Horse, attacked by a lion, breathed forth fire. 'Torrents of real fire,' it was advertised, would issue from its nostrils, ears, and every part of its body.

Incidentally, these performances explain Keats's vow[1] to unbar the gates of his pride and let his 'condescension stalk forth like a Ghost at a Circus.' Ghosts were rare in circuses, but one to fit this reference walked at the Royal Circus in *Halloween; or, The Castles Of Athlin And Dunbayne*, a New Grand Scotch Spectacle by J. C. Cross, the description of which is in *Circusiana*, published 1809. Malcolm, murderous baron of Dunbayne, strikes the rock over his victim's grave. Blood issues from it and crimsons his sword, whereupon the recitative he has been singing continues:

> Well – Athlin – thee I murdered ! and dare brave
> These throes of Conscience ! I thy Pride abhorr'd !
> And could thy form, in arms, stalk from its grave,
> Again I'd meet thee with my blood stain'd sword.

Stalks past the Rock – thunder – the sky is darkened – the Rock opens, and a figure in complete armour appears, pointing to his blood-stained wounds – Malcolm starts, terror struck.

VOICES HEARD in the AIR

> Foul Murderer ! beware – beware !
> Blood will have blood – thy Lot's despair !

The armour drops from the figure, and a skeleton appears – Malcolm shudders, reclines on Edric; who, from alarm, seems scarcely able to support himself – the skeleton sinks.

---

[1] In a letter to Jane and Mariane Reynolds in the September of 1817.

It was such melodrama as this, and not Davis's skill in horse-training, that enthralled Hannah Astley. When the Royal Circus was burned down in 1805, its sign of Pegasus disappearing in flames before a vaster audience than the entertainment had ever brought together, she claimed this to be their opportunity. Melodramas henceforth were regularly acted on the stage at Astley's. They were separated from the horsemanship until the summer of 1806, when Mrs. Astley appeared in *The Fair Slave; or, The Moors And The Africans*, on the subject of Mungo Park's travels. There were views of towns, rivers, forests, plantations, a floating bridge over the Black River, and a Moorish encampment, nightly destroyed. There was also a procession of 'camels and real horses,' with Mrs. Astley as the fair slave in the midst. The same programme included *The Polish Tyrant; or, The Woman Of Ten Thousand*, with Mrs. Astley as the woman of ten thousand.

During the winter season of 1806–7 a company headed by Davis, Mrs. Parker leading lady, performed at the Olympic Pavilion. For the opening of the summer season, John Astley engaged them at the Amphitheatre to test a new invention for dividing the stage into platforms which could be raised or sunk to varying levels, and crossed by a 'Devil's Bridge' so that horses could be put to more elaborate use. He wrote *The Brave Cossack; or, Perfidy Punished* to exploit the new machinery. Unfortunately for his domestic peace, the leading female character, Balsora, was not a heroine but a temptress. Mrs. Astley refused the part: Mrs. Parker, originally engaged as a stop-gap 'for 24 nights only,' accepted it. The plot told a tale of treachery –

against Mr. Hengler as Prince Polotinska – and vengeance that led to such 'tremendous warfare' that it became the topic of the day. Among the spectators was Lady Bessborough, who wrote to Lord Granville:

> Think of my going to Astley's last night. There is a battle on the stage with real horses galloping full speed, and fighting to a beautiful white light like day dawn that is quite beautiful and like one of Bourgignon's pictures animated.

Gratifying as the chorus of praise was to John Astley's pride of authorship, it did not please Mrs. Astley at all. She insisted that *The Brave Cossack* should end; and the bills of June gave out that while Mr. Astley begged leave to return his sincere thanks to the admiring numbers who had assisted 'the present Exercises, Pantomimes, etc.,' he had to withdraw the piece because of 'the multiplicity of appropriate Machinery.' The lame excuse failed. Each of the many times *The Brave Cossack* was withdrawn, it had to be brought back again; and each time the bills advertised 'Mrs. Astley, whose performance in the popular pantomime of *The Fair Slave; or, Moors And Africans* has given such universal satisfaction,' the date of her rival's next appearance had to be named. *The Brave Cossack* was called for directly the Amphitheatre's season opened in 1808, and for two years afterwards. It was not forgotten until *The Blood Red Knight*, staged in 1810, ran for 175 nights and brought the proprietors a profit of £18,000. The plot was simpler, turning on nothing more than the attempts of the Blood Red Knight to seduce Isabella, wife of his brother, Alphonso, the Crusader. Alphonso returns, is defeated once or twice, and calls in the soldiery when, to quote the promise of the play-bills:

> The Castle is taken by Storm, the surrounding river is covered with Boats filled with Warriors, while the Battlements are strongly contested by the Horse and Foot Guards. Men and Horses are portrayed slain and dying in various Directions, while other Soldiers and Horses are emerged in the River, forming an effect totally new and unprecedented in this or any Country whatever, and terminating in the Total DEFEAT OF THE BLOOD-RED KNIGHT.

It was also the defeat of Mrs. Parker, who was merely Columbine in the after-piece, while Mrs. Astley played Isabella. Henceforth John Astley had to write many melodramas with his wife as the heroine, himself as the lover, and the Sagacious Elephant[1] or other animal to keep the interest alive.

That figure of £18,000 inspired the managers of Covent Garden to enlist the aid of John Astley and Davis in reviving Colman's *Blue Beard*, with unequalled splendour, as an equestrian drama to match Sister Ann's cry from the look-out:

---

[1] They set a fashion which affected Keats while he was at work on *Otho The Great*. In a letter of 1819 he wrote, 'We are thinking of introducing an Elephant, but have not historical reference within reach to determine us as to Otho's Menagerie. When Brown first mentioned this I took it as a joke; however, he brings such plausible reasons, and discourses so eloquently upon the dramatic effect that I am giving it a serious consideration.' Twenty years later horses, lions, and tigers were still 'esteemed the worthy successors of Garrick, Kemble, and Kean,' the biographer of 'Monk' Lewis records, and to ensure success a dramatist had only 'to introduce a stage-coach, a live bull, or any other absurdity into his piece.'

I see them galloping, they're spurring on amain !
Now faster galloping, they skim along the plain.

Sixteen beautiful horses, mounted by spahis, suddenly appeared before the spectators, and were seen ascending the heights with 'inconceivable velocity.' In the charge, some of the horses appeared to be wounded, and fainted gradually away. One, who in the anguish of his wounds had thrown off his rider and was dying on the field, sprang suddenly to his feet, on hearing the report of a pistol, as if again to join the battle, and then fell exhausted.

This 'splendid novelty' was declared by *The Dramatic Censor* to be a black epoch for ever. Another critic, stating that the dressing-rooms of the 'new comedians' were under the orchestra, complained that in the first row of the pit the stench was so abominable 'one might as well have sitten in a stable.' But the equestrian drama had come to stay. 'Monk' Lewis (nicknamed after his novel, *Ambrosio; or, The Monk*) wrote Covent Garden's next example, *Timour The Tartar*, which prospered despite hisses and the raising in the pit of placards denouncing the horses. Lewis rightly attributed its success 'above all to the favour with which the horses were received by the Public,' for his story of the long-lost shepherd's son who returns to his native land as a ruthless Tartar chieftan, was too involved to be exciting on its own account. To Davis belonged the chief credit. He won the author's admiration by the way he made a horse obey him, not by using whip or spur, but by steadfastly fixing his eye upon it and then exclaiming in a terrible voice, and with the most horrible contortions of face, 'Ha ! What – will you *dare* – will you *dare* ?' till it trembled. The leading lady also owed to Davis her triumph as an Amazon on a bespangled courser. When African boys in golden chains prostrated themselves and had a cloth flung over them, the courser knelt for her to step upon this human footstool, then paid its homage and withdrew.

Few players are so highly commended by *Biographia Dramatica* as this horse. 'He knelt, he leaped, he tumbled, he danced, he fought, he dashed into water and up precipices in a very superior style of acting.' Others who fought and died also 'climbed up walls perpendicular, or scampered longitudinally, and leaped through breaches with the greatest ingenuity.' After praising the fine compound of cataract and castle at the close, the critic tells how the heroine, threatened by Timour on the battlements, glided from his hand and sprang from a height, 'which really appeared too perilous to give pleasure to the spectators.' When her son rode into the torrent to save her, they rose from canvas wave to canvas wave and ascended the cataract on horseback.

Equestrian spectacles became so feverish a craze that Colman, as guilty an author as any, satirised them in *The Quadrupeds Of Quedlinburgh*; *or*, *The Rovers Of Weimer*, at the Haymarket:

> Dear Johnny Bull, you boast much resolution
> With, thanks to heaven, a glorious constitution,
> Your taste, recovered half from foreign quacks,
> Takes airings now on English horses' backs,
> While every modern bard may raise his name,
> If not on lasting praise, on stable fame.

At Astley's after Wellington's Peninsular Campaign had been celebrated in 1812 with *The Siege And Capture Of Badajoz*, and *The Battle Of Salamanca*, Napoleon's Russian Campaign was celebrated with a revival of *The Brave Cossack*, because Mrs. Astley wanted to play the leading part – Mrs. Parker won fame elsewhere, for at Covent Garden she played Columbine until she was old enough to be Columbine's grandmother. Parker himself had had enough of the stage. In 1817 he retired from Astley's with a handsome fortune in order to settle down on an estate in Norfolk. John Astley and William Davis, on renewing their partnership, invested their fortunes to the greater glory of the equestrian drama, and the stage was again enlarged in mechanical scope. By a contrivance which drew back the flanking doors and the proprietors' boxes over them, as well as the frame of the proscenium, the opening was increased to sixty feet. Across the back of the stage, massive platforms on floors, rising above each other, extended from wings to wings in the guise of battlements, heights, bridges, and mountains. Over them horsemen could gallop and skirmish, or a carriage, equal in size and weight to a mail coach, could be driven. Yet they could be 'placed and removed, in a short space of time.'

Among the first pieces written to suit the new conditions was *Peregrine Pickle; or, Hawser Trunnion On Horseback*, in 1818. On that stage, Commodore Trunnion and Mrs. Grizzle went to the church to be married, their horses joined in the pursuit of the fox, and hounds followed in full cry until the fox clung to a sack of flour as it was drawn up to a mill. In 1819 Astley's contrived to open the winter and was let to

W. Barrymore, a manager with a remarkable flow of language. His season was noteworthy for the first appearance of Dick Turpin in the ring. He was played by Bradbury, a clown famous for throwing himself about in violent falls and tumbles.

Since she had little of her father-in-law's dislike for a life lacking in the zest of rivalry, Hannah was now content: her husband was exhausted. In common with many who began life as infant prodigies, he was burned out in middle age. The doctor diagnosed liver complaint, and ordered him abroad. They left for France in the summer of 1821. The tired, ageing Apollo of Marie Antoinette's Court was drawn to Paris, though it was no longer the city of his memories. On the Boulevard du Temple, noisier now and more concerned with dramas of crime than with feats of activity, the name of Franconi had blotted out all trace of Astley. Another revolution was preparing, but there were no heads as lovely as those of old for the guillotine. John Astley, aged beyond his years, tottered across the lawns of Versailles where once he seemed to fly. Even if ladies-in-waiting had come again to the terrace, they would not have looked his way. Paris was hard, forgetful, but he could not leave. He went to his father's house among the booths of the mountebanks, climbed the creaking stair, where the clown's cries to the crowds on the boulevard beat against the windows, and entered the room where his father had ended his life. There, in the same bed, he died on October 19th, 1821, and was buried close to his father's grave in Père Lachaise. On the stone his wife had the words inscribed, 'The Once Rose Of Paris.'

Davis, who had attended him in his last illness, helped Hannah to face his debts, which amounted to £8,000. When the creditors met, he promised to pay her two-fifths of the profits, which had been her husband's share. His thrift was evident in the equestrian drama of that season. In *The Secret Mine* Russian duck trousers and short black gaiters from *The Brave Cossack* were worn in all the processions, especially on the legs of Persians. But Davis laboured in vain. Hannah wanted to play heroines as before. He questioned her age, and all his good offices were forgotten in an instant. Henceforth there could only be war between them. Hannah went to the Gills and made complaint of Davis's arrogance in changing the title of Astley's Royal Amphitheatre to 'Davis's Royal Amphitheatre.' They made common cause with her against him.

To protect himself rather than for revenge, Davis applied at Kingston Sessions in the spring of 1822 for the renewal of the licence to be made out in his name only. Mrs. Astley attended, in deep mourning, to oppose the change. Pointing at her the finger of scorn, counsel said that at an early period of her widowhood she had appeared all in white, and accused her of 'playing off before the Bench' in order to affect their feelings. But Davis argued in vain that as sole capitalist and director he was responsible for the rent of £1,000 per annum and for all the labours of management; in vain he mentioned his forty years' association with the Amphitheatre; in vain he asked for permission to remove his belongings so that he should be exonerated from responsibility during the remaining period of the contended lease; in vain he swore that he only wished to be rid of the whole concern and her. The Bench granted the licence in the joint names of Astley and Davis.

Money was spent freely at the Amphitheatre that season. The craze for dramatic versions of *Life in London* inspired both the Surrey – as the new Royal Circus was now called – and Sadler's Wells to mount spectacles called *Tom And Jerry*, in imitation of others on the same subject at the Olympic and the Adelphi. Davis joined the contest with yet another *Tom And Jerry*, remarkable for its scene of Epsom Races, which boasted post-chaises, gigs, tilburys, caravans, hackney coaches, carts, and four-in-hand barouches, all drawn by real horses, besides gambling tables, pickpockets, sweeps, piemen, beggars, and ballad singers. It ended with a race between seven 'Bits of Blood' on extensive platforms across the whole width of the house. The succeeding piece, *The Frozen Regions; or, The Treacherous Esquimaux*, included a real bear and two sagacious dogs. The next year, in *The High Mettled Racer; or, Harlequin On Horseback*, after a real horse race and a real fox chase, the actor of the name part suffered itself to be 'drawn up by ropes into the nacker's cart and to be shot again, without betraying the least sign of life.' Thus the equestrian drama reached the point where a horse trained by Davis could gain more glory unsaddled than when bestridden by Mrs. Astley.

At Kingston, in the spring of 1823, Davis repeated his application, but the result was the same. The next year his lease ended, but he was glad enough to renew it for a year, the licence being made out in the names of Hannah Waldo Astley, William Davis, Sophia

Elizabeth Gill, Louisa Gill, and Amelia Ann Gill. After the season of 1824 (when Philip Astley's ground lease had fifteen years to run) the name of Davis was removed from the bills for ever.

The cause of his downfall was the rise of one who had already proved his worthiness to vault into the saddle of Philip Astley. The name of this prodigy of showmanship was Andrew Ducrow.

III

'DEAR, DEAR, WHAT A PLACE IT LOOKED, THAT ASTLEY'S'

– Old Curiosity Shop

I

Andrew Ducrow

From now onwards Astley's, however firm its hold over the emotions of the masses, was to be a stock joke. Journalists, all its life long, laughed at it. Poets made game of it. Novelists sent their most simple-minded characters to it. Artists liked to take it unawares. All ridiculed it because they loved it; otherwise they would have ignored it. Gaudy, inglorious Astley's! No great actor trod your boards – not in the days that matter; no authors, except hacks, wrote dramas for you; no good thing came out of you to enliven Covent Garden or Drury Lane, but was condemned by critics in scorn. Nobody took you seriously but yourself; everybody visited you, but all who went to scoff, remained to scoff, and went away scoffing. That is what happened when you were living. Now you have vanished, all crowd eagerly round a toy theatre when one of the many of your spectacles preserved by the Juvenile Drama in 'Twopence Coloured' form, is performed – not out of sentimental yearnings for the past, but in a spirit that wishes the modern life-sized theatre could show anything like it.

Astleys might come and Astleys might go, but Astley's would go on to the day of destruction. Andrew Ducrow unpacked the whole bag of tricks and performed them as they had never been performed before. In the arena he transformed feats of activity into visions of romance, and on the stage the old horseback spectacles into 'grand military and equestrian melo-dramas,' with dialogue and songs, which were pageants expressive of honesty, chastity, chivalry, courage, self-sacrifice, and patriotism. All this was evident in *The Battle Of Waterloo*, presented throughout his first season. It was written by J. H. Amherst, an actor[1] who specialised in cowardly comic parts, and his sense of what is known in the theatre as 'character' gave guilelessness, liveliness, and heartiness to subjects which otherwise might easily have proved too grand. His technique – it might be called pyro-technique – was masterly. The amount of noise he introduced, and opportunities for picturesque limelight, could not have been increased without bewilderment.

Each act of *The Battle Of Waterloo* ended in a 'general contest' of horse and foot. In a village 'partly illuminated by the moon, partly by torch and fire light,' a peasant woman related her unspeakable wrongs to the Prussian patrols, who commented, 'It's too bad.' On the French side farriers struck sparks from anvils in the moonlight, to the refrain of 'tra la la,' before the call to arms heralded the Grand Entry of baggage, troops, staff officers, and Napoleon. At Marchienne, a trooper was dragged off with one foot in the stirrup, Prussians were rescued from drowning, and Blücher's

[1] 'Invaluable as a prompter' was one summary of his career.

CHARACTERS IN *TIMOUR THE TARTAR*
By kind permission of Mr. Pollock of the Toy Theatre Shop in Hoxton

CHARACTERS IN *THE BATTLE OF WATERLOO*
By kind permission of Mr. Pollock of the Toy Theatre Shop in Hoxton

horse was shot under him, while horse and foot did battle for the bridge.

In the English bivouac, a duet between Corporal Standfast and his Mary, disguised as a Highlander, preceded a grand review by the Duke of Wellington. Ligny went up in flames on the backcloth of Quatre Bras where the Highlanders were shot down among the corn. Blücher brought up cannon to play upon the wood where the French were taking cover, and British and Prussian colours floated triumphantly at the tableau. At 'Quatre Bras by Moonlight,' Corporal Standfast was captured; Napoleon, greatly impressed by his manly bearing, addressed him as 'Sir,' and reflected 'Yes, I may venture to trust everything to England.' Standfast, rescued by Molly Maloney (comic relief), was restored to his Mary. In Mont St. Jean the Guards beat off the attack before Napoleon took to flight amid a volley of Roman candles.

These flames were more crimson, these moons more blue, and these anvils more metallic than any ever seen inside a circus before. Andrew Ducrow could make Bengal lights burn more brightly and gunpowder smell more strongly, than in any play not mounted by a 'greatest showman on earth.' His upbringing had ensured that. As a child he dared all things and endured all things for the sake of the show. His father was the Flemish Hercules who leaped through a hoop of fire at the Royal Circus in 1793. Andrew, born in the Nag's Head, Southwark High Street, on October 10th that year, was an Infant Hercules at the age of four. The next year he was balanced on a slackrope, with orders to stay there or be thrashed. The year after he was sent to Astley's for training in horsemanship. Then Peter Ducrow hired a company and went to Bath, where Andrew earned the nick-name of 'The Little Blackguard.'

All the people living in or near the public house where the acrobats and horsemen lodged believed the frail, sickly boy to be possessed of a devil. In spite of having to practise his feats of trick-riding daily, and to take his part in building their crazy amphitheatre in Bathwick Fields at the bottom of the road, the infant prodigy was never too tired to torment all mankind. The only one spared was Miss Saunders, who had joined them when her father was seized for debt. Being released from his wish to make a lady of her, she jilted the very rich merchant whose suit he had urged, plighted her troth to a vaulter, and was now helping to feather their nest by gracing old Peter's show. Andrew worshipped her, as only a cockney street-urchin can worship, because she was all that existed in his world to still an aching, urgent need of romance. Most of the day he was unworthy of her, but performances changed all that. In his pallor and best Sunday clothes, he knew he might be mistaken for her equal; he did, in fact, suggest to simple-minded spectators who lived not too near, an angel child, not altogether of this world. The pair drew such crowds that Peter Ducrow was satisfied when he locked up his takings, picked up his *chambrière*, and walked to the ring. He was too pleased to notice that Andrew was ardently admiring Miss Saunders's ankles whenever they showed beneath her long skirts as she pirouetted on her horse. Not being checked by a cut from the whip, he overbalanced, fell badly, and could not rise. Peter dashed forwards with a heartbroken cry. No arms but his should pick up his boy and carry him from the ring; no others should be allowed to tend him. Father and child vanished behind a canvas flap, and then there were screams; Peter was horsewhipping the little blackguard for breaking his leg.

When they came back to London in 1807, William Davis engaged them. But Davis had two sons of his own, both horsemen, and his chief reason for keeping Andrew at Astley's was to restrain him from making a name elsewhere. 'Ducrow' was not printed on the bills no matter how powerful might be the Flemish curses. 'Herculean Equilibriums' alone signified their share in the entertainment until they took their benefit in the last week of the season. In the midst of a programme consisting of *The Brave Cossack*, a sketch, a song, horsemanship, and a pantomime, the Ducrows showed what they could do. Besides dancing on the tightrope, Andrew performed the Polander's[1] equilibriums with ladder, table, and chair, and Peter supported on his hands and feet a stage of boards which bore ten persons.

Before Andrew was eighteen, the time came for Peter to take his ease. When they went on tour, he merely haggled over terms for Andrew's performance at theatres. At Edinburgh the great Dr. Bartlett, lecturer in anatomy, was deeply interested. His pupils twitted him with it. 'I beg you to observe,' he answered, 'how the body of the funambulist serves as a striking

[1] Such feats are still called 'polandric,' after the Little Polander, a balance master who performed them during the latter half of the eighteenth century.

example of what the human form can achieve in distortion and balance. I shall send for him to attend our next lecture in order that I may demonstrate the truth of my remarks.' Andrew went to the school. He stripped and stood between two skeletons while Dr. Bartlett fingered his muscles. Peter was scared: he thought they were preparing to cut up the source of his livelihood.

The next night Andrew fell and put out his wrist. Peter prayed for the end of the week. On the last night Andrew fell again and injured his leg. Peter shivered. This being too much in keeping with his worst forebodings, he went out for some grog, rolled home to bed, and lay quaking with only his snuff-box to console him. He left it open under the candle when he slept. Andrew was carried to his lodgings, and laid himself down by the old drunkard's side. He awoke in a fit of coughing. The room was full of smoke, and the table, fired by the snuff, in a blaze. He lowered himself out of the bed, and slid backwards to the door. In the kitchen he found a broom to use as a crutch; he hobbled to the pump, filled a bucket, hobbled back to his room, put the fire out, and went back to bed. Peter did not awake until late the next morning, when he made a blasphemous inquiry for his snuff.

They went to Wales. As Peter still needed snuff and grog, Andrew was not allowed to rest. He danced the rope on one leg, in order to recover before they returned to London, where the Flemish Hercules, with funds raised by his son's performances, took a lease of the Surrey, the theatre which had supplanted the Royal Circus, and restored the ring. James West was engaged with his troop of horses, and Andrew wheeled a boy in a barrow from stage to ceiling. At the second performance the boy was missing, and Andrew ascended the steep slant of the wire with his barrow empty. At the top his boy was leaning against the gallery-rail, chewing an orange, and enjoying the spectacle of danger. An arm trained from infancy to lift heavy weights hoisted him from his seat. 'I've paid my shilling and I'm going to be let alone' – he was wheeled down the wire so quickly that his cry was stilled by fear.

Owing to the cost of adapting the building, the funds left for the show were small and the season failed dismally. Peter Ducrow, declared bankrupt, lived but a few months longer. Andrew could decide his future for himself. As rope-dancing and other such equilibriums had been carried by others to a pitch of excellence that could not be surpassed, he returned to Astley's in 1812 as a horseman. Besides his 'Extraordinary Leap Through a Balloon'[1] he transformed the performance referred to by Mrs. Astley when she wrote that 'John does the peasant' into *The Peasant's Frolic or Flying Wardrobe*. In the disguise of a drunken lout, he rushed from the audience into the ring, and pulled the clown from a horse. The ring-master's dignity was ineffectually tried upon him. People cried, 'Turn him out.' The clown, offering to help him, threw him over the horse's back to the ground, pulled him up again, and sat him on the horse with his face to its tail. The peasant fell off, got astride again, stood up and kept

[1] In circus language 'Balloon' originally meant a cylinder, formed by two hoops covered with paper, which did somewhat resemble a balloon. When this 'property' was simplified into one hoop of paper the name was retained. 'Transparent' was the French name.

HE

his feet even though the horse got into its stride, threw off greatcoat, waistcoat, under-waistcoat, a third and a fourth, and ten other waistcoats – traditional business of First Gravedigger in *Hamlet* – and then his trousers fell down. The next instant, drawing his shirt off in a twinkling, Ducrow revealed his fleshings and classic grace.

Play-acting became a passion with him when he took part in the equestrian dramas of 1812. He went to Covent Garden in 1814 to play Eloi, the dumb boy, in a canine drama from the Boulevard du Temple called, *The Forest Of Bondy; or, The Dog Of Montargis*, where the villain had to wear raw steak round his neck in the last scene so as to be gnawed to death. By combining acting with equilibrium, Ducrow invented 'histories on horseback' which gained him an important place in the bills of Astley's two and three years later. But Davis, lest these should outshine the 'wonderful activity' of the Masters Davis, did not continue the engagement.

With his performing horse, Jack, and accompanied by his brother and two sisters, Ducrow went abroad. At Ghent he joined Blondin's Cirque Olympique, and travelled with the company through Belgium. One of the performances was witnessed by Laurent Franconi, son of Antoine, and even to this master of the horse the *Poses Plastiques Equestriennes* were a novelty. Ducrow represented Mercury, or Zephyr bearing Cupid and waving garlands of flowers, as though the saddle were as secure as a pedestal. To persuade him to appear at the Olympique in Paris, Franconi agreed to share all profits above three hundred francs.

There Ducrow stepped into John Astley's shoes. Soon Franconi's pupils were all riding in his style. As they went into the ring for the first act of horsemanship, he observed that each executed at least one of his feats. With his wife,[1] sister, two boys, and ten horses he set forth on his travels. At Bordeaux and Toulouse his profits were such that he engaged a dramatic company to play musical pieces. At Lyons he formed a replica of Astley's, with equestrian dramas. Unhappily a soldier left the ramrod in his musket, fired it at the gallery, where it pierced the neck of a woman, who died shortly afterwards. For three weeks, Ducrow's performances at Lyons were suspended, and he was allowed to reopen only on condition that no battles were represented. Without his equestrian drama, he could not longer claim the privileges of a theatrical manager; he had, legally, dwindled into the proprietor of a mere *spectacle de curiosité*, and, as such, was compelled by law to pay one-fifth of his receipts to the Theatre Royal and a quarter to the poor. He effected a compromise by paying to his rival the *redevance* demanded, and to the *hospices* of Lyons only the tithe required from a theatrical company.

Directly peace was thus restored, the crowds thronging to the circus blocked every avenue. As a rival attraction, the Theatre Royal engaged Mazurier, famous for his imitation of animals. 'Whatever Mazurier does on the stage,' vowed Ducrow, 'I'll do in the saddle.' Mazurier presented himself as the man-monkey, Ducrow as a monkey on horseback. Mazurier played

[1] He married a Miss Griffith, horsewoman, of Liverpool, on May 24th, 1818.

Polichinelle, Ducrow a *Carnival Of Venice* in which Punch was merely the first character in a series created by quick changes of costume while the horse galloped. Crowns of laurel were flung into the ring when he made his bow. The Duchesse d'Angoulême presented him with a gold medal. And when at last the time came for his departure, women entered his house, strewed his bed-chamber with flowers, and left presents, including silver spurs.

After travelling as far as Milan, Ducrow came back to London. The next year he went to Nantes and Paris before spending the summer at Astley's, where he was given the small part of St. Anthony of Italy in *St. George And The Dragon; or, The Seven Champions Of Christendom*. After his name appeared the words, 'His first appearance here.' The next year the bills announced, 'For first time in England, Mr. Ducrow will ride his two wild coursers at one time at racehorse speed without saddle or bridle.' At Covent Garden his troop played during the autumn of 1823, in *Cortez; or, The Conquest Of Mexico*. The part of a wild warrior needed an expert tumbler, since he had to fall from a great height: dropping from the flies, Ducrow rebounded from platform to platform until he disappeared beneath the stage. *Cortez* was not very successful, but a revival of *Timour The Tartar* made amends, and that led to the appearance of Ducrow in Covent Garden's Christmas pantomime, of *Harlequin And Poor Robin; or, The House That Jack Built*. As Squire Sap he entered riding on a pony seven or eight hands high, before being transformed into the Dandy Lover of the harlequinade.

In the spring of 1824, Elliston engaged Davis's stud for Moncrieff's *The Cataract Of The Ganges; or, The Rajah's Daughter*, which was to give the public both real horses and real water. This opened at Drury Lane on March 29th, 1824, and drew crowded houses with its field of battle, burning forest, gallopings, burnings, marchings, countermarchings, speeches, and heroine who rode on a real horse up a cataract of real water.

On that Easter Monday when Hannah Waldo Astley had Davis at her mercy, Ducrow eyed the situation very shrewdly. He agreed to be engaged at the Amphitheatre on condition that he was virtually manager, which meant a programme plastered with his spurious claims to French nationality. It began with a Grand Amazonian Entrée, headed by Madame Ducrow and Mademoiselle Ducrow. Monsieur Ducrow was billed to give his 'unique performances of scenes in the circle, concluding with his matchless feats on two uncaparisoned horses.' In the equestrian drama, the evolutions were 'under the superintendence of Mr. Davis and Mons. Ducrow.' This spectacle was not dumb-show, but J. H. Amherst's play with dialogue, *The Battle Of Waterloo*, described at the opening of this chapter.

In the autumn of 1824, Elliston prepared to stage at Drury Lane *The Enchanted Courser*, by George Croly, the reverend Irish poet. Ducrow's stud was engaged. At the first rehearsal his horses were on the stage, but he was absent. As nothing could be done without him, Elliston sent a note begging his instant attendance. Some time within an hour he arrived.

'What, Mr. Ducrow, is the meaning of this?' asked Elliston.

'Anan ! Miss t'Elliston,' was the only reply.

'Why, sir, have you not been here to your engagement ?'

''Gagement, Miss t'Elliston ? *I* have no 'gagement. There's the 'osses – punctual creatures.'

Elliston at once saw that it was a case where the Newmarket Club would have given the verdict against him, but the stud of horses was about as useful without the aid of Ducrow himself as a conjurer's rabbit without the conjurer. *The Enchanted Courser* was at a stand until Ducrow was finally engaged to superintend rehearsals.

Then James West came back from America with a fortune, which he was willing to put, with his horses, into Astley's. Davis had to go, and the most amazing period of Astley's when the ring was transmuted by a showman's alchemy from sawdust to gold, began.

2

Mazeppa, And The Wild Horse

Concerning Ducrow's life behind the scenes many a wildly comic story is told. Even when full allowance has been made for the exaggerations which flamboyant people always inspire, we still see him as a character more improbable than any of those Dickens was inventing. In Louisa Woolford, he had a partner who, brought up like himself to be both wire-walker and trick-rider, danced on the back of a horse as it circled, as confidently as if she had the power to float on air. In the centre of the ring stood Mr. Widdicomb, paragon of riding-masters, whose portly dignity subdued the rowdiest catcalls from the Olympians' orange-scented heights. In the equestrian dramas, Gomersal's glory, especially when giving his celebrated impersonation of Napoleon, was more glamorous than that of any hero of military history, while the hoarse roaring of Cartlitch wafted lines of defiant verse to the back of the gallery and out into the street. Comic relief came from the antics of John Ducrow, brother of *the* Ducrow, whose style stamped the stock jests of circus clowns for years to come.

COLONEL NEWCOME'S BOX AT ASTLEY'S
From Richard Doyle's illustration to *The Newcomes*, 1854

In *The Battle Of Waterloo*, Ducrow, as the Duke of Brunswick, had little more to do than die effectively on horseback. Gomersal, however, had a stirring time as Napoleon; Grierson was Wellington, and Widdicomb carried the Eagle to victory as Marshal Ney. Though one critic might dub Gomersal 'the gentlemen *with* the fingers and *without* the handkerchief,' we have to remember what Colonel Newcome said of his performance when, in the midst of little people, 'all children together,' lavishly supplying them with sweetmeats and eating an orange himself with perfect satisfaction, he laughed delighted at Mr. Merryman's jokes in the ring, and beheld *The Battle Of Waterloo* with breathless interest: he 'was amazed – amazed, by Jove, Sir – at the prodigious likeness of the principal actor to the Emperor Napoleon.' Likewise Bon Gaultier pays a handsome tribute, even in jest, to the actor in the ballad beginning:

It was the Lord of Castlereagh, he sat within his room,
His arms were crossed upon his breast, his face was marked with gloom.

At midnight he receives a visit from THE MAN, in the famous hat that waved along Marengo's ridge, the spurs of Austerlitz, and the boots of Lodi's bridge. Boasting that his name has been thundered in England's capital by men within the Surrey side who know to do and dare, Napoleon swears that to-morrow he will plant his standard before Castlereagh's ashen cheek, to-morrow another town will sink in ghastly flames while he crosses the Thames as he crossed the Borodin. Before leaving, he lays a paper on the table:

With trembling hands Lord Castlereagh undid the mystic scroll,
With glassy eye essayed to read, for fear was on his soul –
'What's here? – "At Astley's every night, the play of Moscow's fall!
NAPOLEON, for the thousandth time, by Mr. Gomersal."'

There was enough truth in the boast for a newspaper to complain: 'The French management of the ci-devant Astley's perhaps discover that the tone and spirit of those unlicensed compliments to Bonaparte, are not quite palatable.' To Ducrow, thoroughly cockney though his upbringing had made him, this was the finest of compliments. In his determination to be French, he wholeheartedly adopted the Emperor worship which was the soul of the equestrian drama of Franconi's, the circus founded by Philip Astley in Paris. *Buonaparte's Invasion Of Russia*, which drew more spectators than Astley's could comfortably hold, was written by Amherst, who allowed Ducrow the greatest part of the merit and praise because of the last scene, where a naked Frenchman and revengeful Russian opposed each other to the last gasp of life. 'This contest,' Amherst said, 'causes even gentlemen of the military profession, to shudder and lift up their hands.' Perhaps this occurred at the moment when the French Horse entered Moscow, headed by Napoleon. The half front of a house gives way and 'a woman is seen with child in agony, the Officers attempt to enter, but the flames prevent them. Napoleon dashes through everything and brings them out in safety.'

From 1818 to the fifties, Gomersal acted many heroes, but never one more heroic than Napoleon. Waterloo was constantly lost and Moscow burned night after night to enable the public to admire his exact impersonation. While the noble volunteers of the French army, superbly accoutred and mounted, performed evolutions on the stage, he inspected them from the corner a few yards away, through an immense telescope. When they halted, he addressed the 'flower and nobility of France' who were eager to avenge the insults received from the over-weening arrogance of Russia. 'I, in common with all the good and great,' he said, 'admire that true nobility which prompts ye to spurn inglorious ease and enjoyment while an enemy presumes to exercise a haughty influence over the affairs of Europe.'

Another of Gomersal's triumphs was *The King Of Tartary*, celebrated in *Don Fernando Gomersalez*, which Bon Gaultier derived 'from the Spanish of Astley's.' Gomersal, as the Spanish knight, was captured by the Moorish monarch Al-Widdicomb, early in the play, after leading the Christian army in a charge across the footlights. Since then he had been wasting in a dungeon, until brought forth to grace a Moslem feast, by fighting the monarch's champions. Scarcely from tumultuous cheering could the galleried crowd refrain:

But they feared the grizzly despot and his myrmidons in steel,
So their sympathy descended in the fruitage of Seville.

Yet Gomersal does not appeal so powerfully to our fancy as Mr. Widdicomb. Lord of the grooms, who stood in line by the stables' barrier, in scarlet jackets, white breeches and shining boots, he proved that the gentility of a riding-master could be as perfect as that of a knight of chivalry. No initials sullied his name. Until the announcement of his death, at the age of sixty-six, on November 2nd, 1854, the public did not know he was christened John Esdaile. Life fitted him for the part he was called upon to play. He had always, as far as living memory could retrace, had the same immaculate appearance. That seems natural when you read in the playbills of Grimaldi's pantomime at the Coburg in July 1822, 'Lover, Mr. Widdicomb.' In the November of that year, the playbills of Astley's, giving details of

Harlequin Achilles; or, A Trip To Hyde Park, repeated, 'Lover, Mr. Widdicomb.' Yet in *St. George* he was merely a courier, and in the next year's show a servant. But after he had been a marshal at Waterloo, his rank seldom subsided except when, in *Paul Pry On Horseback*, at Bath, he dwindled into 'Sambo (Black Servant to the Nabob).' It was in 1825 that he first appeared as Master of the Ring and his peculiar genius was recognised. Shapely legs rigid, right foot well forward, shoulders erect under epaulets, waist corseted under the tasselled sash, chest swelling under *décolleté* shirt and lancer's tunic or mess jacket, he advanced his whip gracefully when not in use, holding the stock vertically in his right hand while with the fingers of the left he delicately caressed the thong. His face was ornamented either with curling moustache or tapering points of an imperial, and his head of flowing hair which graced the very centre of the 'Scenes in the Circle,' was oiled and scented. No emotion stirred him, except when Signora Cavalcanti coyly disposed her floating draperies to hide the too maddening symmetry of her limbs. On that occasion he betrayed some excitement; at all others he exerted his power with proud imperturbability. 'Widdicomb,' a critic declared, 'is a great man, a clever man – a good man, if you will – but experience proves that he will never be an old man – no, never !' Though not so old, or so long at Astley's, as Gomersal, he ever inspired this widespread legend of great age and perpetual youth. It appears in *The Ingoldsby Legends* –

> Well, the Knight in a moment recover'd his seat –
> Mr. Widdicomb's mode of performing that feat
> At Astley's could not be more neat or complete,

– It's recorded, indeed, by an eminent pen
Of our own days, that this *our* great Widdicomb, then
In the heyday of life, had afforded some ten
Or twelve lessons in riding to Alured Denne –

as well as in less permanent records, all of which was not without effect. After rehearsals, he turned into an eating-house at the foot of Westminster Bridge, and sat in a box facing the fire. 'So-ho they have an ordinary at one here, have they?' he exclaimed. 'Aha,' he continued with his well-known chuckle, looking significantly at the clock, 'and now – now, they've got an extraordinary at two.' When served with a plate of beef he muttered for all to hear, 'So-ho. Is this the way they treat me – me, Methuselah Widdicomb?' Drawing himself up to his full height, and stretching out his mouth to its full width, he asked, 'Roast beef – and where is the equestrian radish?' Though his son, Harry Widdicomb, was with the company from 1836 to 1841, the father still maintained the appearance of youth in age; in fact, he was the strapping Corinthian Tom when his boy was Bob Logic. What he was like in his heyday, Dickens describes:

> We defy anyone who has been to Astley's two or three times, and is consequently capable of appreciating the perseverance with which precisely the same jokes are repeated night after night, and season after season, not to be amused with one part of the performances at least – we mean the scenes in the circle. For ourself, we know that when the hoop, composed of jets of gas, is let down, the curtain drawn up for the convenience of the half-price on their

ejectment from the ring, the orange peel cleared away, and the sawdust shaken, with mathematical precision, into a complete circle, we feel as much enlivened as the youngest child present; and actually join in the laugh which follows the clown's shrill shout of 'Here we are!' just for old acquaintance sake. Nor can we quite divest ourself of our old feeling of reverence for the riding-master, who follows the clown with a long whip in his hand, and bows to the audience with graceful dignity. He is none of your second-rate riding-masters in nankeen dressing-gowns, with brown frogs, but the regular gentleman-attendant on the principal riders, who always wears a military uniform with a table-cloth inside the breast of the coat, in which costume he forcibly reminds one of a fowl trussed for roasting. He is – but why should we attempt to describe that of which no description can convey an adequate idea? Everybody knows the man, and everybody remembers his polished boots, his graceful demeanour, stiff, as some misjudging persons have in their jealousy considered it, and the splendid head of black hair, parted high on the forehead, to impart to the countenance an appearance of deep thought and poetic melancholy. His soft and pleasing voice, too, is in perfect unison with his noble bearing, as he humours the clown by indulging in a little badinage; and the striking recollection of his own dignity, with which he exclaims, 'Now, sir, if you please, inquire for Miss Woolford, sir,' can never be forgotten. The graceful air, too, with which he introduces Miss Woolford into the arena, and, after assisting her to the saddle, follows her fairy courser around the circle, can never fail to create a deep impression in the bosom of every female servant present.

When Miss Woolford, and the horse, and the orchestra, all stop together to take breath, he urbanely takes part in some such dialogue as the following (commenced by the clown): 'I say, sir!' 'Well, sir?' (it's always conducted in the politest manner) – 'Did you ever happen to hear I was in the army, sir?' – 'No, sir.' – 'Oh, yes, sir – I can go through my exercise, sir' – 'Indeed, sir!' – 'Shall I do it now, sir?' – 'If you please, sir; come sir – make haste' (a cut with the long whip, and 'Ha! done now – I don't like it,' from the clown). Here the clown throws himself on the ground, and goes through a variety of gymnastic convulsions, doubling himself up, and untying himself again, and making himself look very like a man in the most hopeless extreme of human agony, to the vociferous delight of the gallery, until he is interrupted by a second cut from the long whip and a request to see 'what Miss Woolford's stopping for?' On which, to the inexpressible mirth of the gallery, he exclaims, 'Now, Miss Woolford, what can I come for to go, for to fetch, for to bring, for to carry, for to do, for you, ma'am?' On the lady's announcing with a sweet smile that she wants the two flags, they are with sundry grimaces, procured and handed up; the clown facetiously observing after the performance of the latter ceremony – 'He, he, oh! I say, sir, Miss Woolford knows me; she smiled at me.' Another cut from the whip, a burst from the orchestra, a start from the horse, and round goes Miss Woolford again on her graceful performance to the delight of every member of the audience, young or old. The next pause affords an opportunity for similar witticisms, the only additional fun being that of the clown making ludicrous grimaces at the riding-master every time his back is turned; and finally quitting the circle by jumping over his head, having previously directed his attention another way. . . . Can our friend in the military uniform ever appear in threadbare attire, or descend to the comparatively unwadded costume of every-day life ? Impossible ! We cannot – we will not – believe it.

To Ducrow, Louisa Woolford meant the quieting of the fierce desire for romance which devoured his strange, fantastic, almost grotesque soul. Though devoted to Madame Ducrow, he could not regard her as ethereal no matter how her spangles might sparkle in the light of gas-jets and chandelier. Louisa Woolford was the fit object of his worship when she joined his company as a child. Her father was a horseman of Bristol, named George Woolford, who had trained his daughter in the arts of balancing on horse or wire. When Ducrow was touring with his company in the West Country in 1826, he leased the Theatre Royal, Bath, where George Woolford joined him and obtained an engagement for 'Miss Louise,' then twelve years of age, to play Columbine in the pantomime that brought the performance to its close. Two years later her 'graceful riding on a single horse' was one of the attractions of Astley's, where, in 1829, she was promoted to play the heroine in a revival of *Timour The Tartar*; she was too artless to be an actress, but she was a partner worthy of Ducrow on the double tightrope. Such exquisite girlhood, aglow with radiant health, had not been known in the circus. When she stood on horseback, with the lightness of a *ballerina* and the sureness of a rope-dancer, perilously (so it seemed) aslant through the centrifugal force of her steed's circling race, the audience imagined her to be enchanted. 'Gauzy and roseate dream' is how D. L. Murray has described her in an inspired flight of fancy. Looking on her as she appears, with her lustrous orbs a trifle exaggerated, at the foot of an illustration by Doyle to *The Newcomes*, he feels the true Astleian rapture:

She is the Taglioni of the ring, the *écuyère de panneau* in her classical quintessence. It was not for her to vault on and off like a tomboy, to throw somersaults from the pad, or hang inverted (Mercy on us, my dear!) with tresses dabbling in the tan as Mazeppa. She might by condescension flit across the outspread 'garter' or the 'banner,' or even burst through the wrack of a paper 'balloon,' like Phoebe piercing the clouds with silvery visage. But for the rest the art of the *ballerina* sufficed, *entrechats*, attitudes and arabesques. What man (what schoolboy) with a soul could ask more? Was the hand that looked so ethereal on the neck of the great white horse, curved like a chess knight's, really claimed in mortal marriage by the intrepid Ducrow? History says so, and surely he deserved the prize, the tremendous fellow, who rode his three horses abreast right on to the stage of Drury Lane.

There is only one voice that withholds its praise. When Barbara asked 'if Miss Nell was as handsome as the lady who jumped over the ribbons,' Kit answered, 'Double as handsome,' and when she declared that Woolford was the 'beautifullest creature that ever was,' Kit answered, 'Why, *you* are a good deal better-looking than her, Barbara. You are, any day – and so's your Mother.'

Louisa Woolford's clown was that 'Prince of Pyed Jackets, yet no fool,' John Ducrow. He was the perfect fool of the ring. Though lost under the chorus of praise for Woolford and Widdicomb, Gomersal and Andrew Ducrow, evidence enough can be found to show that he was to the circus what Grimaldi[1] was to the pantomime. While no more the inventor of Mr. Merryman than Joey was of the clown, he perfected the part. In the golden age, before the costume of the French grotesque had become general, he had a pliant queue nodding over his whitened scalp, red cheeks and enormous mouth, red and white dress, with huge pockets, and red-clocked stockings. On being told that the top of the rope was chalked, 'to prevent the performer from slipping down, sir,' he insisted on chalking the bottom of the rope 'to prevent the performer from slipping up, sir.' After chalking Miss Woolford's shoes, he chalked his own nose to prevent his foot from slipping when he should tread on it. He drank the contents of a bottle of wine, after throwing a somersault, because he had been told to 'pour it into a tumbler.' He would quarrel with the Master of the Ring concerning who should leave first.

[1] Although the circus clown has been named 'Joey' after him in all parts of the world, especially America, Grimaldi never entered the ring.

If the Master said, 'I never follow the fool, sir,' he would reply, 'Then I do,' and tell the audience, with a wink, 'The dust always goes before the broom.' 'Now I'll have a turn to myself,' was his cry after the horse had ceased from circling, and then he turned cart-wheels round the ring. Falling flat on his face, he made a loud outcry, gathered sawdust in his hands, poured it from his head, and said his nose bled. Or he would try to make the rope-dancer's balance-pole stand on end by propping it up with sawdust. When Mr. Stickney, the American horseman who joined Ducrow's company early in the thirties, was about to jump over the banners, Mr. Merryman pulled aside a groom who was holding one end, took his place, and found great difficulty in holding it at the proper level until, having at last received the answer, 'Yes,' to his oft-repeated question, 'Will that do?' he put his hands in his pockets and walked away saying, 'I'm glad of it.' Picking up a piece of straw, he would exclaim, 'There. I might have fallen over it,' and run about with it balanced on the end of his nose. Odd sayings such as, 'Our horses are as clever as the barber who shaved bald magpies at twopence a dozen,' or (this to the grooms), 'Rub them well down with cabbage-puddings, or they'll get colly-wobbleums in their pandenoodles,' also appear to be his, for they are attributed to the clown who was with Mr. Stickney. Occasionally there were bursts of anger in the newspapers about the behaviour of Astley's clowns, particularly when one sprang among the spectators in the pit and 'took the liberty of kissing a respectable female' (possibly put there, as nowadays, for the purpose). But as on each of these occasions a second clown was in the ring, Ducrow may be alike deserving of all praise and free from all blame. Life was not very merry for him. He was consumptive. And so, one day in the May of 1834, the two little ponies that had often preceded him in the ring, led the way to the burial ground of Old Lambeth Church.

Prints of John Ducrow's 'Tea and Supper Party' and other *entrées* make it clear that those two ponies sat for their portraits when Vincent Crummles described the parents of 'the strange four-legged animal' which drew his four-wheeled phæton. The mother ate apple-pie at a circus for upwards of fourteen years, fired pistols, went to bed in a night-cap, and, in short, took the low comedy entirely. The father, rather a low sort of pony, had been originally jobbed out by the day, and never quite got over his old habits. He was clever in melodrama too, said Mr. Crummles, 'but too broad – too broad.'

'When the mother died he took the port-wine business.'

'The port-wine business !' cried Nicholas.

'Drinking port-wine with the clown,' said the manager; 'but he was greedy, and one night bit off the bowl of the glass, and choked himself, so his vulgarity was the death of him at last.'

No other spectacle mounted at Astley's, no other play staged in any theatre of the world, was acted so far and wide and so persistently as Andrew Ducrow's *Mazeppa, And The Wild Horse; or, The Child Of The Desert.* It was not a new piece but an adaptation of *Mazeppa; or, The Wild Horse Of Tartary,* dramatised

JOHN DUCROW'S TEA AND SUPPER PARTY

ANDREW DUCROW AND HIS DANCING HORSE, PEGASUS

From Prints in the Collection of Mr. W. S. Meadmore,
by whose kind permission they are here reproduced

ANDREW DUCROW AS THE GOD OF FAME
From a Print in the Author's Collection

from Byron's poem by H. M. Milner,[1] the regular playwright of the Coburg (now the Old Vic), where it was first acted on November 3rd, 1823. It would probably have been forgotten but for Ducrow, who, on April 4th, 1831, launched it on a universally triumphant career of half a century – without acknowledging the author's name on his bills. Not even the representation of the locomotives on the Liverpool and Manchester railroad exhibited in the Amphitheatre at the time, excited such a shout of welcome. From the first performance it was destined to satisfy all that audiences could demand of the equestrian drama. Nothing, it was said, could surpass the magnificence of the costumes, or the gorgeousness of the scenery – as if that mattered.

In the courtyard of the Castle of Laurinski, as dawn is extinguishing the lights in the windows, Cassimir, a Tartar who serves as a page, climbs a buttress to kiss the hand of Olinska, the Castellan's daughter, who enters on a balcony. But when he pleads with her to fly to the deserts of Tartary, she answers, 'How, with barbarians? sworn foes of my country – never, never!' Meanwhile, at the head of a splendid cavalcade of knights, Premislas, Count Palatine, comes to wed Olinska. In his honour a tournament is held: 'first a small sword combat, between two of the Pages – then a tilt of mounted and armed Knights, with spear and battle-axe, of whom Cassimir is one – then a sword combat on horseback, between Cassimir and his opponent – in both of these Cassimir is successful –

[1] Milner was also the author of *The Jew Of Lubeck; or, The Heart Of A Father*, staged in 1819 at Drury Lane. In 1836, when sent for to adapt *Zazezizozu*, a French burlesque, for Covent Garden, he fell on entering the theatre, and died soon afterwards.

then a broadsword combat of four, in which Cassimir is also the victor.' That night the Tartar challenges Premislas to a duel and wounds him, but is secured by servants and sentenced by the Castellan to the punishment inflicted on rebel slaves:

Lead the vile Tartar hence – strip him of the garb he has degraded – let not the arms of my house be sullied by adorning a traitor who raises his assassin arm against my friend, under the very roof that gives him shelter. Lead out the fiery untamed steed – prepare strong hempen lashings round the villain's loins – let every beacon-fire on the mountain's top be lighted, and torches like a blazing forest cast their glare across the night.

After the comic character named Drolinsko 'discovers his small-clothes torn' by the fiery untamed steed, Cassimir is bound to its back. Amid masterly groupings, the horse, bearing the helpless victim, gives a sudden plunge of fright and is seen, in the red glare of torchlights, tearing through a long avenue of rocks:

He presently reappears on the first range of hills, from L. to R. all the spectators rushing to the L. and as he crosses again from R. to L. they take the opposite side – when he has reached the third range of hills, they commence pursuing him up the hills, and as he progresses they follow – when he has disappeared in the extensive distance, the whole range of hills is covered by the servants, females, guards, and attendants, shouting, waving their arms and torches, forming an animated tableau – Olinska, who has fainted is supported by Agatha and Premislas, in the front, whilst the Castellan expresses exultation.

A 'Moving Panorama Of The Course Of The Dnieper River' is unrolled during a tremendous storm of thunder and lightning, hail and rain. The wild horse stops while Mazeppa describes how 'yon group of ravening wolves scare the affrighted beast from the bank – already have their gnashing teeth been buried in my flesh; and I could almost wish again to feel their horrid grip.' An enormous vulture hovers above him as the horse bears him off. At length he arrives in the steppes of Tartary where the Abder Khan is mourning his long-lost 'angel babe.' During another storm Mazeppa – 'extended motionless, and apparently lifeless, upon the body of the exhausted horse' – is recognised as the angel babe itself. 'Again,' he cries, 'I stand erect, again assume the godlike attitude of freedom and of man.' He rescues the Khan from a conspiracy of cowards and villains – 'in the course of the conflict several interesting pictures are formed by the mutual efforts of father and son to save each other' – and is acclaimed 'Mazeppa, King of Tartary.' After a grand review of his forces, he sets out to win Olinska. In disguise he enters the castle of Laurinski, and denounces her betrothal to Premislas as perjury and pollution, before the ceremony is interrupted by Tartar hordes, who 'like the whirlwind's blast sweep opposition into dust.' Tartar cavalry encounter Polish cavalry on the upper terraces. Agreeably both to Byron and circus custom, 'all the horrors of battle, carnage and confusion' follow, but instead of

turrets in a blaze,
Their crackling battlements all cleft,

it is only the forest which burns. Subdued Poles and magnanimous Tartars are united by the love of Olinska for Mazeppa.

While Gomersal was merely the Abder Khan, Cartlitch played the hero. Critics had described him as 'one of the grinning buffoons who wait upon Mr. Ducrow and assist him in destroying the King's English,' and referred to his elocution as a 'nightly howling.' Formerly he had been principal tragedian to Old Richardson, the Penny Showman, in whose booth he learned to bawl. Many who had seen Mr. Cartlitch at Astley's, it was explained in the Press, had been much puzzled to account for the strength of his lungs, which admitted of his 'being heard occasionally by persons standing beneath the outside portico.' In the booth he was very popular indeed. Once when a piece was going badly, Richardson called for Cartlitch to go on again.

'He has just been killed in the presence of the audience,' said the stage manager.

'Has he?' answered Richardson preparing to strike the gong and light blue fire, 'then the piece is saved. On with his bleeding ghost.'

After his success in *Mazeppa*, he stepped into Gomersal's shoes, by impersonating Napoleon in *The Wars Of Wellington*, which, because it contained the gist of *Seringapatam*, *The Repulse at Corunna*, *Badajoz*, and *Waterloo*, was billed as 'four pieces in one.' While praising this richness, a critic mentioned that 'Napoleon was most inhumanely murdered by a Mr. Cartlitch.' Against this we have to set the opinion of

Mr. C. J. Yellowplush, who could never forget Cartlitch's acting on a certain memorable night: 'Talk of Kimble! talk of Magreedy! Astley's for my money, with Cartlitch in the principal part.' And later Frederic Altamont's acting of anger was 'very near as natural and as terrybl as Mr. Cartlitch's in the play.' In *Todgers' Table Talk*, published in *Punch* in 1856, Cartlitch is credited with the loudest voice ever known. Whenever he called for vengeance on the stage, he always called for a pot of porter off. Were the windows open, he could be heard on the far side of Westminster Bridge. 'I do not say,' said Todgers, 'that I caught the exact word *vengeance* or *beer*, but I knew it was Cartlitch calling for either one or the other.'

At seventy years of age Cartlitch became a member of the equestrian drama company at the Amphitheater, Philadelphia (where the stage-manager was Joseph Foster from Astley's). One day he came into the greenroom, agitatedly asking, 'I hear they are going to play *Mazeppa*. Is this true?' He went over to the cast-case, looked at it in mute bewilderment, took out his spectacles, wiped the glasses, put them on, and stood for a long time gazing at the names. Joseph Jefferson (famous in later years as Rip Van Winkle) saw there were tears in his eyes, and followed the old man as he walked to a dark corner of the stage:

> He took out a large handkerchief, and, burying his face in it, began to sob. After he had recovered himself he said, 'Foster has cast me for the *Khan*.' Then turning on me with his eyes full of tears and a retrospective look in his face, he continued, 'Young

ASTLEY'S
ROYAL AMPHITHEATRE OF ARTS.
Proprietor & Manager, Mr. WILLIAM BATTY, Bridge Road, Lambeth, Surrey
LICENSED BY THE LORD HIGH CHAMBERLAIN.

GRAND SPECTACLE

EXTRAORDINARY!

CONTINUED SUCCESS OF MAZEPPA!
FOR SIX NIGHTS LONGER!
In compliance to the demand for places to witness MAZEPPA, and on account of the Extensive Preparations for the New Military Spectacle, Lord Byron's magnificent Drama of the **Wild Horse** will be **repeated for**

PLAYBILL HEADING FOR *MAZEPPA*
From a Playbill in the Author's Collection

man, I was the original *Mazeppa* fifty years ago, and now I am cast for *Mazeppa*'s father. Why should I not play *Mazeppa* still? I may be a little too old for it, but . . .' Here he broke down again, and as he sat there with his eyes and his spectacles both full of tears he looked more like *Mazeppa*'s grandfather than like *Mazeppa*.

But he recovered from that broken heart. John Cartlitch died on December 12th, 1875, at the age of eighty-two.

By then *Mazeppa* had been acted on practically every stage and everywhere on earth where the sawdust ring could lay its fence. According to Charlie Keith, the Roving English Clown, the piece was a favourite among Polish players, though 'performed by them without a horse, the hero being bricked up in a room to starve.' This is strange considering that the wild horse is one of the few things in the spectacle at Astley's, which tallies with the passage quoted by Byron from Voltaire as a matter of Polish history.

How Ducrow's influence spread may be understood by reference to *Pictures From Italy*, when Dickens describes a Paris circus company on the road. As he came out of the dim cathedral of Modena, he was suddenly 'scared to death by a blast from the shrillest trumpet that ever was blown.' Immediately, the riders came tearing round the corner, marshalling themselves under the walls of the church, and flouting with their horses' heels, the griffins, lions, tigers, and other monsters in stone and marble, decorating its exterior:

> First, there came a stately nobleman with a great deal of hair, and no hat, bearing an enormous banner, on which was inscribed, MAZEPPA! TO-NIGHT! Then, a Mexican chief, with a great pear-shaped club on his shoulder, like Hercules. Then, six or eight Roman chariots: each with a beautiful lady in extremely short petticoats, and unnaturally pink tights, erect within: shedding beaming looks upon the crowd, in which there was a latent expression of discomposure and anxiety, for which I couldn't account, until as the open back of each chariot presented itself, I saw the immense difficulty with which the pink legs maintained their perpendicular,

over the uneven pavement of the town: which gave me quite a new idea of the ancient Romans and Britons. The procession was brought to a close, by some dozen indomitable warriors of different nations, riding two and two, and haughtily surveying the tame population of Modena: among whom, however, they occasionally condescended to scatter largesse in the form of a few handbills. After caracolling among the lions and tigers, and proclaiming that evening's entertainments with blast of trumpet, it then filed off, by the other end of the square, and left a new and greatly increased dulness behind.

When the shrill trumpet was mild in the distance and the tail of the last horse 'hopelessly round the corner,' the people who had come out of the church to stare went back again. One old lady, who had watched the circus without leaving the spot where she knelt, now crossed herself and went down, full length on her face, before a figure in a fancy petticoat and gilt crown, 'which was so like one of the procession-figures, that perhaps at this hour she may think the whole appearance a celestial vision.' When Dickens arrived at Verona, an equestrian troop had been performing in the Roman amphitheatre a short time before – 'the same troop, I dare say, that appeared to the old lady in the church at Modena' – and had scooped out a little ring at one end of the arena, where the marks of their horses' feet were still fresh. He pictured to himself a handful of spectators gathered together on one or two of the old stone seats, and a spangled Cavalier being gallant, or a Policinello funny, with the grim walls looking on. He thought how strangely those Roman mutes would gaze upon the favourite comic scene of the travelling English, where a British nobleman (Lord John), with a very loose stomach – dressed in a blue-tailed coat down to his heels, bright yellow breeches, and a white hat – came abroad, riding double on a rearing horse, with an English lady (Lady Betsy) in a straw bonnet and green veil, and a red spencer, and carrying a gigantic reticule, and a put-up parasol.

There is another link with this history when Dickens recalls 'the delights – the ten thousand million delights' of the old fairs, in the introductory chapter to *The Memoirs Of Grimaldi*. He had been taken as a schoolboy to see the play and the pantomime presented by Richardson, next but one to the booth where the lady with the green parasol supported herself 'on one foot, on the back of a majestic horse, blotting-paper coloured and white.' Judging by the date, the baron in the pantomime was Cartlitch. The clown, who caused him such 'indignation and surprise' by saying his speech of thanks before the curtain was all gammon, also went over to the ring. 'We saw him only the day before last Bartholomew Fair, eating a real saveloy, and we are sorry to say he had deserted to the illegitimate drama, for he was seated on one of "Clark's Circus" waggons.'

3

Queen Victoria Rides In The Ring

Whatever critics might say of the influence on the drama, Ducrow argued, 'In the theatre half a pint of pison is diluted to fill out five acts.' In his world there was very little use for words except when one big scene had to be changed for another. The climax was always a battle . . .

> Where a dozen of scene-shifters, drawn up in rows,
> Would a dozen more scene-shifters boldly oppose,
>   Taking great care their blows,
>   Did not injure their foes,
> And alike, save in colour and cut of their clothes,
> Which were varied, to give more effect to 'Tableaux,'
>   While Stickney the Great
>   Flung the gauntlet to Fate,
> And made us all tremble, so gallantly did he come
> On to encounter bold General Widdicomb.

On the stage or off Ducrow was no respecter of words. Partly through his love of posing as a Frenchman, which caused him to say 'champignion' for champion, and partly through his cockney delight in verbal substitutions, which caused him to say 'dialect' for dialogue, his language was picaresque even without his mastery of oaths. Thus he enriched the English tongue with the proverbial phrase, uttered while he was watching *Hamlet* at a rehearsal, of 'Cut the dialect and come to the 'osses.'

When Amherst wrote patriotic speeches for life-and-death struggles, Ducrow cut out all lines about such things as 'Nelson's orders that every man should do his duty, even by his enemies,' and boiled the battle of words down to:

– Yield thee, Englishman.
– Never.
– Obstinate Englishman, you die.

with the unexpectedly happy result that when *The Burmese War* was published, the author gave credit to Ducrow for having 'invented and introduced two scenes of remarkable tact and talent – "the Equestrian conflict at the Mountain pass," and "the Storming a Fort" – both of which never were, and probably never will be, surpassed.'

There was about Ducrow's everyday behaviour an air of vagabondage strangely at variance with his grace in the circle. In consequence, no matter what the public thought of his heroics, the critics were mostly derisive.

There was an outcry at Christmas 1833, when he brought his company to Drury Lane. The Poet Bunn, so called because no one could understand how a manager without any ideals should publish a volume of verse, had control then: being also in charge of Covent Garden at the same time, he was unwilling to pit pantomime against pantomime at his two houses.

Accordingly he contracted with Ducrow for the equestrian spectacle of *St. George And The Dragon; or, The Seven Champions Of Christendom.* Bunn was impressed when Ducrow – the St. George, by the way – rehearsed supers for the scene where the Princess's nuptials were interrupted by a dismayed neatherd's news that the sea serpent had been seen again. Though Ducrow carefully explained how they all should rush to the feet of the Emperor, then to the Chancellor, then to the flaming altar of their gods, the Egyptians moved from one party to the other at a smart trot of happy unconcern. In a fever Ducrow ran hither and thither, shouting, 'Look here, you damned fools! You should rush up to the King – that chap there – and say, "Old fellow, the Dragon is come, and we're in a mess, and you must get us out of it." The King says, "Go to Brougham." Then you all go up to Brougham and he says, "What the devil do I know about a dragon? Go to your gods." And your gods is that lump of tow burning on that bit of timber there.' Later he burned his foot on their 'gods' and had to direct all the rest of the rehearsals while hopping about on one leg.

Whatever the public thought of this 'most effective piece of pageantry,' a critic 'who had the honour to yawn through it' could only say in its praise that it was 'quite good enough for horses to paw, champ, and neigh to.' On the other hand, Queen Adelaide sent Ducrow a hundred pounds, whilst Count D'Orsay gave him an ivory-handled dirk and a pair of gilt pistols. 'Insufferably tedious' and 'very inferior' were the comments of a critic who advised:

If we are to be imprisoned in these large houses until nearly one o'clock in the morning, to see cast-off exhibitions from the minor theatres, we ought to be provided, at the expense of the management, with easy chairs and warm nightcaps.

Bunn recollected that the representation of Shakespeare's noblest plays by Mr. Kemble, Mr. Charles Kemble, and Mrs. Siddons had been supported by *Blue Beard* and *Timour The Tartar*, with Astley's whole stud of horses at Covent Garden Theatre, and could not see that he 'was so very much to blame.' Five years later he presented Ducrow at Drury Lane in *Charlemagne; or, The Moors In Spain*.

To perform at Drury Lane was no great honour to an impresario who had assisted at the coronation of William IV. Ducrow had been invited to teach the King's 'Champignion' how to 'currycomb' – meaning caracole – while backing gracefully out of Westminster Hall after he had flung down the gauntlet; and in acknowledgment of his services he was presented with two tickets for the ceremony. Furnishing himself and Madame Ducrow with Court dresses out of the wardrobe of the Amphitheatre, he entered the best carriage the equestrian drama could boast, and harnessed to it a pair of Hanoverian Creams which had once belonged to the Royal Stud. Thus the 'Emperor of all Horseflesh,' attended by Little Dick and Joe Chafe, dressed as magnificent flunkeys in royal liveries hired from Nathan's, drove across Westminster Bridge before a wondering populace. Not content with the honour of taking a place in the queue of notables' carriages, their equipage broke the line, way being made for them partly because of the royal colour of the team, and partly because Dick was cutting figures of eight with his whip. Inside Westminster Hall the pageant made no impression on the critical eye of Ducrow. The horsemanship of the 'Champignion' aroused in him nothing but disgust.

'Why,' he asked in a voice loud enough to startle all his noble neighbours, 'isn't he puffing?' – by which he meant piaffing.

When the bridle was pulled too hard, he roared to Madame, 'That's vone of the best performing 'osses we've got in the whole stud; that's our Mazeppa mare. I dare say he's spiled the poor h'animal's mouth. If he has, he'll pay a pretty penny for it, I can tell you.'

He got up to go. Meanwhile his magnificent flunkeys had been joining in a dispute at the King's Arms over the abnormal armorial bearings upon their property coach which none of the coachmen of the House of Peers could interpret. Curiosity on this point was natural. Having belonged to Napoleon in *The Burning Of Moscow* before being prepared for the Count Palatine in *Mazeppa*, not to mention other equally illustrious personages, the coach bore savages, dolphins, dragons, swans-with-two-necks, and elephants-and-castles, above the motto, rudely scrawled by some impious hand, 'Widdicomb, Biddicomb,' or words to that effect. Yet its magnificent flunkeys resented questionings. By the time 'Mons. and Madame' had decided to assist no longer at the ceremony, Dick lay sprawling in the kennel, and Joe was squaring, in his shirt-sleeves, at his own shadow. Dick was drunk, and the only place for him was inside the coach next to Madame. His coat was given to Joe, who was ordered to step up behind. Ducrow himself mounted the box, and drove off amid the cheers of a crowd who mistook them for some outlandish emperor.

Two years later he was commanded to perform before King William at the Pavilion, Brighton. Old Stager, whose reminiscences were published in 1866, was stage-manager when the riding-school there was being turned into a circus. 'A young lady, mounted on a white cob pony, and with a groom in attendance,' took two or three turns round the newly made ring before the noise of thirty hammers and saws hard at work proved too much for her. Soon afterwards four of her servants brought the workmen 'a couple of large trays filled with cold beef, mutton, and bread, and also with two large flagons of Windsor home-brewed ale.' Old Stager discovered 'the kind young lady' to be the Princess Victoria, daughter of the Duke of Kent, 'and now, need I say, her most gracious Majesty the Queen of England.' When she came each day to take a turn or two round the ring, she 'never would have the ring door opened, but made her pony leap[1] into the circle, and leap out again when leaving.'

At the start of the command performance, the curtain rose upon *Raphael's Dream*, a long piece, written for Ducrow to exhibit 'the Grecian Statue sort of business.' It pleased the younger branches of the Royal Family and most of the visitors well enough, but Queen Adelaide had a hard task to keep 'Royal Billy'

[1] Assuming Old Stager refers to the movable part of the low 'fence,' this sentence may be taken simply as an expression of loyalty.

awake. Coffee was needed to enliven him during the performances on the stage, but the scenes in the circle went exceedingly well, especially Ducrow's *Vicissitudes Of A Tar*, which the 'Sailor King' now wide enough awake, energetically explained to the Queen:

There was first the future sailor leaving his native home, then drill on board the school-ship, followed by his first cruise, with the successive incidents of mounting the rigging, heaving the lead, approach of a storm, and boatswain's piping to quarters. Then an engagement – loading and sighting the gun for the broadside, a mate wounded and carried to the cockpit, victory and rejoicing, sudden change to grief for his shipmate's death, with the funeral of the latter, and throwing him overboard. Then the vessel is ordered home – arrival in port, paid off, purchase of presents for Polly, including a pair of trousers for the first boy and a frock for the first girl that are to bless their union, and mounting the coach for home.

In future Ducrow scorned lesser lights. At Sheffield his labour in erecting an immense temporary structure was lost because he considered civility wasted upon local dignitaries. The Master Cutler and Town Council, wishing to patronise the circus officially, arrived at the head of a *cortège* of between forty and fifty carriages, containing the principal manufacturers and their families. When the Master Cutler's card was presented, Ducrow sent word that he only waited upon crowned heads, and not upon 'a set of dirty knife-grinders.' The cutlers drove off to the town hall, where a ball was improvised. Ducrow's season was ruined.

Another sop was given to his vanity by Disraeli – cutting a figure on the stage of politics as highly coloured and 'foreign' as that of the Astley's ruler in make-believe – when he spoke at High Wycombe, in 1836, on the subject of Lord Melbourne's Reform Ministry:

> I dare say some of you have heard of M. Ducrow, that celebrated gentleman who rides on six horses. What a prodigious achievement! It seems impossible but you have confidence in Ducrow. You fly to witness it.

So far the reference was complimentary, but in order that the state of Lord Melbourne might be deplored Disraeli added:

> Behold the hero in the amphitheatre, the spangled jacket thrown on one side, the cork slippers on the other. Puffing, panting, and perspiring, he pokes one sullen brute, thwacks another, cuffs a third, and curses a fourth, while one brays to the audience and another rolls in the sawdust.

This proves how celebrated the *Poses Plastiques Equestriennes* had grown since the day Mons. and Madame Ducrow first appeared in England as Cupid and Zephyr, while the playbills boasted that he would represent 'Le Chasseur Indien On Two Naked Horses!' These histories on horseback, performed with the aid of a steed whose build is suggested by his name of John Lump, were always springing from his fertile imagination. There was little of the old system of horsemanship in his trick-riding. As the Chinese Enchanter

ANDREW DUCROW AS THE YORKSHIRE FOX HUNTER
From a Playbill in the Author's Collection

he stood astride three horses bareback, and as the Yorkshire Fox Hunter he stood astride two while leaping the bars. He acted Paul Pry in the saddle, and struck attitudes as a Roman Gladiator, Mercury, Fame, Two Greek Brothers, Adonis, and all the characters of a harlequinade, including Columbine, at a gallop. His masterpiece was *The Courier Of St. Petersburg*, in which he would ride first one, then two, then three, then four, and then five horses abreast, and finally conduct and manage six horses, while acting the story in this way:

> Upon the backs of the Coursers are supported Banners inscribed with the names and other insignia of the Countries the Courier has to pass through in the pursuance of his Journey with Dispatches. The tinkling of the Bells and the other characteristics of

the Foreign Post Horse – the zealous ardour with which the Courier impels his Horses – his reposing on their backs when he becomes fatigued – the chiming of the distant Village Bell – his stoppage at the Relay, and his arrival at his Destination within the time that his exertions would bespeak him to be limited to, are strongly marked and cannot be misconceived.

When the sixth horse arrived, he would ride two, lead one, and drive the rest, while 'elegantly displaying the British Ensign.'

Reviving one of his earliest fancies, he appeared in 1831 as Zephyr, with the 'Infant Equestrian Prodigy' as Cupid. Two years later this child took a benefit, executing his 'two favourite parts of Bacchus, the God of Wine, and the Pigmy Sportsman On Two Ponies,' and disclosed his name as Master Ginnett. His father, a trainer of performing horses, whose 'Barbary Courser' was exhibited at Astley's in 1835, was said to have fought in the ranks of the French cuirassiers at Waterloo, and to be able to argue that the French then won – on points. Thus the Ginnetts of Brighton took to the circus. Master Ginnett, the Infant Prodigy, made one of his earliest appearances in the command performance at Brighton.

Ducrow's impersonations, Christopher North told the Ettrick Shepherd, proved that he was a man of genius. To the Shepherd's inquiry whether they were 'a' his ain inventions,' North answered:

> Few or none. Why, if they were, he would be the greatest of sculptors. But thus to convert his frame

into such forms – shapes – attitudes – postures – as the Greek imagination moulded into perfect expression of the highest states of the soul – *that*, James, shows that Ducrow has a spirit kindred to those who in marble made their mythology immortal.

This is only a part of the praise bestowed upon Ducrow in *Noctes Ambrosianæ* to prove that his impersonations of ancient statues were as perfect as his horsemanship:

Tickler. The glory of Ducrow lies in his Poetical Impersonations. Why, the horse is but the air, as it were, on which he flies! What godlike grace in that volant motion, fresh from Olympus, ere yet 'new-lighted on some heaven-kissing hill'! What seems 'the feathered Mercury' to care for the horse, whose side his toe but touches, as if it were a cloud in the ether? As the flight accelerates, the animal absolutely disappears, if not from the sight of our bodily eye, certainly from that of our imagination, and we behold but the messenger of Jove, worthy to be joined in marriage with Iris.

Shepherd. I'm no just sae poetical's you, Mr. Tickler, when I'm at the Circus; and ma bodily een, as ye ca' them, that's to say, the een ane on ilka side o' ma nose, are far ower gleg ever to lose sicht o' yon bonny din meer.

North. A dun mare, worthy indeed to waft Green Turban,

> Far descended of the Prophet line,

across the sands of the Desert.

Shepherd. Ma verra thocht! As she flew around like lichtnin, the sawdust o' the amphitheatre becam the sand-dust o' Arawbia – the heaven-doomed region, for ever and aye, o' the sons o' Ishmael.

Tickler. Gentlemen, you are forgetting Ducrow.

Shepherd. Na. It's only you that's forgettin the din meer. His Mercury's beautifu'; but his Gladiawtor's shooblime.

Tickler. Roman soldier, you mean, James.

Shepherd. Haud your tongue, Tickler. Isna a Roman soldier a Gladiawtor? Doesna the verra word Gladiawtor come frae the Latin for swurd? Nae wunner the Romans conquered a' the warld, gin a' their sodgers focht like yon! Sune as Ducrow tyuck his attitude, as stedfast on the steed as on a stane, there ye beheld, staunin afore you, wi' helmet, swurd, and buckler, the eemage o' a warriour-king! The hero looked as gin he were about to engage in single combat wi' some hero o' tither side – some giant Gaul – perhaps himself a king – in sicht o' baith armies – and by the eagle-crest could ye hae sworn, that sune would the barbaric host be in a panic-flicht. What ither man o' woman born could sustain sic strokes, delivered wi' sovereign micht and sovereign majesty, as if Mars himself had descended in mortal guise, to be the champion o' his ain eternal city?

No one knew where Ducrow got all his knowledge. How he studied history and mythology was a mystery, since he never read. Nor could anyone understand how he had become so finished a draughtsman although in childhood he preferred drawing horses to riding them. Accordingly to his biography in *Actors By Daylight*:

> Whenever missed (and that not seldom) he was certain to be discovered in some obscure corner, colouring insignificant designs with an equally insignificant box of paints, which he always carried carefully concealed about his person, from the prying and unartist-like eyes of his cruel father who phlegmatically destroyed his pictorial efforts whenever he could lay hands on them.

To suggest the setting to a scene-painter, he would throw himself on the stage, and sketch – 'always cleverly, often beautifully' – his design on the boards in chalk. All his groupings, classical or medieval or martial in any age, were masterly. Scorning all the old conventions of the equestrian drama, apart from the inevitably besieged castle, he would copy no ideas – except his own. That was his weakness. He delighted to repeat pet tricks, in place or out of place. Like Old Astley's partiality for a heroine's narrow escape from death, and old Richardson's for a bleeding ghost in a red or blue light, Ducrow's fondness for a blacksmith's shop by night, with the red glare of the forge contrasting with the blue limelight of the moon, as in *The Battle Of Waterloo*, never cooled. When an author brought him a piece called *Harry Of England; or, The Trumpeter's Horse And The Conquest Of Harfleur*, Ducrow was thinking only of his anvil when the reading began:

> *Playwright.* Scene the first is the Countess's bedchamber. She is discovered watching, when a

ANDREW DUCROW AS THE WILD INDIAN HUNTER
From a Print in the Author's Collection

THE VICISSITUDES OF A TAR
From a Print in the Author's Collection

ASTLEY'S AS REBUILT IN 1843
From *The Illustrated London News*

messenger brings her news of a victory by her lord over the rebels.

Ducrow. Don't you think that we had better open with a representation of a blacksmith's shop by moonlight? Couldn't you make the horses of the *cuaier* that is a-bringing the news lose a shoe on the road, and stop at the blacksmith's shop to have another put on? But you needn't have it, if you don't like it. I only suggested it.

Playwright. The next scene is a wood, wild and secluded.

Ducrow. Here will be a capital place for a blacksmith's shop.

This time the author's objections were emphatic. Waving the point, Ducrow allowed him to continue until he came to the next scene, 'The Ocean, between Dover and Harfleur: Quarter Deck of the *Royal Harry*, man-of-war.' At this Ducrow pricked up his ears.

'Now here,' he said, 'will be a capital place for a blacksmith's shop.'

Again the author protested. Ducrow argued, 'They have blacksmiths' shops on board ships, I believe,' but allowed him to continue as far as 'Grand tournament at the Court of France in Paris.'

Ducrow breathed a sigh of relief. 'Well here,' he pronounced, 'we have a situation for the blacksmith's shop at last. All the knights come the evening afore to have their armour fastened on.'

The playwright lost patience. 'Why, that blacksmith's shop's been in every piece you've brought out since you were a manager,' he shouted.

Ducrow agreed. He went so far as to promise not to insert it into *Harry Of England*. But when the piece was performed, there was a blacksmith's shop at the opening and another before the tourney.

In Ducrow's character the affectations of Mantalini, the cockneyisms of Sam Weller, and the trickery of Montague Tigg, went with the kind-heartedness of the Cheeryble Brothers, the whimsicality of Dick Swiveller, and a brand of courage more 'Dickensian' than any trait of hero, villain, or comedian the novelist ever drew. When the Amphitheatre's elephant[1] broke loose from the stables one day and overturned everything in his way, Ducrow got up from a couch where he had been lying ill, rushed into the yard, seized it by the trunk, led it back to its stall, fastened a cable round its leg, locked the door – and fainted. When the much-vaunted Herr Cline, who came to Astley's in 1832 in order to ascend a rope from stage to gallery, found fault with the apparatus at rehearsal, Ducrow, in his duffel dressing-gown and loose slippers, seized the pole, and exclaiming, 'You're afraid of your pretty face, sir; but *I'm* not pretty,' rushed up and down as rapidly as if he

[1] While making his first appearance at Astley's in the melodrama of *Blue Beard* this elephant took fright, made a plunge towards the pit and got his fore legs and trunk over the panels around the ring. 'The screams of the females,' reported the Press, 'were terrific – a general rush took place towards the doors, and the confusion that took place is almost impossible to describe. Several ladies were slightly injured by the elephant's trunk, and one lady was so much hurt, that she was taken to a surgeon's and bled immediately. With some difficulty the elephant was secured and taken out of the circle, when it was announced that he would again be brought in to proceed with his performance; upon which a general cry of "No, no!" resounded through the house, and he was at last brought out on the stage when he went through his tricks with the greatest docility imaginable.'

had been wearing his dancing garb and 'opera' shoes. That he was 'passionate to excess' there can be no doubt, but that his temper was ungovernable was questioned by one who knew the secret of his behaviour at rehearsals. When the company were fractious, Ducrow put himself in a rage and spoke 'in a mixture of *con furore* and *sotto voce*.' Directly his loudest notes were reached, a lounger named Jem, whose usual tasks were to go on the stage in mobs and to sweep the stables, would sidle into view.

'Oh *you* are there, are you, sir,' Ducrow would shout. 'I'll pay *you* off at all events. I've long threatened I'd give it you and now you shall have it.'

Seizing a horse-whip from one of the subdued and abashed company, he would make his way after Jem, who retreated hastily. His cries of 'Murder! Mercy! Oh Lord!' could be heard in the distance. But Jem uttered these cries while Ducrow worked off his fury on the nearest water-butt. When he returned, panting for breath, 'even the illustrious Methuselah himself, though vaulted high in the saddle, would shake in his magnificent pantaloons.'

On the other hand, Ducrow's flow of language, 'generally indelicate and often revolting,' was undoubtedly ungovernable, no matter how eloquently an apologist might plead, 'he was indulging in no vicious propensity whilst shocking the ears of modest women; habit had made such expression to him mere words of course.' Certainly this needs to be borne in mind when reading an account in MS. of the burial of his first wife, who died on January 16th, 1837, aged thirty-nine. Ducrow was anxious to spare no expense. From

Liverpool, her body was brought to Kensal Green cemetery, where he intended to raise a lasting monument. The funeral was conducted in a seemly manner until the party reached the grave-side. Examining the pit with a calculating eye, Ducrow saw water at the bottom.

'B—— the b—— thieves,' he shouted.

When the parson protested that he would discontinue the service if such language were used, Ducrow declared that he cared nothing for 'swindling parsons,' and the body was placed in the catacombs until 'The Family Vault Of Andrew Ducrow Esq.' had been built and suitably adorned with the head and wings of Pegasus in honour of horses.

Having settled this in a worthy fashion, he married Miss Woolford, who was now twenty-three years of age. She presented him with a daughter, Louisa. Ducrow, 'a dutiful son, a kind brother, a tender husband, and a doting father,' loved all children. 'From him the beggar's babe could at any moment command a smile, a kiss, and a shilling. In the torrent of his rages, which were awful, a child could always tame him.' And his happy family was increased by infant prodigies, particularly Ducrow's adopted son, Master Chafe, who was known in the ring as Le Petit Ducrow. Mrs. Peter Ducrow was still alive, and one of her daughters was married to W. D. Broadfoot, stage-manager of Andrew's company while it held together (then he left her). We also hear further news of Woolford's father; he went to New York with Cooke's company, and in 1837 played Mazeppa at the American Theater, Bowery.

Much, if not all, that has the essential flavour of the

circus can be traced back to Ducrow. That he presented 'liberty horses' is evident in an account of his Olympic Games at Vauxhall Gardens in 1839, when 'a course of wild horses,' pranced, and scampered, and rushed round the arena 'with the wildness with which they would rush through their native plains, uncurbed by the hand and power of man.' The same programme included chariot races; horse races, with women jockeys; pony races, with small boys on mounts 'scarcely as large as Newfoundland dogs'; and courier races, with each rider standing upon the backs of two horses while driving two more 'at full speed round this extensive arena, each with the full determination to win.'

4

Again Burned Down

Like Young Astley, Andrew Ducrow began to be exhausted in middle age. Although too weak for equilibriums in the ring, he took companies on tour besides directing the seasons in town. Before the audiences of Astley's could tire of the equestrian drama, he sprang upon them the leonine drama. Its first hero was the American tamer, Van Amburgh. His performances were particularly admired by the Duke of Wellington, who asked whether he was ever afraid – 'When my pupils are no longer afraid of me I shall retire from the wild beast line,' was the answer – and bought Landseer's Royal Academy painting of the performance, for Apsley House. Van Amburgh appeared at Astley's in the October of 1838 as the hero of *The Brute Tamer Of Pompeii; or, The Living Kings Of The Jungle*. Coveting this great attraction, Bunn secured the hero of it for Drury Lane, where he announced:

ROARS of laughter intermingled with *roars* of lions. The public will naturally observe that although the performances are most successfully carried on without the works of Shakespeare, yet Mr. Van Amburgh's edition of Dry-den[1] is in a state of the highest request every evening.

While his lions and tigers were in the pantomime of *Harlequin Jack Frost*, early in the January of 1839, Queen Victoria went to see Van Amburgh, and attended six more performances within two months, when the Christmas piece gave place to opera without disturbing his run. After the fall of the curtain one night, she went on the stage to see them fed. 'And is that,' she asked Bunn, 'the trainer, Von Humbug?' In Bunn's account of what happened, he says the beasts had not eaten for thirty-six hours. When Van Amburgh performed his famous Biblical feat of making the lion lay down with the lamb and a panther as well, hunger was subdued only by ferocious use of the lash. The first chunk of meat seemed to appease the lion until it was swallowed. In an attempt to gain the last scrap of the panther's meal, he caused an uproar which made the den shake until the bars seemed likely to snap. Although many faces blanched, the Queen remained unmoved.

Nor was that the end of her interest in his pride of lions. She commissioned Sir David Wilkie to paint them: and Van Amburgh was called to Windsor Castle when on tour in 1844. While he was performing at Warminster, one of the lionesses had four cubs.

---

[1] Lions were always caged in what was called a 'den,' in the hope that its Biblical sound might overcome the strong Puritan bias against public entertainment.

LE

Wallett, 'the Shakespearean clown' of Astley's, says that Her Majesty sent word that she was not well enough to visit the 'dear little creatures,' as she called them. As soon as the show had pitched on Batchelor's Acre, Windsor, he took them to the Castle, and ever afterwards styled himself the Queen's Jester.

Ducrow engaged Carter, another American lion king, at Astley's in the October of 1839, to put a whole menagerie through its paces on a stage protected by a network of strong wire, in *Afghan*, which was called an 'Egyptico-Hindu-Arabian Spectacle.' Horses, ponies, zebras, ostriches, and crocodiles, besides other beasts natural and unnatural, paraded in 'endless variety' up and down the stage. Carter was discovered fast asleep in the wilderness. A leopard sprang upon him from a rock, and he subdued it. He was thrown into a den of lions, tigers, leopards, panthers, and subdued them all. He also drove a lion, harnessed to his car, up a mountain-side. One night the car fell off the mountain. Only the lion was injured.

Critics said that Carter's lions and tigers were too tame; their spirits had been so severely broken that he appeared to be quite safe from harm. About the beasts of Van Amburgh there had been 'a savageness, an uneasiness, an air of offended dignity, and they sent forth growls which infused throughout the spectators the satisfactory feeling that the life of a fellow creature was in danger, and thus gave a zest to the scene which excited even Royal curiosity.' But spectators were thrilled when Carter, in Astley's next drama, *The Lion Of The Desert; or, The French In Algiers*, ascended, with one of his leopards, in a balloon.

After touring the lions that had 'attracted the repeated presence of Our Most Gracious Sovereign,' Van Amburgh took over the Royal Lyceum Theatre and English Opera House for Carter and himself to act 'lion brothers' in *Aslar And Ozines! or, The Lion Hunters Of The Burning Zaara*, and later noble Bedouins in *Mungo Park! or, The Arabs Of The Niger*.

These were the heroes who tried to step into Ducrow's shoes when he retired from acrobatics and trick-riding and turned actor – he had long played anguished mutes as minor parts, but now they were leading parts – in that long-popular melodrama, Benjamin Rayner's *The Dumb Man Of Manchester*, which first saw the footlights on the stage of Astley's in 1837. The hero, wrongfully convicted of murder, was brought to the foot of the gallows; but there he seized the chance to reconstruct the crime in dumb-show so as to expose the real criminal. That play became a stock success, overshadowing his production, in 1838, of *The Poor Idiot! or, Souterain Of Heidelberg*, with Ducrow as the blank-witted youth, Kaspar Hauser of Nuremberg, whose story had recently been published as *An Account Of An Individual Kept In A Dungeon For Years*.

While acting these pedestrian melodramas in town and on tour with equal success, Ducrow gave up his place in the ring at Woolford's side. It is Gomersal who rides with her in Bon Gaultier's *The Courtship Of Our Cid*, when Donna Inez Woolfordinez fires Roman candles and Catherine wheels as she circles the ring before Gomersalez bounds, man and courser, over Master, Clown, and all:

>   Donna Inez Woolfordinez !
>   Why those blushes on thy cheek ?
>   Doth thy trembling bosom tell thee,
>   He hath come thy love to seek ?
>   Fleet thy Arab, but behind thee
>   He is rushing like a gale;
>   One foot on his coal-black's shoulders,
>   And the other on his tail !

Flinging trunk, cloak, and vest to the Clown, he now – as Shaw the Lifeguardsman – cuts a path through imaginary foes:

>   Woolfordinez ! speed thee onward !
>   He is hard upon thy track –
>   Paralysed is Widdicombez,
>   Nor his whip can longer crack;
>   He has flung away his broadsword
>   'Tis to clasp thee to his breast.
>   Onward ! – see he bares his bosom,
>   Tears away his scarlet vest.

Leaping out of his trousers, Gomersalez appears as a London dustman, nimbly cutting and shuffling, over the buckle heel and toe;

>   Flaps his hands in his side-pockets
>   Winks to all the throng below.

While Woolfordinez bounds over garters, Gomersalez, wild with passion, casts 'clouds of somersets' and tosses his feet in the air while he holds on by the mane. Wings burst from his head and heels as he doffs his smalls to stand transformed as Mercury. All is hushed, 'save where a starting cork gives out a casual pop,' as our noble Cid alights with a bound by Woolfordinez' side, and raises her in his arms just before the stable barriers close behind them.

Ill health also caused Ducrow to leave the devising of new spectacles to others, but there was no danger that the public's interest would tire: and, to crown his success, the Queen and Prince Albert, three months after their marriage, witnessed a performance at Astley's on May 20th, 1840. In his house, separated only by a thin wooden partition from the amphitheatre, Ducrow lived in a style after his own heart, surrounded by what he called 'costly articles of virtue and bigotry' that he had not troubled to insure. Records of his career, newspaper-cuttings of praise in prose and verse, besides prints of himself in equestrian attitudes, were treasured in a vast scrapbook. In the amphitheatre were other venerated relics, from the carefully cherished chandelier presented by the Duke of York, to the vast wardrobe, containing armour from the Eglinton tournament and costumes from the Shakespeare Jubilee. In the stables surrounding the arena was his stud of performing horses, unrivalled not only in England but throughout Europe, besides his zebras, ponies, and a jackass who was now ready to make himself the hero of the amphitheatre. In the storerooms were other properties and other materials to maintain the supremacy of the equestrian drama. Yet it was these very spectacles that threatened to overthrow his reign. There was a warning in 1841 which was ignored; the fire which started was soon put out, but no precautions were taken against the outbreak of another. The family of Ducrow continued to sleep unafraid in their bedrooms over the entrances to pit and boxes – and the insurance company's night-watchman to doze in his lodge at the entrance to The Ride instead of making hourly rounds.

Ducrow's circle was about to be overtaken by the fate that destroyed Shakespeare's Globe. Guns were fired in the midsummer of 1841 during *The Wars Of Cromwell; or, The Royal Oak*, a spectacle arranged by West's son. Charred wads, blown from their muzzles, dropped into the mezzanine below the stage, and there smouldered, unobserved, in sawdust. Amid entranced shouting, the spectacle gave place to *The Correo; or, Spanish Bull Fight*, with the bull 'personated by one of Mr. Ducrow's broke horses, tutored by him for the purpose, enveloped in an Elastic Skin, and so managed as to deceive the nicest eye.' There were 'scenes in the circle,' including an exhibition of the Charmed Charger; then the band played the audience out and the horses were tethered for the night.

'Beings of light and elegance, in milk-white tunics, salmon-coloured legs, and blue scarfs, who flitted on sleek cream-coloured horses' before the eyes of Kit Nubbles and Colonel Newcome, now dwindled into pale, dirty shabby-genteel men in checked neckerchiefs, and sallow linen, walking home to their lodgings in Stangate, one or two carrying under their arms stage shoes loosely wrapped in old newspaper. The night watchman exchanges 'Good nights' with them, keeps the last for a chat, and says it is a fine night. Underneath the stage a wad is turning to ashes in a flame without light that scorches the planks. Past midnight there is not a sound. Towards dawn, the night-watchman stirs. Hoofs are restive. He shouts for quiet and dozes again. Once more he is awakened, this time by a constable from his beat in Stangate Street, who has seen smoke rising from the roof over the stage. The watchman drags himself from his seat, and together they hurry along The Ride to the main building. Beyond the footlights smoke is gathered in a cloud. The watchman unrolls the hose, but the constable, instead of manning the pump, has left to give the alarm. The last chance of saving the building is gone. The watchman realises that as he hurries to the house in Stangate where the grooms live, to shout at the windows of Signor Hillier, Master of the Horse.

Woolford, stirring in her sleep, smells smoke. She awakens Ducrow, and gathers her child to her while he calls Le Petit Ducrow to collect the servants, musters his household, and marshals them down the stairs to the box-holders' entrance. The door is locked, and, batter as they will, it does not move. 'We shall be burned to death,' whimpers an old servant, but he marches them all upstairs again, past the partition, blistering in the heat, to the door on the far side, where they all, through the smoke and flames that fill the courtyard, reach the street in their night clothes. Hillier dashes from his house in shirt and trousers, and tells them to use his house for shelter. When Ducrow leads his flock that way, he does not notice that his wife is vainly trying to restrain the servant from going back to fetch her mistress's birds and her own savings-bank book. At last Woolford answers her husband's urgent command to take charge of the children, and leaves the servant to her own wilful desires.

'Let me see my horses out; I care nothing for the building,' cries Ducrow.

Now the horses, liberated from the stables, are madly

galloping down Stangate Street, Amphitheatre Row, and Westminster Bridge Road, the clatter of their hoofs sounding the first alarm to the whole neighbourhood. Inside the amphitheatre, the grooms are untethering as fast as the frenzy of the stud will permit. Some horses and most of the ponies turn inwards at once, through habit, for the ring. The greatest danger is on the south side where the fire started. To get to the horses and donkey stabled there, the arena must be crossed. Hillier dares this journey four times. Thrice he brings out a horse, but the fourth drops dead from heat in the centre of the ring. Another horse, the donkey, and a pony are left to perish, for all further efforts are vain. Only eight minutes have passed, yet flames are surging from the windows. Old Astley's crazy structure of ship's spars and fir-poles burns like matchwood. The insurance company's fire brigade and five others, summoned by constables who saw the light while patrolling the bridges, are manning their hand-pumped engines, but every hose is empty – twenty minutes pass before water can be tapped. Hacking down the doors reveals nothing but a vast furnace within, except at the box-holders' entrance. Crouched against the inside of this door is a blackened mass, barely recognisable as the body of a woman until a bystander remembers the servant who went back for the birds and her savings-bank book. As they drag the charred thing aside there is a threatening rumble. The walls give way. The roof falls in with a crash that sends sparks flying over all Lambeth.

Always highly strung, as the twitching of his face had long shown, Ducrow was racked not only by the memory of this fiery ordeal, but by his fevered imagination which pictured the horrors of his family's fate if he had slept but a few minutes longer. Throughout Tuesday his mind was darkened. On Wednesday morning he read the reports of the fire, and learned for the first time of the death of the old servant, huddled beside that unyielding door.

Benefits were arranged. At Drury Lane a German company lent him the stage for a performance of *Charlemagne*, while Anderson, the Wizard of the North, at the Adelphi, and Rouse of the Grecian Saloon, raised funds for the company. Thus financed Ducrow took his stud on tour. As the news of the fire was an advertisement that added to his renown, his return to Hull, and other cities where he had long been popular, was triumphant. In the next six months a fortune was amassed. But his exertions were the last brilliant flicker of a guttering flame; he knew that his life was burning too fast. After an engagement at the Olympic, he was due to appear in *The Dumb Man Of Manchester* at Liverpool. The stud had gone on ahead. When it was time for him to follow he gave Le Petit Ducrow a crown and kissed him. 'Attend to your duty. Be a good boy. You'll never see your papa again,' he said.

There is a distressing account of his last days. While unable to speak or move, because of seizures, Ducrow was removed to a mad-house at Peckham Rye. When Old Stager went to see him there 'he caught hold of my hand with both of his,' and tears rolled down his cheeks. 'They call me mad,' he said; 'do you think I am ?' By threatening to procure a warrant, Old Stager was able to take him back to the house in York Road, Lambeth, that had been his home ever since he lost Astley's:

> His wife was not at home when we arrived, and as did not particularly care about meeting the lady, I soon took my leave. Next morning I received a letter asking me to come to the house in York Road at once, as Mr. Ducrow had been suddenly taken ill, and was anxious to see me. When I got to the house, I found Dr. Brooks in attendance, who said that his patient was suffering from severe internal inflammation. His mind, too, was now wandering in earnest, and I found what he wanted to speak to me about was the plans for a new theatre, which he insisted I should see about at once.

In this state he lingered for only a few days longer, until the evening of January 27th, 1842. Thus he died so soon after the centenary of Astley's birth that they should ever be commemorated together.

Louisa Woolford was left, besides the Unrivalled Stud, £47,000 in Three-and-a-Half per cents, which even allowing for insurance, Drury Lane benefit funds, and savings not hitherto mentioned, seems to reflect his gallant resolve not to leave the earth until his family was safe. Like a true showman, he had also taken thought for his funeral, and his friends, including Oscar Byrne, the ballet-master, Anderson, the wizard, and Hillier, the master of horse, carried out his wishes faithfully except in one detail. Old John Lump, whom he had ridden for seventeen years in the *Poses Plastiques Equestriennes*, died of old age or grief while they were arranging his place in the burial pomp. Nevertheless the procession was imposing enough for a national hero. After the mounted police, mounted undertaker, mounted porters, and pages bearing feathers, his favourite horses, Vienna, Beauty, and Pegasus, were led in caparisons of deep mourning. The hearse, drawn by six horses with four postilions and ten pages, bore the coffin in an 'open coffin' of purple velvet, studded with silver-gilt nails, and bearing a plate representing Genius weeping over her favourite son. Afterwards came eleven coaches drawn by four horses apiece, seven drawn by two horses apiece, and actors on horseback. There were spectators in thousands. He was laid inside his vault at Kensal Green, behind this *diminuendo* epitaph:

> Within this tomb repose
> in the humble hope of a blessed hereafter
> Through the merits of his Redeemer,
> The mortal remains of
> ANDREW DUCROW
> Equestrian.
> Many years lessee of the Royal Amphitheatre.
> In him
> the Arts and Sciences have to deplore the loss
> Of a generous patron;
> His family
> an affectionate husband and father
> His friends
> a boon companion
> and
> the world
> A strictly Honest Man.

In the following June, Woolford gave birth to Peter Andrew Ducrow. Meanwhile, after the grooms had been put in suits of mourning, Ducrow's 'Pre-eminent And Peerless Treble Stud' again galloped before the public from Easter Monday onwards. Under the leadership of Hillier and Broadfoot, the company, with Le Petit Ducrow as its star, and Widdicomb and Stickney as lesser lights, accepted hospitality in the minor theatres that had once housed their rivals. For six weeks in the early summer of 1842 they were at Sadler's Wells, which they fitted with a contrivance which caused the stage to disappear after their drama so that their 'scenes in the circle' could be performed in a large space, somewhat resembling a basin, underneath. At the Wells, they acted *Harry Of England; or, The Trumpeter's Horse And The Conquest Of Harfleur*, duly introducing the 'Armourer's Cave in the Village of Marsonielle,' and a fight for the Oriflamme with 'The Dying Steed.' In July this gave place to *The Moor And His Horse; or, The Passage Of The Pyrenees*, again introducing 'Troopers' Smith and Armourers' Forge.'

In September the company were at the Royal Surrey, where they performed *The Battle of Blenheim; or, The Horse Of The Disinherited*. The bills declared Blenheim to be 'the Waterloo of the Eighteenth Century,' in order to borrow glory from Ducrow's famous spectacle, and the resemblance was to be remarked in the scene described as 'Night Bivouac and Suttler's Tent.' After the victory, the return to England was celebrated with a

Magnificent, Military and Rustic Allegorical Procession, including a Goddess of Agriculture on a bull,

Peace and Plenty on 'Living South America lama'; Commerce on a zebra and four continents in a state coach, concluding with the Horse of the Disinherited surrounded by captured flags and heroes on the pyramid of fame.

In the November the company was merged into Batty's at the National Baths in Westminster Bridge Road. Ducrow's stud went to Germany.

Thus ended the golden age. What had once been the haunt of gilded youth and pickpockets, wild rakes and Cyprians, and all other types you meet in *Life In London*; what had been the scene of squabbles and fights, occasionally ending in duels, had changed in Ducrow's tenancy to 'an establishment to which all the first families in England took their children in the season.' Both Thackeray and Boz celebrate the glories of the boxes. Later on Dickens made the gallery seem still more dear to our affections when Kit took his mother, Barbara, and her relations, there with 'one handkerchief full of oranges and another of apples':

> Dear, dear, what a place it looked, that Astley's! with all the paint, gilding, and looking-glass, the vague smell of horses suggestive of coming wonders, the curtain that hid such gorgeous mysteries, the clean white sawdust down in the circus, the company coming in and taking their places, the fiddlers looking carelessly up at them while they tuned their instruments, as if they didn't want the play to begin, and knew it all beforehand! What a glow was that which burst upon them all, when that long, clear,

KIT IN THE GALLERY AT ASTLEY'S
From Hablot Browne's illustration to *Master Humphrey's Clock*, 1841

brilliant row of lights came slowly up; and what feverish excitement when the little bell rang and the music began in good earnest, with strong parts for the drums, and sweet effects for the triangles! Well might Barbara's mother say to Kit's mother that the gallery was the place to see from, and wonder it wasn't much dearer than the boxes; and well might Barbara feel doubtful whether to laugh or cry, in her flutter of delight.

Then the play itself! the horses which little Jacob believed from the first to be alive, and the ladies and gentlemen of whose reality he could be by no means persuaded, having never seen or heard anything at all like then – the firing, which made Barbara wink – the forlorn lady, who made her cry – the tyrant, who made her tremble – the man who sung the song with the lady's maid and danced the chorus, who made her laugh – the pony who reared up on his hind legs when he saw the murderer, and wouldn't hear of walking on all fours again until he was taken into custody – the clown who ventured on such familiarities with the military man in boots – the lady who jumped over nine-and-twenty ribbons and came down safe upon the horse's back – everything was delightful, splendid, and surprising !

That equestrienne passed out of sight of Kit and Barbara into another existence, strangely unlike 'behind the scenes' at Astley's. After the burial of Ducrow, Louisa Woolford appeared once more before the public, this time as a rider *en haute école* during her company's season at the Surrey. She had a devoted admirer in John Hay of Wycombe (where Disraeli made his Ducrow speech), and as he was but seven years older than herself, and represented the world of comfort and social graces she had never known, her heart became wholly his. All the garish glories of the show were left behind with a shudder by Mrs. John Hay. Though her children bore the name of Ducrow, she was resolved they should not belong to sawdust and tan. Her daughter, Louisa, was married to Surgeon Major Henry Wilson, who served with distinction in the Indian Mutiny. Peter Andrew, an ensign in the 40th Regiment, was ordered to New Zealand for the Maori War in 1863. In the attack on the stockade at Rangariri, he was 'if not the first, certainly one of the first, to enter the enemy's entrenchments.' They brought him home, a pale shadow that faded almost as his mother's lips touched him: and at Christmas-time they buried him beside his father. John Hay, devoted husband, died in 1873. Lovely Woolford, with her daughter and two granddaughters, lived for many years. Perhaps, as the world changed around her, she remembered Astley's only as a remote and whimsical dream. Or perhaps that noisy, blustering dream became more real – so the visions of youth appear in old age – than the peace of her house where the rose of the ring was now white-haired (but not at all ethereal, for photographs show her to be a determined-looking old lady), and in black skirt and shawl instead of gauze. She died at the age of eighty-six, after straying twenty-five days into a new century. For sixty years she had lived out of sight and hearing of the spot where she inspired those Astleian verses –

>   Like a beautiful Bacchante
>   Here she soars, and there she kneels,
>   While amid her floating tresses
>   Flash two whirling Catherine wheels –

which yet contrived to breathe the spirit of adoration that all her holders then felt, and some who never saw her feel yet.

But then again, in the way of Astley's, we may be wrong.

IV

THE ASTLEY'S OF PARIS

I

Antoine Franconi

UNDER the name of Franconi's, the amphitheatre which Astley founded in France had become of far greater significance than its London twin. Coming revolutions had cast their shadows in its circle. What was a harmless craze or childish amusement in London, became a political influence when installed in Paris. The circus crossed the Channel as a sinister omen of the impending downfall of Louis XVI. A generation later it grew into the equestrian drama, which by glorifying the career of Napoleon, undermined the thrones of Charles X and Louis Philippe. Under Napoleon III it did much to create the garish glamour of the Second Empire – so much so that a joke of the day was to deny Louis Napoleon's betrothal to Mademoiselle Cirque Olympique, daughter of the Maréchal Franconi, 'who won his spurs in the most distinguished military circle of the Empire.'

Historians have overlooked this significance of the showman. Carlyle makes no mention of Marie Antoinette's delight in the English trick-riders who visited Paris in 1782, though he does declare that the passion for English horsemanship was 'prophetic of much.' Jockeys, saddles, top-boots, and redingotes were proofs of the French nobles' love of neighbouring freedom: 'Nay, the very mode of riding; for now no man on a level with his age but will trot *à l'Anglaise*, rising in the stirrups; scornful of the old sit-fast method.' Before the year was out Marie Antoinette had brought the Astleys back to Paris. Thus Anglomania, while fertilising the revolution, was planting in Paris the equestrian spectacles destined to play a part in French politics for many years.

When war brought Philip Astley's enterprise to an end, there was no one in France to represent his interests. But he contrived to appoint someone. Formerly he had had an apprentice named Laurent who ran away, was recognised among the puppet-shows of the Pont Neuf, and brought to London, where he became a famous clown at Astley's and a man of means. A message was smuggled to his mother to take possession of the Amphithéâtre Anglais and the dwelling-house attached to the property in order to protect it from what Decastro calls the univeral devastation of the ravages committed by the people of the French nation.[1] This

---

[1] This from *Picture Of Paris*, 1814, will serve to show the difficulties showmanship had to endure during the reign of terror:

The inhabitants of Vineuil, a village exactly opposite to the place where the château formerly stood, resolved to shoot the wild beasts in the menagerie, as agents in the conspiracy of Condé to starve the people. But they were apprehensive that these animals might make a sally, and wage a war of extermination against them; upon which consideration, feeling their courage to be unequal to the shock *d'une battaille rangée*, or of a pitched battle, and being afraid to butcher the animals in detail, they determined in solemn council to call in the revolutionary army, as their auxiliaries. As soon as their allies arrived,

she did, as well as she could, but the building was commandeered for barracks before it passed into the hands of a showman who made it famous under another name.

The Franconi became to Paris what the Astleys were to London. The first of the family to turn showman was Antonio (later Antoine), who was born in 1738 of a noble family of Venice. When he was twenty years of age his father killed a senator in a duel, was condemned to death, and lost all his family possessions to the State. As an exile, Antonio arrived in France without money or friends, and in desperation offered himself to the owner of a menagerie at Lyons as a tamer of wild beasts. The same night he entered the cage of a lion, and was seized by the arm in a grip that left its mark throughout his long life; but he triumphed until his violent temper made enemies. After a quarrel, he left Lyons for Bordeaux, where he made the acquaintance of the Duc de Duras, under whose patronage he journeyed to Spain and back to fetch bulls and bullfighters. The show was the delight of the country for miles round. But the toreadors, being jealous of the wealth Franconi was accumulating, refused to appear in the ring, and threatened to set up on their own account. He turned bull-fighter, and by appearing in

---

and had stationed a couple of pieces of artillery on the neighbouring height, a general action commenced. A heavy fire was opened on the imprisoned sovereigns of the forest. After a breach had been effected, the drums beat a general charge; the centre of the revolutionary army advanced to the *pas-de-charge*, bayonets fixed, while the right and left wings kept up a smart fire of musketry upon the invisible enemy. The inhabitants of Vineuil were in the rear. At length the revolutionary army entered the breach, and the whole garrison was put to the sword.

black silk without the cuirass, then customary, he startled the spectators with his courage.

For a long time he practised as a toreador, for half the season at Bordeaux and for the other half at Lyons But the public tired of bull-fighting, and ran after another new thing. When Franconi was not using his ring at Lyons, he had let it to a famous horseman, Balpe, who set a new fashion in entertainment. Franconi accepted the challenge, bought a horse at once, and trained it himself. After a month he exhibited his horsemanship at Lyons amid cries of admiration, and from that time devoted himself to horsemanship. In 1783 he joined Astley in the amphitheatre of the Faubourg du Temple, afterwards returning to Lyons with Young Astley as his partner, to display new ideas of showmanship in his wooden bull-ring. His enterprise was noted by a nobleman, who advanced funds for an amphitheatre. Here profitable shows were given until 1791, when it was burned down.

On returning to Paris, Franconi found the Amphithéâtre Anglais deserted. There had been a company, *Les Comédiens Sans Titre*, bold enough to open its doors on March 20th, 1791, but they closed down three days later. In that year a decree of the National Assembly proclaimed the freedom of the theatres, and the Boulevard became crowded with new shows. At mid-day the parades began. First there would be a harangue, spoken by a type of clown who was called, because he wore a garment like the covering of a mattress, *le paillasse*.[1] Hardly had one finished than another began

[1] Not derived from the name of the Italian mummer *pagliaccio*, literally 'chopped straw.'

two steps away. Cries of orange-sellers and others mingled with the banging of the big drum, the ear-splitting clash of cymbals, and the shriek of shrill trumpets. As part of this wild carnival, Franconi reopened the amphitheatre from April 14th until June 5th. While every theatre was free to open, no spectators were free even as much as to listen to the cry of the *paillasse* to walk up. If any man stopped, he had his pocket picked.

Events were too stirring to let the need of entertainment make itself felt. The mob swarmed into the Tuileries; what theatres survived closed during the massacres of September. Some – but not the amphitheatre – opened at the end of the month, playing to audiences intoxicated with blood. A refugee, the nobleman whose purse had enabled the *cirque* to be built at Lyons, asked Franconi for shelter and was not refused. After hiding for a month, he was tracked down and captured. Franconi was absent at the time; on his return he knew that he would be arrested. Determined not to be taken alive, since the punishment for harbouring an aristocrat was the guillotine, he fortified himself in the *foyer* of the amphitheatre. Fortunately for him the local Committee of Public Safety consisted of friendly neighbours. When kept in the street by his threat to shoot the first to cross the threshold, they promised to return in force – and forgot to. Their minds were distracted by more momentous matters. At nine o'clock on the morning of January 21st, 1793, a show began in the Faubourg that drew the people from all other shows. To loud rolling of drums, Louis XVI came out of the gate of the Temple on his way to the guillotine. At three o'clock in the morning of August 2nd, 1793, in a carriage with closed blinds, Marie Antoinette was taken away from the Temple to the Conciergerie, a stopping-place for a month or two, on her way to the guillotine.

On March 21st, Franconi again opened the Amphithéâtre d'Astley. On the bills of July 27th, the historic 9th Thermidor – when Old Astley was serving as a volunteer with the dragoons at the siege of Valenciennes – *le citoyen* Franconi announced that he would celebrate the *fête civique* with all possible pomp, winding up with the entry of a car bearing an illuminated *tente nationale*, drawn by four coursers.

Patriotic spectacles, with speeches by patriots wearing tricolour cockades on their breasts and Phrygian caps on their heads, were now the only entertainments to be given with safety. Franconi had a great advantage over the companies of actors, particularly those of the Théâtre Français, who had narrowly escaped the guillotine. While they were in prison their theatre was empty. Here was the chance for Franconi to occupy the centre of the town. Taking his horses and men to the Théâtre National before the end of the year, he presented there a spectacle called the *Constitution À Constantinople*, suited to the temper of the times.

Three years later the combats and tournaments in his pantomimes at the Théâtre de la Cité highly gratified the martial ardour aroused by Napoleon's first years of victory. The most celebrated was not Franconi's handiwork. After the Peace of Amiens, a manager named Gougisbus presented at the Théâtre de la Cité a spectacle on the subject of the *Knights Of The Sun*.

It was performed before the First Consul Bonaparte, and ran for two hundred successive nights – an unprecedented success. Then it was exported to Astley's Lambeth house, where the bills boasted of its 'grand uncommon Combats, Military Evolutions, Siege by Land and Sea, widespreading Conflagration, etc.,' and of the opening exhibition of a 'Splendid and Nouvelle Tournament.' In the spring of 1803, *The Knights Of The Sun; or, Love And Danger*, was performed by the French company at Astley's Amphitheatre in Dublin, still in celebration of the happy return of peace. In that spring, war broke out again.

Franconi had moved his circus in 1802 to the ancient garden of the Couvent des Capucines. When it was destroyed four years later to make way for the Rue de la Paix, he handed over the reins to his sons, Antoine Laurent (called Laurent), now twenty-nine years of age, and Henri, who was a year younger. They erected a Cirque Olympique between the Rue Saint-Honoré and the Rue du Monthabor in 1807, where they played *La Lanterne De Diogène*. The subject was simple but enthralling. Diogenes sought a man and could not find one. In vain there were set before his eyes the heroes of each century; he fanned his flame and continued to search. When, at last, the bust of Napoleon was exhibited, surrounded by the trophies of victory, the philosopher, snuffing his candle, cried, 'I have found him.' This increased the Emperor's regard for Antoine, who found high favour, partly because he was an Italian, and partly because he was a horseman. Also he was a fine dandy. The Emperor told Murat of the furred and embroidered pelisse, snow-white plume and diamond aigrette, crimson morocco boots, white kid gloves, and jewelled riding-switch, that he looked far less a king than his superior in elegance, the riding-master.

Every evening, Antoine Franconi rode several times round the ring at full gallop as if to demonstrate that he had not yet lost his horsemanship. Every evening the sons performed the *grand écart* and the *saut des rubans*. Every evening Laurent's horses did new tricks: his *Cheval gastronome* opened a bottle of champagne, and his *Jument coquette* displayed her airs and graces. Old Franconi conducted grand manœuvres of cavalry *en haute école*, and four horses danced a minuet. In his *drame à cheval*, the horse was the leading performer. In *Don Quichote*, both the player of the name-part and Sancho Panza were eclipsed by Rosinante and the faithful ass. In the *Voyages De Gulliver*, the chief scene was the isle of the houyhnhnms, where men were humble valets of noble beasts. Even in the military spectacles, horses monopolised the heroics. While, in the *Bataille D'Aboukir*, the troops of Franconi laid siege to a fortress with cannon, shell, and grenade, and fought against Arabs in the arena, the horses acted a very moving drama of devoted courage. One saved his master by offering him his croup as a means of scaling a wall, found him wounded and restored him to consciousness with the warmth of its breath. Another 'died' so thoroughly that an army corps passed before mount and rider as before two corpses. In *Les Français En Pologne*, a piece celebrated for the immense amount of gunpowder discharged, an equine villain enabled a Cossack to carry off an innocent girl beloved by a

French officer. Speech was forbidden, and (as in England) statements were exhibited on scrolls: but horses overcame the ban. 'Thanks to their trainers, they spoke.'

On May 27th, 1816, the family returned to the Faubourg du Temple, and on February 8th, 1817, they reopened Astley's old haunt as a new Cirque Olympique of grand size.

Little is recorded of the distaff side save that Minette was noted for her acting in the pantomimes and Lucie for her horsemanship. Among the Franconi, glory was for the males. Laurent was renowned as a rider and as an animal-trainer. In all the capitals of Europe he exhibited the accomplishments of his mare Blanche in the 'High School of equestrianism' without the stirrup or bridle hand. Blanche would fence, smoke, defend her master, waltz, strike academic poses, exercise as the horse of Alcides, fire cannon, and mount stairs in a shower of fireworks. Coco, Laurent's masterpiece, was a stag who leapt over eight men and four horses, and stood while a pistol was fired between its antlers. Prints were engraved to show how the 'Incomparable cerf du Nord Nommé Azor' ascended the cord 'in a manner challenging comparison with the most famous rope-dancers.' What he actually ascended seems to have been a pole: round his waist was fixed a girdle attaching him to a shield, bearing Astley's motto of *Vide et Crede*, which served as a guide by running along a rope fixed parallel to the pole. There were also canaries who held *conseil de guerre* and an elephant who balanced himself on a wooden disc. Henri Franconi saw to the *mise en scène* of the pantomimes and mimodramas, and wrote several himself. The brothers played the principal rôles, and Minette Franconi the heroine, though all were outshone by the elephant Kiouny in *L'Elephant Du Roi De Siam*.

As ambitious as Astley's in its spectacles, the *Cirque Olympique* revelled in fireworks and conflagrations; and, as at Astley's, a mimic fire was fanned one night, while the family slept, into a real fire. After a performance of *L'Incendie De Salins* on March 15th, 1826, the circus was burned down. Both the Court and the public subscribed to help the Franconi raise a new building, and benefits were given at every theatre. The Cirque Olympique was reconstructed on the boulevard near the Ambigu. The building, so large that it covered the site formerly occupied by the Théâtre de la Malaga, Ombres Chinoises, and Théâtre des Nouveaux-Troubadours, opened on March 31st, 1827, with *Le Palais, La Guinguette Et Le Champ De Bataille*. It was run first by Henri and then by his son, Adolphe, for Laurent perferred to travel with a company which included his son, Victor, and blazon the name of Franconi far and wide.

As his age advanced, Antoine lost his sight through cataract. During this time he amused himself by constructing one of his *voitures nomades*, a new type of caravan containing dining-room, bedroom and galley. For seven years he was blind until he underwent an operation. With restored sight he used to watch, from a special armchair in the first circle, every performance. By now his old apprentices had built permanent circuses in every country of Europe, as well as in America, and pitched their tents in strange outlandish parts. The chief of these pupils was Jacques Tourniaire.

That his grandson should become famous as a geographer is but natural considering Jacques' travels along the unending road traversed by the show, while founding the German circus whose branches were to extend throughout Scandinavia.

Jean-Baptiste Auriol, a favourite of London as well as of Paris, was Franconi's clown. Laughter broke out directly the bells of his motley tinkled before he entered the ring to take a standing jump and pirouette three or four times in the air. From the *tremplin*, he would vault over eight horses and their riders, over twenty-four soldiers with fixed bayonets, or over twelve horses flanked by soldiers who fired during the leap. He would dive through fireworks, or through a circle bristling with 'churchwarderns' without breaking a stem, and march, drill, and fire his musket while balancing on the tops of a dozen wine bottles. He could climb walls 'like a fly' and throw himself, seemingly with foolhardy recklessness, from the topmost frieze of the Cirque Olympique. Or he would somersault in the air and let his feet fall straight into the slippers he had left on the ground. In *Zazezizozu*, a Chinese spectacle staged by the Franconi in 1835, concerning three princes named Zizi, Zozo, and Zuzu, who all loved the Princess Zaza, Auriol was tied to the wings of a windmill which whirled him round at breakneck speed. 'What,' it was asked, 'is lighter than a feather? Dust. Than dust? The wind. Than the wind? Auriol.' His son became Auriol II, his daughter married Flexmore, the English clown, and his nephew, Thomas Belling, invented the new type of clown, called Auguste, who wears not motley but suits much too large for him.

Outliving both Philip and John Astley, Antoine became, before his death in 1836 at the age of ninety-eight, the patriarch of the circus. While he feebly moved his shrivelled hands together with the delight of watching horses obey the crack of the *chambrière* in his grandson's establishment, showmen who had learnt their trade from the pupils of his sons' apprentices were risking death from cold in the northern regions of Russia, and from tomahawks on the outposts of civilisation across the Atlantic.[1]

[1] Even to-day his influence is to be found in every circus of the world. Every ring is of his regulation size – thirteen metres in diameter – because wherever horses are taken they must be on familiar ground.

2

Napoleon's Circus Wars

Long before the death of Antoine Franconi the minds of Frenchmen had become filled with disgust for their rulers and regrets for the Empire. Both in London and Paris, the glories of that epoch of warfare were being resurrected out of the circus until Napoleon was the hero of Europe. Although time had more to do with the change of feeling than Astley's, the glamour of the past was intensified by the glitter of gaslight. If this was so on 'the Surrey side,' how much more powerful must the spell have been on the Boulevard du Temple? Hearing old grenadiers' boasting of the past, the younger generation were so roused when they smelt powder at Franconi's that the equestrian drama played no unimportant part in the return of the Bonapartes to the throne of France. The truth of this was plain enough to inspire a *Punch* artist to caricature Louis Napoleon as a juggler balancing his illustrious uncle's hat and boots on his nose while treading insecurely on the tops of bottles in the manner of Auriol.

In 1830, Charles X was forced to abdicate, and the people's triumph over their ruler immediately caused all to burn with republican or Bonapartist ardour. Napoleon was again their idol. Whereas the Cirque Olympique had hitherto staged sieges for the sake of fiery spectacles, the Franconi now staged such pieces for the sake of fiery patriotism. Every theatre was looking for an actor who could be praised for bearing an astonishing likeness to the *Grand homme*. Frédérick Lemaître was emperor at the Odéon; Cazot, emperor at the Variétés; Génot, emperor at the Opéra-Comique; Gobert, emperor at the Porte-Saint-Martin; and Edmond, emperor *chez* Franconi. 'All those who had known the Emperor,' says Georges Cain in his *Anciens Théâtres De Paris*, 'all the veterans who had served under him, all the bourgeois who had seen him in profile on a medal, were thrilled to see him again in Cazot, Edmond and Prudent.'

These actors took their mission seriously on or off the stage. Gobert gravely paraded the boulevard with knitted brows, hands behind his back and *le chapeau en bataille*; Edmond smoothed his lock and nobly took snuff from his leather waistcoat-pocket; Cazot solemnly pinched the ear of the *costumier* when his breeches of white cashmere were well cut, and murmured, 'Soldat, je suis content de vous.' In the autumn of 1830, the Vaudeville was presenting *Bonaparte – Lieutenant D'Artillerie*; the Variétés *Napoléon À Berlin Ou La Redingote Grise*; Nouveautés, *L'Ecolier De Brienne Ou Le Petit Caporal*; Ambigu, *Napoléon*; Porte-Saint-Martin, *Napoléon*; Cirque Olympique, *Passage Du Mont Saint Bernard*. Georges Cain knew an old artist's model who played Sir Hudson Lowe in *Sainte-Hélène*. One night a mob, lying in wait at the stage door, seized him and threw him in the basin of the Château d'Eau amid cries of 'Vive l'Empereur!' During the run of this sad spectacle of the Last Phase at the Cirque, one veteran was carried out dying. Georges Cain's grandfather, who fought at Waterloo, went to the theatre only when he might see the *redingote grise*.

In the eighteen-thirties the municipality took the Cirque Olympique off the hands of its founder's family. Though still called Franconi's, its official name was now the Théâtre du Cirque Olympique. No longer were Scenes in the Circle displayed there. Both stage and arena were required solely for equestrian dramas such as *Murat*, *L'Empire*, and *Le Cheval Du Diable*. With singular unwisdom, the Government directly encouraged displays of Napoleon's victories. Liking to hear himself called the Napoleon of Peace, Louis Philippe forgot that by patronising performances mainly devoted to the glory of the First Empire he was keeping alive the Napoleonic legend to the detriment of Orleanist prestige. Should you wish to understand what was passing in the minds of the ardent worshippers of the Emperor, read *Les Misérables*, particularly this snippet of conversation between two young men who have just met:

By the way, do you hold any political opinions?
Of course.
What are you? – Bonapartist, democrat.

And it was at the time this creed was germinating that 'In the Council of Ministers the question was discussed whether the woodcuts representing tumblers, which seasoned Franconi's bills and caused street urchins to crowd round, should be tolerated.' But at the time of Fieschi's attempt to kill Louis Philippe on the Boulevard du Temple, by firing twenty-five barrels charged with various missiles, no Napoleonic spectacles were billed at the theatres near by. At the Cirque Olympique martial ardour had temporarily run short of inspiration. Under various names, the drama of Napoleon had been performed nearly four hundred times. All the fame he had won on earth had been summarised, and his glory had been followed to the skies in order to reveal the apotheosis of the heroes of France beyond the grave; their horses, taking wings, had flown with them through the air. But now drum-majors became sailors, *sacré nom d'une pipe* was exchanged for *mille sabords*, standards gave place to ensigns, the prompter's *cabane* represented a rock, and the drums that once beat to arms now sounded the swish of water.

La Traite Des Noirs was a sea-piece, setting forth how the cargo of a wrecked slave-trader turned pirates and successfully waged war against ships manned by Europeans. As this was the first of the naval dramas which were a feature of the Cirque Olympique, the secret of the wild waves should be told. Alexandre Dumas was the inventor of the scheme; when he first brought the Mediterranean upon the boards of the Odéon he admitted a journalist to rehearsals. In consequence, this turbulent ocean was now declared to be nothing more remarkable than a painted canvas covering *tous les gamins du 12° arrondissement*. From time to time the director, by well-directed kicks, stirred what was literally the angry sea. At Franconi's Thackeray witnessed *Le Maudit Des Mers*. A celestial vessel, with angels on deck and cherubs in the shrouds, received the Flying Dutchman's soul, saved by a maiden's prayer. The critical comment was: 'An angel-ship was introduced in place of the usual horsemanship.'

When *Napoléon Bonaparte* was again presented, *la Mer, cette grande actrice*, appeared in the fourth act. This time she was agitated by an equinoctial gale so powerful that the women aboard the ship enacted a real tragedy. Complaining that the *dénouement* of this spectacle even upset him a little, the critic of the *Monde Dramatique* said he seemed always to see the director's redoubtable feet exciting the waves.

When Heine visited the theatres of the 'Boulevard du Crime,' in 1837, he decided that the stage of Franconi's could not be placed in rank with the others, as 'the pieces given there are more fit for horses than for men.' But all the stirring incidents were not acted in the saddle. In *Le Soldat De La République* inspiration was drawn from Fieschi. While in charge of a post, the corporal found that his men had been drugged; by laying all their muskets on a table, he defied the enemy with this new *machine infernale*. In every performance the clatter of arms and explosion of powder mattered more than dialogue. The company could not be said to consist of actors; they were rather sham soldiers. Thackeray, at this time, described how there was as regular gradation in the ranks of the mimic army at Franconi's as in the real Imperial regions:

> After a man has served with credit, for a certain number of years in the line, he is promoted to be an officer – an acting officer. If he conducts himself well,

he may rise to be a Colonel, or a General of Division; if ill, he is degraded to the ranks again; or, worse degradation of all, drafted into a regiment of Cossacks or Austrians. Cossacks is the lowest depth, however; nay, it is said that the men who perform these Cossack parts receive higher wages than the mimic grenadiers and old guard. They will not consent to be beaten every night, even in play; to be pursued in hundreds by a handful of French; to fight against their beloved Emperor. Surely there is fine hearty virtue in this, and pleasant childlike simplicity.

This was the year when Louis Napoleon attempted to stir such enthusiasm into an insurrection at Strassburg, and failed.

Was the time of the First Empire, asked Heine, really as beautiful and happy a time as the Bonapartists, great and small, represented? He was thinking of his neighbour, the old grenadier, sitting pensively before his door. 'From time to time he begins one of his old Bonapartist songs; but emotion intercepts his voice: his eyes are red, and to all appearances the old fellow has wept.' It was because he had been to Franconi's and there seen the battle of Austerlitz. In Elizabeth Sharp's translation the passage continues:

He quitted Paris at midnight, and the recollections so dominated his soul that he marched back during the night as though in a state of somnambulism, and reached the village this morning to his great astonishment. He enumerated all the faults of the piece to me; for he had himself been at Austerlitz, where the cold was so intense that his rifle froze to his fingers;

at Franconi's, on the contrary, the heat was unbearable. He was quite pleased with the powder smoke, and also with the smell of the horses; only he affirms that at Austerlitz the cavalry had not such well-groomed horses. He could not verify exactly if the manœuvres of the infantry were correct, for at Austerlitz, as in every battle, the smoke was so thick that it was scarcely possible to distinguish what was happening in the neighbourhood. But at Franconi's the smoke, according to the old man was perfect, and it came so agreeably on his chest that it cured him of his cough.

'And the Emperor?' Heine asked him. 'The Emperor,' answered the old soldier, 'he was exactly the same as when in life – in his grey coat, with his little three-cornered hat, and my heart beat in my breast. Ah, the Emperor!'
Not only the old Bonapartists, but also the great mass of the people, delighted to cradle themselves in these illusions. The heroism of the imperial domination was the sole pride of the French and Napoleon their only hero. In any of the little vaudevilles of the Boulevard du Temple there had only to be a scene of his times for applause to be assured. The audience wept over such words as *Aigle Français, soleil d'Austerlitz, Jena, les Pyramides, la grande armée, l'honneur, la vieille garde, Napoléon* . . . or when *l'homme* made his appearance at the end of the piece, as *Deus ex machina*. He always had the magic hat on his head, his hands behind his back, and spoke as laconically as possible. Songs were sung of his glory and tragic end. The music of these

Napoleonic refrains was heard everywhere. 'It seems,' wrote Heine, 'as though they are floating in the air or sung by birds in the trees.' Here are the first and the last lines of one of them:

> *Te souviens-tu*, disait un capitaine
> Au veteran qui mendiait son pain,
> *Te souviens-tu* qu'autrefois dans la plaine
> Tu détournas un sabre de mon sein?

The Pyramids, Italy, Germany, Russia, and then:

> Mais si le mort, planant sur ma chaumière,
> Me rappelait au repos que m'est dû,
> Tu fermeras doucement ma paupière,
> En me disant: Soldat, *t'en souviens-tu*?

The passion for the Emperor was fanned by the spectacles of the Boulevard du Temple until Louis Napoleon, in the summer of 1840, again tried to excite a rebellion and again failed. The flame still burned vigorously. Mimic show gave place to imperial pomp on December 15th, when the coffin from St. Helena was brought to the Hôtel des Invalides. All the relatives of the Emperor were absent, for (having been proscribed) they were either in exile or in prison. No further insurrections were attempted, and nothing was feared from the continued popularity of the Napoleonic drama. While the public thronged to Franconi's, society patronised the Cirque d'Été, in the Champs Élysées, founded by Antoine Franconi's grandson Adolphe. At first, performances were given in the open air, and on mild summer evenings the ring was the favourite resort of all those for whom the opera had no more mysteries; of all the fashionable ladies, 'beautiful exiles from the Italian theatre,' who were content to watch horses leap while awaiting the return of Lablache, Rubini, and Madame Persiani. In 1840, a roofed building arose on the spot, adorned by Pradier. This sculptor had a very large family; he wanted to take them to the circus, but found it too expensive. He gave Dejean, the manager who succeeded Adolphe Franconi, a stone group in exchange for a permanent pass for himself and his children. It was of 'a beautiful amazon breaking an unruly horse for mere amusement.'

Meanwhile Laurent Franconi's son, Victor, had come back, after serving his apprenticeship throughout the world, and was inventing a new type of circus. On a site beyond the barrier of l'Étoile, he erected seats for ten thousand spectators around a large track in the open. The arena was oblong with rounded corners. Neither in shape nor in size could it be described as a circus ring; it was unsuited for equestrian feats relying upon centrifugal force, or for close acquaintance between clowns and public. This he called – helping another ancient word on a tortuous modern career – the Hippodrome. It opened in 1846 with the spectacle of the *Camp Du Drap D'Or*. At the moment of the meeting between Francois I and Henry VIII, a heavy rainstorm burst, so that lords in rich armour and ladies on palfreys floundered in a lake of mud – yet thousands of voices called for the show to continue. Thus happily begun, the Hippodrome prospered under Victor Franconi until political disturbances caused him to sell out.

When the grand reform banquet was prohibited in 1848, barricades were thrown up, the Tuileries ransacked, and the prisons opened. In February, Louis

Philippe abdicated; in June, the Red Republicans fortified themselves in the Faubourg du Temple and surrendered only when cannon were brought against their positions; in December, Louis Napoleon was elected President, and at last, in 1852, Emperor.

With renewed ardour, Napoleon's victories were won all over again in Franconi's ring, while the Cirque in the Champs Élysées – now called the Cirque National but soon to be called the Cirque de l'Impératrice – was the spot chosen by Louis Napoleon to distribute crosses of the Legion of Honour, just as his illustrious uncle – in the person of Gomersal – made field marshals amid the sawdust at Astley's. It had to be said for ourselves, commented *Punch*, 'that in England we only give the dramatic versions of history at our amphitheatres, while in France, they are the places in which the great events of national interest take place.' In that jest, the difference between Franconi's and Astley's is indicated. The only history made on the Surrey side of Westminster Bridge was the history of showmanship; but on the Boulevard du Temple changes of politics were often anticipated, if not created, and were always reflected. This can be noted in the titles given to Franconi's. In 1842 it was the Théâtre Imperial du Cirque, in 1848 the Théâtre National (*Ancien Cirque*), and in 1852, the Théâtre Imperial once more. Whether national or imperial, its glory was still the Emperor. It regularly supplied the hungry public with such intoxicants as *La République*, *L'Empire Et Les Cent Jours*, *Les Pages De L'Empereur*, *Le Prince Eugène Et L'Impératrice Joséphine*, *Austerlitz*, *Murat*, *Masséna*, *L'Enfant Chéri De La Victoire*, and *Bonaparte En Egypte*.

In 1854 the military drama was brought up to date at the Hippodrome, where a force was occupied three or four times a week in resisting the *Siege Of Silistria*. It was got up with such splendour that *Punch* doubted whether the real thing could have been half so good as the imitation: it was quite certain that nothing in the British Army could compare with 'the Scotch regiment of little men with long black beards, which strikes terror into the Russians at the Hippodrome.' In order to give as much reality as possible to the siege, the troops were commanded by real French officers:

> We can hardly imagine Lord Raglan galloping backwards and forwards on Astley's stage; or H.R.H. the Duke of Cambridge dashing up a platform on his richly caparisoned steed, and inviting six mounted supernumeraries to follow him through the upper entrance O.P. side to death or victory.

The Théâtre Impérial du Cirque was still loyal to Napoleon. Here, in 1860, was staged *L'Histoire D'Un Drapeau*, by Adolphe D'Ennery, which aroused as much enthusiasm as the earliest of the series. This grand military drama was in twelve tableaux, whose very names revealed the generous nature of the plot. After being embroidered in a French workshop, the flag saw service on the plateau of Rivoli, on the bridge of Arcole, in the battle of the Pyramids; it was carried from the feast of the Nile to a Russian cottage; it survived the snows of the north, welcomed the Emperor on his return from Elba, and survived to triumph at Solferino – the year before these performances were given.

In the large space created by joining arena to stage,

three or four hundred soldiers and troops of horse manœuvred. Bayonet charges were delivered, redoubts taken and retaken, the flag saved by horses, bivouac fires lit, batteries carried by assault, traitors shot, and nations subdued. National pride, says Georges Cain, was carried to such a pitch that each super – as in former days – agreed to play a French soldier for a franc, although fifty centimes extra was paid to every man willing to represent a Russian, Austrian, or Englishman. It was in such a piece that Colbrun, a diminutive actor who looked like a boy of fourteen, won glory. In answer to a voice which cried: 'Surrender, brave Frenchman,' when he was surrounded by Cossacks, he cried, before dispersing his enemies, 'If General Cambronne were here, I know what he would have to say to that.'

While these deeds of heroism were being enacted, the doom of the Boulevard du Crime was sealed. Its seven theatres were pulled down in 1862 to make way for the new boulevard, which Louis Napoleon inaugurated in the December of that year. But the old Franconi's had already been replaced by a circus near by. Twelve years after the building of the Cirque d'Été, Dejean looked around him for the opportunity of establishing another circus. Arguing that Franconi's was now a theatre, because scenes in the circle were no longer performed there, he obtained permission to replace the Cirque Olympique. Once again he commissioned Hittorf to draught plans, this time for a Cirque d'Hiver. Pradier adorned the entrance with statues; the Amazon on one side was entirely his, but the warrior on the other was finished by another, for

Pradier died that June. On December 11th, 1852, the building was opened as the Cirque Napoléon by the Emperor himself. After the surrender of the Emperor at Sedan, the revolution in Paris, and the declaration of a republic, it became the Cirque National, while the Crown Prince of Prussia awarded Iron Crosses beneath the statue of Louis IV on the spot where the Astleys had performed at Versailles. In times of peace the Cirque d'Hiver, resuming its original title, lived to be the oldest circus building in the world.[1]

In Genoa Dickens saw marionettes from Milan act *St. Helena; or, The Death Of Napoleon*, a faint echo of those circus campaigns. Although Bonaparte's boots might skate away with him when he was in full speech with settled melancholy depicted on his face, and although when he bent over a book his sentimental eyes were glaring obstinately into the pit, the audience applauded him and execrated Sir Hudson Lowe. 'It would be hard to say why; for Italians have little cause to sympathise with Napoleon, Heaven knows,' was Dickens's comment. The explanation could probably be traced to the circus.

[1] The oldest in London, which now houses the Stadium Club, was opened as the Holborn Amphitheatre in the June of 1867.

V

EQUESTRIAN DRAMA

I

The Terrible Fitzball

TWICE before now Astley's had risen from its ashes, and it would do so again. In the circuses throughout the country which carried on the traditions of Astley in amphitheatres of brick or wood, as well as in those performed under canvas (according to the new-fangled fashion for tenting) or in arenas marked out in fields by cross-roads, many a showman had cherished the hope of ruling over the Amphitheatre, no matter what it might cost, and several had the means in money, horses, wild beasts, and men to take over Ducrow's command. Yet the task of rebuilding was not lightly to be undertaken. Showmen used to the perilous hazards of transport by sea or land feared a public which would not walk up – and we have Dickens's word for it that Londoners were hard to please:

Astley's has altered for the better – we have changed for the worse. Our histrionic taste is gone, and with shame we confess that we are far more delighted and amused with the audience, than with the pageantry we once so highly appreciated.

Although peers of the realm waited upon wasp-waisted *écuyères* from Paris when they rode *en haute école*[1] at Astley's, London society never thronged the stables there as Paris society did at Franconi's.

One showman instantly decided to seize the chance to rebuild Astley's. This was William Batty, the horseman, well known as 'Mons. Batty' as far back as 1828, when his Olympic Circus was at the Royal Pantheon, Norwich; ten years later it had two zebras, a wild ass, and an elephant to display in performances of *Mazeppa*. Batty was described by Fitzball, the hippo-dramatist, as a most extraordinary man, endowed with a natural intellect, 'so penetrating, so microscopic, that it would have required a very powerful mind indeed to have deceived him on any point'; his calculations were incredible, and Fitzball preferred his opinions on all subjects 'to those of a Lord Chancellor.' Yet Batty owed nothing to education, for he was born in humble circumstances, and worked his way up from boyhood by sheer industry in spite of ill health. When Astley's was burned down, he was with his circus in Dublin. While others hesitated, he crossed by the first steamer, set out for London without resting, and bought the site directly he arrived. Before his rivals had heard the news he had completed arrangements for the rebuilding and was on his way back.

Several architects had been recommended to his notice, but to all such offers he had answered, 'Dicky Usher is the only man to do it.' The news was startling

---

[1] This denotes skill in the saddle as distinct from *basse école*, defined by Littré as 'exercises by which pupils learn to mount' – *basse* in the riding-school being an incline for training.

except to the few who knew the old clown, a performer of Philip Astley's stamp in his knowledge of showmanship. While travelling with his father's mechanical exhibition round the north of England and Ireland, he was trained how to 'mould' (collect coppers) until old enough to perform at street-corners himself. After catching the eye of the manager of the Royal Amphitheatre, Christian Street, Liverpool, in 1807, he graduated in two years to Astley's. Here the Mr. Merryman was supplied with jokes by Westminster scholars in rivalry to see which were most applauded. In time there was a stock of these, but Dicky Usher's own were best. The bills of a benefit he took at the Surrey in 1829 announced:

> It being the request of numerous Persons who witnessed Mr. Usher's eccentric Aquatic Excursion, in triumph, like Neptune in his Car (on the River Thames) drawn by his four favourite Geese.
> Gibble, Gabble, Gobble and Garble.
> Then proceeding on the High Road from Waterloo Bridge, drawn by
> His Four Thorough-Bred Mousers,
> who won the Wager by performing the distance of 951 yards within 8 minutes and a quarter, off the Turnpike Road at Liverpool, he will this night, by desire, mount his vehicle and drive his favourite Cats,
> Four In Hand Several Times Round The Stage.

That voyage was in a washing-tub: he sailed in it from Westminster Bridge to Waterloo Bridge, where the crowd was so great that his little chariot was held up until several jolly young watermen carried him and his cats to the Coburg Theatre shoulder high.

Miss C. Usher was 'the only female Infant Prodigy of the present day,' and acted General Bombastes at the age of five with universal and unparalleled success. With his second wife, a sister of James Wallack, for partner, he fought in *Albert And Elmira; or, The Dumb Boy And His Horse*, through fire and real water at Sadler's Wells. That he was also an architect the new Astley's proved. A few months after it had opened, he died at Hercules Hall on September 23rd, 1843, aged fifty-eight. Three weeks before this, Mrs. Hannah Waldo Astley had died. Thus the last links with Philip Astley snapped.

Six months after the fire, Batty's Royal Circus was housed at the National Baths, Westminster Bridge Road, which in the spring of 1843 became 'Batty's Equestrian Arena,' where he impersonated *The Cockney Sportsman; or, The First Of September*, and Romanzoff carrying the Emperor Nicholas's dispatches to the Sultan. At the end of March, he took his company to the Surrey, where they remained while he also ran a dramatic and operatic company combined with 'equestrian artistes and double stud' at the Olympic Arena, White Conduit Gardens, Islington.

Astley's New Royal Amphitheatre of Arts opened on Easter Monday, 1843. The exterior had two fronts; while the entrance to the boxes still faced Westminster Bridge Road in the only wall that survived the fire, the gallery doors were in a new street from the main road to Stangate. Inside, over fifty boxes were ranged in tiers, each with a chandelier in front, forming three

horseshoes of lights, while from the dome hung a
massive chandelier of crystal and gold. Amid these
glories Batty's company, reinforced by what remained
of Ducrow's, performed *The Afghanistan War! or,
The Revolt Of Cabul! And British Triumphs In India*,
Lord Ellenborough having the honour to be represented by Widdicomb, and a comic Irishman enabling
Thomas Barry to reveal powers which made him one of
Astley's famous clowns – how famous we may gather
from the mention W. S. Gilbert makes of him in a
foreword to Rutland Barrington's reminiscences:

> I remember that when I was a boy of thirteen I
> followed Mr. Tom Barry (the then well-known
> clown at Astley's Amphitheatre) all the way from
> Temple Bar to Westminster Bridge, trying to make
> up my mind to ask him the time. Unfortunately,
> however, just as I had screwed up my courage to the
> sticking point, Mr. Barry baffled me by turning
> suddenly into a public house of refreshment, whither
> I had not the enterprise to follow him.

Barry was the second to ride the Thames in a goose-
drawn tub, and two others, Nelson and Twist, did likewise only a few months later in 1844, when the secret
was disclosed that the tubs were attached to a rowing-
boat some distance ahead by a rope under the water.
Another good publicity measure was undertaken by
Emidy, Batty's 'Master of Horse,' when tooling
fourteen pairs, harnessed to a coach containing the
band, from the Amphitheatre to Greenwich and back
in two and a half hours. Twist in his motley had his
portrait painted on a service of china, each piece

inscribed, 'The Trampolinist and great Herculian Wonder. Astley's Royal Amphitheatre 1843.'

A PIECE OF ASTLEY CHINA
From *The Listener*, 1937

By royal command 'A Grand Equestrian Day Representation' – this was before matinées were invented – was given at Astley's in the April of 1846. As the life of the Queen had recently been threatened, and as she had twice been fired at, the building was strictly searched and strongly defended, although such precautions were not usual during Her Majesty's habitual playgoing. Footguards now lined the passages of the theatre, posted sentries at the stage door, garrisoned The Ride, and occupied the main entrance in force. The auditorium, though empty, was 'gorgeously embellished.' The Queen, with Prince Albert, the Prince of Wales, and the Princess Royal, watched the performance from a box in the centre of the first circle, where the Royal Arms were superbly emblazoned on the hangings of crimson and white silk.

Circuses always attracted Queen Victoria. To use her name as a label for the activities of her most solemn and portentous subjects is unjust. She does not come into this history by accident. If Diderot was right in dividing humanity into the drab and the flamboyant, she must be classed with the flamboyant. When the Panoptican in Leicester Square was assisting 'by moral and intellectual agencies, the best interests of society,' she stayed away even though she had granted it a royal charter; but when, as the Alhambra, it housed an American circus, she attended with Prince Albert and their children, a private performance, as at Astley's. Her character is revealed in the records of showmanship as spontaneously light-hearted, especially in an episode at the Princess's when the manager fell while walking backwards along the passage to the box with lighted candles, and became 'covered with confusion and candle-grease.' Although Prince Albert was shocked at her levity, she leant against the wall to laugh 'long and loudly.' She opposed the rigid etiquette of Colonel Phipps, her equerry, especially when he ordered the player of a blacksmith not to act the part before her in his shirt-sleeves.

Madame Pauline de Vere, the Lady of the Lions, otherwise Ellen Chapman, who became George Sanger's wife, was commanded to appear at Windsor Castle. Queen Victoria sat at a window overlooking the courtyard where the 'den,' containing a lion, a tiger, and the tamer, was drawn up. Afterwards Madame Pauline was conducted into the castle, where the Prince Consort patted her on the back, and the Queen gave her a gold watch and chain. Tears of gratitude poured down the girl's cheeks. 'I am sure you are afraid,' said the Queen.

Barnum did not find admittance to Buckingham Palace difficult when he wished to present Tom Thumb, whom the Queen took by the hand and asked many questions, 'the answers to which kept the party in an uninterrupted strain of merriment.' After the dwarf had sung and danced, the conversation, with Prince Albert taking part, lasted for more than an hour. When running to the door in an unorthodox attempt to 'back out,' Tom Thumb was barked at by a poodle, which he attacked with his cane, while the fight 'renewed and increased the merriment of the royal party.' There was another visit to meet the Prince of Wales. Then there was another visit to meet the King of the Belgians, when the Queen's interest was still unabated. On each occasion Barnum placed on the door of his room at the Egyptian Hall in Piccadilly, 'Closed this evening, General Tom Thumb being at Buckingham Palace by command of Her Majesty.' And so it happened that in 1846, when Haydon, painter of huge Biblical and classical canvases (of the kind that are supposed to represent Victorian taste), was exhibiting a picture he became so desolate at being ignored by the crowds which Tom Thumb was drawing to another part of the hall, that he committed suicide.

At Astley's the royal family saw Mr. Widdicomb, 'all uniform,' in the centre of the ring. There were acrobats, performing horses, the celebrated elephants, and a grand tableau from *The Rajah Of Nagpore*. And, while they watched, they were being watched by one spectator who had eluded the search-parties. James Lloyd, a son of the Lloyd who had been a clown at Astley's since 1830, had climbed a rope to the dome, where he lay looking through a hole in the matchboarding. When the Queen had gone he discovered that the rope had been removed; he jumped and caught another rope four feet away.

There was embittered rivalry at this time between the clowns. While Barry kept to the old ways, Wallett invented a new style to express his own character – devoid of all those qualities of modesty, gentle kindliness, and simple goodwill that endear clowns to all generations – which is expressed in an autobiography so vainglorious as to cause playgoers who read it to grope instinctively with their free hands for something to throw. He called himself 'The Queen's Jester,' wore pedantic costumes inspired by 'perusal of mediæval missals,' and decorated his face with a ponderous moustache. When the critics objected, he rebuked them in a learned lecture on jesters of the olden times. He was no circus clown, but a *Shakespearean* Jester. His jests were long recitations, sometimes in prose, sometimes in verse, studded with political and moral sentiments, from the lists of toasts at the end of old song-books. On his bills, he quoted the praise of *The Nottingham Journal*, which had said that Mr. Wallett was in everything *the perfect gentleman*; 'his actions betrayed him as such immediately.' He inspired a whole school of clever clowns. All who grew too fat to tumble or too stupid to play the fool in the ordinary way turned Shakespearean – this was contemporary criticism – and bored the public with set speeches. There was no Mr. Merryman now to ask Widdicomb, 'Does your mother know you're out?' or pass 'rare old imbecile remarks.'

Wallett appealed so strongly to his generation that Mr. Merryman was exiled. Albert Smith, the phenomenally successful travel-lecturer, saw one in the tent of the Grand Circo Olympico at Pera. When he jumped into the ring, and cried out, in perfect English: 'Here we are again – all of a lump! How are you?' it fell flat:

I looked at the bill, and found him described as 'Grottesco Inglese,' Whittayne. I did not recognise the name in connection with the annals of Astley's, but he was a very clever fellow, notwithstanding; and, when he addressed the master of the ring, and observed, 'If you please, Mr. Guillaume, he says, that you said, that I said, that they said, that nobody said, nothing to anybody,' it was with a drollery of manner that at last agitated the fezzes, like poppies in the wind, although the meaning of the speech was still like a sealed book to them.

Barry left Astley's when his right to choose his own parts in the dramas was taken away. Wallett, to show how observant he had been, played the character of a rollicking Irishman, for which his rival had been famous, at a moment's notice. Barry found a welcome at Drury Lane in the autumn of 1853 as clown to Mlle. Ella, born in Louisiana of French parents. While riding a horse at full gallop, she leapt over the Stars and Stripes nine feet wide. All the young bloods of the town worshipped her shapely legs and tiny feet, and she returned to Drury Lane with her own company in 1857. She rode upright upon her horse while it jumped hurdles, and flew through fifty balloons before performing an 'aerial vault to the throne of fame.' All were astounded at her courage. At length it was known that she was a husband and a father. He had for years dressed with actresses in their rooms, and been received into private families, says Wallett, on terms of the greatest intimacy with the ladies.

When the great exhibition was held in Hyde Park in 1851, Batty opened a Grand National Hippodrome opposite Broad Walk in Kensington, to attract the crowds from the Crystal Palace. Covered seats surrounded an arena 'of enormous dimensions' for chariot races, tournaments, steeplechases, and a pageant of the Field of the Cloth of Gold. There was a race between two ostriches ridden by Arabs, one of whom was thrown. This Hippodrome had a short life in the rain.

Astley's in itself was a difficult enough task. Whereas Ducrow had presented one new spectacle each season, Batty brought out novelties every month, including *Buonaparte In Egypt* (popular in Paris) and an equestrian version of *Uncle Tom's Cabin*, without finding one to rival *Mazeppa*, which he revived season after season. There was very little fame for playwrights at Astley's.

The only hippo-dramatist of note was Edward Fitzball, born plain Ball, the son of a farmer. The 'brave Fitzball,' the 'terrible Fitzball,' he was called by Bon Gaultier, because, while mild and inoffensive of person, his melodramas were sulphurous and sanguinary:

Then said our Queen – 'Was ever seen so stout a knight and
    tall ?
His name ? – his race ?' – 'An't please your grace, it is the
    brave Fitzball.
Oft in the Melodrama line his prowess hath been shown,
And well throughout the Surrey side his thirst for blood is
    known.'

A LAMENT
ON THE SUBSTITUTION OF "THE SCENES IN THE CIRCLE" FOR "THE HISTORIC DRAMA" AT ASTLEY'S.

FROM BATTY'S boards the Tartar hordes
    Have vanish'd like an idle dream;
Our history's page and Astley's stage
    Identical no longer seem.

To Indian wars, in gilded cars,
    No more the British chieftains jolt;
No horsemen fly o'er platforms high,
    Secur'd by mortice, screw, and bolt.

Its eager course *Mazeppa's* horse
 No longer runs with wild career;
And Mister Hicks no longer sticks
 To bare-back'd steed 'mid shout and cheer.

That aged man, the weeping *Khan*,
 Has ceas'd to hug his long lost son;
The *Tyrant Greek* his pound a week
 Has lost—his occupation gone!

Drawings by Tenniel, from *Punch* in 1851

He has been described by Mr. D. L. Murray as the 'happy adapter of anybody's work,' but he was not so happy that he could not complain, 'Dibdin could dramatise a novel in a day or two; I was compelled to take a week.' Although this handicapped his output, he turned out plays enough to be dubbed 'The English Dumas, in quantity, not quality, of melodrama.' Despite their unchanging atmosphere of gloom, distraction, and despair, some were staged at Drury Lane, and his *Idiot Boy* was – so he mentions in his *Thirty-Five Years Of A Dramatic Author's Life* – commended by 'the benevolent Bishop of Norwich – the *best of bishops*.'

In Fitzball's *The White Maiden Of California* at Astley's, according to his own account, a scene of startling interest was represented. This he thought had never been surpassed. A young man, shut up in a cavern where the bones of Indians were buried, dreamed that not only the spirits of the dead Indians, but the *horses* which they rode, appeared to him. The Indians, 'clad perfectly in white, mounted on their war steeds, cream coloured every one, rose on traps, the horses as collected and still as the statue at Charing Cross.'

Besides adapting *Marmion* and *Peter The Great* for Batty, Fitzball turned *Azael The Prodigal*, his Drury Lane version of Scribe and Auber's *L'Enfant Prodigue*, into *Azael; or, The Prodigal Of Memphis*, with Stickney as a priest and Widdicomb as Theophas, a noble. While the Memphian games were being held a procession came in sight introducing the unrivalled collection of wild animals which was always dragged, kicked, poked, and pinched through every quarter of the globe. 'Our old refractory friends, the two stags without tails,' commented *Punch*, 'writhe through the ground square of Memphis as uncomfortably as they wriggle over the Steppes of Tartary in *Mazeppa*, or sidle about among the thumps and shoves of a hostile

THE TERRIBLE FITZBALL

BRITANNIA's brow no longer now
 Is crown'd with fresh historic bays;
In mimic field no Frenchmen yield
 To six dramatic Scottish Greys.

NAPOLEON has pass'd and gone!
 The part has left Astleyan hands;
But LOUIS B. they run to see,
 Burlesquing it in foreign lands.

The hat and snuff, the small-clothes buff,
 Once so familiar to the town,
Are on the shelf; BARRY himself
 Must lay aside his stage renown.

Drawings by Tenniel, from *Punch* in 1851

soldiery in the *Wars Of Afghanistan*.' After losing all he had at dice, Azael was tempted by a young lady in pink and spangles, and at length condemned to be thrown to the Nile's crocodiles. In the scene of the

'Mighty Desert' he reappeared and saw visions. On arising and going to his father, he caused so great a shock to the old man that a galleryite shouted, 'Come, come, hold up, old man, hold up,' before the story continued. Then, by means of a magic lantern, there was a 'grand superhuman reappearance of the nocturnal vision in the desert.'

Fitzball died at the age of eighty-one in 1873, with a vast number of dramas, melodramas, Christmas pantomimes, and burlettas to his credit, besides the libretti of operas, including *Maritana,* and dramatised versions of Scott's novels. 'One likes to take leave of him,' says Mr. Murray, 'in the scene he himself narrates, when, on entering the Puseyite church at Brighton to pray (and be shocked) he was, while kneeling in a low pew, enveloped in the descent of a colossal crinoline and so snuffed out for ever.' Not completely, for his mildness of person still comes to mind whenever *Pretty Jane,* the song he wrote for Sims Reeves, voices his appeal to her to meet him when the bloom is on the rye and 'never to look so shy.' It is a song that lingers so plaintively on 'meet' that, when sung in the home, it would often raise false hopes in the stomach of the Victorian cat.

2

Shakespeare On Horseback

ONLY on condition that it should be kept open year in and year out every day except Sundays, Christmas Day, and Good Friday, was Batty willing to let Astley's. That scared away all prospective tenants except William Cooke. With circus profits of £50,000 in hand, he felt secure in taking a seven-years' lease of the Amphitheatre at a weekly rental of £50, to be collected every Saturday night in person by William Batty, who now retired with riches to Bridge House, Golders Green.

That was how, on the Easter Monday of 1853, Astley's came into the possession of the oldest circus family, which deserves to be called *the* circus family, since it is related by marriage to the circus families of the world. It was founded by Thomas Cooke, who travelled from fair to fair in Scotland round about 1752. The history of Cooke's Royal Circus, published in 1897 and sold wherever the company went, was written by Harry S. Lumsden. This rare little book says that, at Mauchlin, Robert Burns heard Peter McNab, then first fiddle in Cooke's circus, play *The Braes of*

Invermay and *Roslin Castle* after the performance, and listened with 'rapt attention and delight.'

Thomas Taplin Cooke, born at Warwick in 1782, succeeded his father as head of the circus. While returning from Lisbon in 1816, he lost forty horses during a storm in the Bay of Biscay. These were soon replaced when he used his Portuguese takings to build wooden amphitheatres in the chief cities of north England.

With forty members of the family, including his seven sons and five daughters, among the company, he sailed in 1836 for New York, where he erected an amphitheatre of stone and brick to seat two thousand. For six months his enterprise was well rewarded: then the building was destroyed by fire. Thankful that his stud had been saved through being stabled elsewhere, Cooke moved on to Philadelphia, raised fresh funds, and built a vast amphitheatre in Baltimore. There was another fire, and this time all his horses and ponies perished. But, with funds readily subscribed, he formed a new stud, gave a season at Boston, and sailed for Scotland after a year in America. He was proud of his spectacles, which included, besides *Mazeppa*, *Alexander The Great's Entry Into Babylon*. He played parts in these until his death at the age of eighty-four.

He had nineteen children altogether. Thomas Edwin, the eldest, stayed behind in America. William, the next, and James, who came third, were showmen. Ducrow said he had seen only one rider, and that rider was James Cooke – he had run circuses at the Rotunda in Blackfriars Road, and in Great Windmill Street, Haymarket, and his horses had been engaged for the revival of *Timour The Tartar* at Drury Lane in 1831; he had also performed before King William in the ring marked out at the Brighton Pavilion for Ducrow. With the talented equestrian prodigy, Emmeline Marguirette, he excelled in *The Games Of Cupid And Zephyr*, Miss Emmeline enacting the God of Love disporting with Flowers, while borne in a flying attitude upon one foot on the shoulder of Zephyr, at the height of fourteen feet, during the 'rapid circuition of the Steeds.'

Since James was such a paragon among horsemen, William did almost everything in his brother's circus except ride. Sometimes he played the clown, sometimes the strong man and rope-walker, sometimes the vaulter. While hanging head downwards with his ankles strapped to the slack-wire, he would uphold on the soles of his feet a board bearing six children, or seize the girths of a horse placed beneath him and lift it from the ground. He celebrated his powers in verse:

While on the Rope – (to give his friends a treat) –
He will support Six Persons on his Feet.
Through a Balloon he'll go six yards in the air,
And catch a child which will be slumbering there.
His slack Rope Feats will not be done before
He turns one Hundred Tourbillions,[1] or more.
He'll go over Garters and through a Drum;
And another miracle – (it is no hum) –
He'll make a Leap, most wondrous – I declare
Thro' a Hoop of real Daggers in the air.
Over three Horses he'll go, indeed 'tis true.
One being placed on the Backs of the other Two!

[1] Before acrobats adopted this term, the *whirlwinds* of showmanship were spirally-ascending fireworks.

PE

And last take – (by particular desire) –
A terrific Leap through a Circle of Real Fire.
He's the Slack Rope Wonder, his Leaping view,
And lifting a Horse is surely something new.
And you'll see W. Cooke as Simple Jerry
He'll tell of his last place – his Friends to please,
Where he was turned away, 'cause he gnawed the cheese.'

In 1834 William had a circus of his own. He gave up acrobatics in order to direct equestrian dramas and train performing animals. Alfred Cooke, his younger brother, struck the poses of *Cupid and Zephyr*, with his infant daughter, La Petite Emile; and Boswell, their brother-in-law, was the 'Phenomenon Elastique Merryman.' At the Royal Circus, Hull, James Cooke played St. George in a grand combat and encounter with a dragon whose triple tongue, terrifying eyes, and wings of towering grandeur, invested it 'with enough of verisimility to convey proportionate illusions of ideal nature.' He also performed the magnificent treble equestrian act of Sir John Falstaff, Shylock, and King Richard III.

Many Cookes now came to Astley's, all expert in scenes in the circle, with actors from the Theatre Royal, Edinburgh, to roar on the stage. The clowns were Lloyd and Crouestre, whose stock-in-trade, having to conform to the Wallett fashion of the day, consisted of 'Hints at the Times, Pleasing Puns, Play on Words.' This company first played *Amakosa! or, Scenes Of Kaffir Warfare*. Despite the terrific leap on horseback of Amakosa and his bride over the falls of the Umtata, and their flight on Kaffir steeds through the burning forest, it had to give place in the May of 1853 to *The*

Chase; or, Life On The Turf, which ran for a hundred and four performances. From June 18th to October 22nd *The Battle Of Waterloo* was acted – with Widdicomb as Monsieur Maladroit. This was the revival Tom Robertson had in mind when he made Polly exclaim in *Caste*:

Oh ! here's a beautiful brother-in-law. Why didn't you come in on horseback as they do at Astley's ? – gallop in and say Soldiers of France, the eyes of Europe are a-looking at you ! The Empire has confidence in you, and France expects that every man this day will do his – little utmost.

The Crimean War was very speedily dramatised as *The Battle Of The Alma* in the autumn of 1854. There was an unfortunate mishap on the first night. The British Army, represented by a hundred men from the Guards, had orders to capture the heights manned by Russians – mere supers. Following their instructions for actual warfare, the Guards reserved their fire until they saw 'the whites of the enemy's eyes.' Then they delivered a devastating volley. At such close range the wads injured so many that Cooke paid out almost as much in compensation as he could hope to take in profits.

Menschikoff, the Russian commander, was a leading character. What he lacked in height he made up in feathers, which shot up from his cocked hat and fell upon his shoulders. Epaulettes, as yellow and almost as big as bird-cages, hung on his sides like panniers on a donkey. He had long jack-boots, and his buff gloves, which he was continually pulling back, reached to the elbows. The sound of cannon set all these ornaments shaking like a rickety cabinet of china, and, if he heard the French or English were coming, he instantly ran the other way. He was principally opposed by a British war correspondent, armed with note-book, umbrella, and eye-glass, and an Irish soldier, who waged a little war against the Russians on their own account. Ruffianly Cossacks, who seized a cart belonging to market women of very superior appearance, threw away the vegetables and ate a parcel of candles, were driven off by the war correspondent's umbrella and the Irishman's shillelagh. When these two were at last captured, Menschikoff treated them in a rough but not ill-natured manner, even though the war correspondent, objecting to the diet of tallow candles and train-oil which composed the Russian army's rations, said he could not think of 'taking all the fat of the land and leaving all the lean to the Russians.' They escaped from prison with a Highlander and a sailor in time to see the Allied Army advancing. While the infantry fought on the stage, the horsemen in the ring crossed swords, and went round and round an imaginary point, until the Cossacks retreated up the inclined plane in order to form part of a tableau in the glare of red lights while the Union Jack was waved to the accompaniment of 'Rule, Britannia.'

Representations of the battles of Balaclava and Inkerman were added to the spectacle. It was a season that made Astley's a favourite topic of the quidnuncs again. But it was also Widdicomb's farewell. He died on November 2nd, 1854, at the age – despite his nickname of Methuselah – of sixty-five.

SHAKESPEARE ON HORSEBACK

> The comic man no longer can
>   Defiance at the foeman fling;
> But now he pokes his ancient jokes
>   At WIDDICOMB, within the ring.

> The clever hack his bivouac
>   Upon the stage no longer takes;
> At side-scene fount the wearied Count
>   His thirst no more in action slakes.

> Yes, history now has made her bow,
>   And leaves the scene of other days;
> The horses claim the wreath of fame,
>   The laurels will adorn the bays.

Drawings by Tenniel, from *Punch* in 1851.

    These were difficult times for William Cooke. That clause which compelled him to keep open all the year round doomed him to financial failure. Since the public could not be kept constantly excited, there were losses in the bad seasons to exceed the profits of the good.

How well he struggled to overcome this handicap is proved by his discovery of the first serious rival to *Mazeppa*. He equestrianised Shakespeare, and fired enthusiasm for *Richard III*. The wonder was not why this happened, but why it had taken so long. While at Birmingham in 1815, Charles Kemble wrote to Elliston that conditions were hopeless 'unless some extraordinary means be resorted to,' and offered to bear half the expense if real horses were brought on in a spectacular production of *Richard III*. At that time a mocker, as so often happens, proved a true prophet. In a facetious commentary on the appearance of horses on the stage of Drury Lane in *The Enchanted Courser*, Thomas Wooler wrote to Elliston:

> 'Saddle White Surrey' in good earnest. Instead of niggardly furnishing *Richard* and *Richmond* with armies that do not muster the force of a sergeant's guard, give them an efficient force of horse and foot. Richard should march to the field in the full panoply of all your cavalry, and not trudge like a poor pedlar, whom no one would dream of interrupting in his expedition. Think of the thunders which would echo from the vaulted roof of Drury, when 'Falstaff' should attempt to mount his cob! for surely he must have ridden, or we should find him even to this day on his road to Coventry.
>
> There may be some hypercritics who would tell you that there were no horses north of the Tweed in the days of *Macbeth*, because Shakespeare has fallen into some anachronisms about guns and so forth. But you must be above all this.

SHAKESPEARE ON HORSEBACK

Cooke carried out each suggestion. First he saddled White Surrey in good earnest by presenting on August 4th, 1856, *Richard III* in the form of an equestrian drama. His alterations had been 'approached, considered and effected with all the deference and reverence for the immortal author, that the subject so peculiarly and imperatively demanded.' In accordance with the stage custom of that time, he used Colley Cibber's text, which consisted not only of Cibber and *Richard III* but also of extracts from other plays by Shakespeare, including this adaptation of Warwick's lines from *Henry VI* –

> Richmond, I say, come forth, and singly face me,
> Richard is hoarse with daring thee to arms.

– which proved particularly apt to the elocutionary school of Astley's. Richard was played by James Holloway from the Theatre Royal, Edinburgh. He had been a barnstormer for by far the greater part of his career, and his children – one of whom was now playing Richard, Duke of York – were born under the flapping canvas of a mummer's tent. However new to the saddle, he conducted with credit the scene where White Surrey fell under his master in the midst of a combat against superior numbers. When many dead horses were dispersed about the stage, he obeyed the time-honoured custom of rolling every 'r' with redoubled force as his end drew near, Gomersal, in the rôle of Ratcliffe, offering him a swift horse 'below yon thicket,' while his enemy was visibly approaching. The docility of the stud was shown by 'the pertinacity with which they retain the semblance of death, while the swords of Richard and Richmond are clashing over their heads.' After stabbing Richard, Richmond hacked him about the neck until he put an end to him and the piece at the same time. It was an unquestionable success. Ninety consecutive performances were given. After a very short break, the run was resumed. It was repeatedly revived.

Macbeth, with Holloway in the lead, opened on December 1st. Critics who expected much in illustration of the lines –

And Duncan's horses (a thing more strange and certain)
Beauteous and swift, the minions of their race,
Turn'd wild in nature, broke their stalls, flung out,
Contended 'gainst obedience –

were disappointed at being given too much Shakespeare and not enough Cooke. One who had a 'perfectly vivid notion of the way the late Mr. Ducrow would have ridden over the difficulty,' suggested a scene. After supper, Duncan would express a wish to 'just go round the stables,' where the 'minions of their race' would stamp and clatter, with grooms and horseboys wildly hanging on in every sort of straggling attitude, now dragging them one way, now backing them another, according to the vigorous pantomime exhibited in *Mazeppa* as the proper method to manage wild horses. What actually happened was that even when Macbeth cried, 'Send out more a-hor-r-ses,' none appeared, although the last scene was thrilling – Dunsinane in a stage of siege, terrific encounter of horse and foot, sortie of the garrison, Macbeth rushing about without his hat, 'like a maniac in the front garden.' The cream-coloured horse on the 'prompt side' was tapped under the knees until he fell down dead, and then the white horse on the O.P. side was served in the same way, and fell down dead, too; then Macbeth met Macduff; and then Macbeth smeared some rose-pink over his countenance, and was finished off in a grim and ghastly manner. Mr. W. Cooke, Junr., was hoisted on a shield, the warriors all shouted 'Hail, King of Scotland !' and the curtain fell.

This was followed by Garrick's version of *The Taming Of The Shrew*, in which the audience saw 'how her horse fell, and she under her horse,' and how the horses ran away. Then *King Henry IV, Part I*, was arranged with 'equestrian illustrations.'

In the March of 1857, Cooke announced 'extraordinary equestrian and scenic effects' for grand opera. Wits seized the chance to prophesy that every prance must cause a '*tremolo* concerted movement of the voice together with the body of the rider'; that in the execution of a *rondo* round the circus, there would probably be many more shakes introduced than the most florid composer dreamed of; that *The Beggar's Opera* should be so presented that Macheath might sing 'How happy could I be on either, were the other fair charger away,' while continually tumbling from two horses. But the actual performances afforded no scope for ridicule. Meyer Lutz conducted *Il Trovatore; or, The Gypsy's Vengeance* with Rebecca Isaacs as Leonora and Augustus Braham as Manrico. It was followed by *Maritana* and *La Sonnambula*.

Though Shakespeare and opera had now had their day, Cooke's resources had not given out. With *The War Trail; or, The White Horse Of The Prairie*, in the

October of 1857, and *Jibbenainsosay; or, The White Horse Of Nick Of The Woods*, in the February of 1858, he exploited the vogue of the Wild West. The Indian Mutiny inspired *The Storming And Capture Of Delhi*, and the war in China *The Bombardment And Capture Of Canton*. But still *Mazeppa* put in his regular appearance.

Cooke also tried to excite interest in his horsemanship. When J. S. Rarey, the American professor, tamed the most vicious horses to be found in London, and even zebras from the Zoological Garden, by methods of kindness known only to a few besides himself, Cooke announced that he would demonstrate the secrets of Rarey's system, and invited the public – despite Rarey's protest – to bring wild horses. The one Cooke practised upon did not reveal vicious propensities. A canvas band, passed over its back, was fastened to two legs so that the horse was hobbled; then it was turned round and round until stupefied and exhausted. As no one else saw fit to praise this exhibition, the trainer himself composed a verse in his own honour:

> Bucephalus was once by Alexander tamed,
> At least the feat is in some Hist'ry named;
> But William Cooke, why he has done much more,
> Alec. tamed One Bucephalus, and Cooke a score.

He was asked for advice in the arrangement of Christmas theatricals at Tavistock House, and his arrival was one of the finest things of the kind Dickens had ever seen. The open phaeton was drawn by two white ponies with black spots all over them (evidently stencilled), who came in at the gate with a little jolt and a rattle, exactly as they came into the ring when they drew anything, and went round and round the centred bed of the front court, 'apparently looking for the clown.' A multitude of boys, who felt them to be no common ponies, rushed up in a breathless state, twined themselves like ivy about the railings, and were only deterred from storming the enclosure by the glare of the Inimitable's eye. Some of these boys had evidently followed from Astley's. The account Dickens gives of this in a letter, ends:

> I grieve to add that my friend, being taken to the point of difficulty, had no sort of suggestion in him; no gleam of an idea; and might just as well have been the popular minister from the Tabernacle in Tottenham Court Road. All he could say was – answering me, posed in the garden precisely as if I were the clown asking him a riddle at night – that two of the stable tents would be home in November, and that they were '20 foot square' and I was heartily welcome to 'em. Also, he said 'You might have half a dozen of my trapezes, or my middle-distance-tables, but they're all 6 foot and all too low, sir.'

From Golders Green Batty had kept a watchful eye on the fortunes and dignity of Astley's, and read John Oxenford's attack which *The Times* published in the July of 1857 on Cooke's mid-day performances of *Richard III* and *Mazeppa* – matinées, the critic prophesied, possibly forgetting that the first had been given at the Queen's command, would lower theatres to the standard of a penny gaff. A more serious scandal was feared when Cooke was accused of employing a dyed

Black Bess in *Dick Turpin*. Batty came down to investigate, but ended by apologising with, 'I ought never to have believed if of you, William.'

The drama acted during Cooke's farewell season was written by Tom Taylor, professor of English literature, barrister-at-law, assistant secretary to the Board of Health, and secretary to the Local Government Act Office, who was fast knocking up his century of plays. There is no humanising the facts of his career. They are as hard as iron railings. Still, he was not quite such a conscientious worker as they make out, for his dramatic output becomes less astonishing when you find how habitually he stole his plots from the French. His trouble was that as every scribbler was at liberty to do likewise, he had to sell his plays for a song for fear managers might employ a mere hack to do the stealing for them. Such rivalry was so serious a threat to Taylor that when authors strove to get the copyright laws amended, he took a leading part in this anti-plagiarism movement. One of the jokes of the day ran:

Knowall: Ah, Taylor! *Comment vous trouvez-vous ce*——
Taylor: What's that?
Knowall: French, of course! Don't you know the language?
Taylor: As a boy – as a boy I did!

The probability is that his Astleian drama was original, since it is difficult to imagine where else such a plot could have been staged. The title was *Garibaldi*, and the story was supposed to have been about him too.

But passion in it was stronger than patriotism. A villain tries to seduce the hero's wife, and fails. To revenge himself for this repulse, he abducts her daughter instead. This angers Garibaldi, who, in a duel, slays him picturesquely at the Stelvio Pass.

At last William Cooke had fulfilled the labours of his seven-years' lease. When it began he had £50,000; when it ended he had £10,000. Had it not been for the profits of his tenting shows, he would have been bankrupt. Yet Batty resumed control in 1860 without any misgivings. He brought *The History Of A Flag*, from the Théâtre Impérial du Cirque, and staged *Fair Rosamund* to show how the queen was doomed to be torn in pieces by wild horses. After yet another revival of *Mazeppa* in 1862, the Amphitheatre came under the management of Dion Boucicault, the 'Shakespeare of the nineteenth century,' who considered that a playhouse on the south side of the Thames opposite the new Houses of Parliament wanted only a new name and a new policy to make it 'a lounge for lazy legislators.'

Boucicault was born in Dublin on December 22nd, 1822; his first play, *London Assurance*, was staged at Covent Garden on March 4th, 1841, and has ever since ranked as a minor classic in the traditional manner of comedy. After that first attempt, he decided, like Shakespeare, to write for audiences instead of academic principles. Ten years later his *The Corsican Brothers* acclimatised the French *drame* so suddenly that an outraged voice, during the duel with broken swords, shouted, 'Un-English.' When he wrote *The Colleen Bawn*, one of the finest of melodramas, it was declined two or three times until he was given a grudging salary for his play, as well as for himself and his wife, Agnes Robertson, as the leading players in it, by Ben Webster at the Adelphi. The scene of sea in a cavern, with incidents of plunging, swimming, drowning, and fishing up, caused excitement that left no doubt that the manager's fortune was made. Early in the run the author and his wife sent word that they were too ill – whatever the ailment was, it made the fortunes of successful playwrights in the future – to act again. There was hope of a cure when Boucicault was asked to name his terms. Like Shakespeare, he took a share of the profits. That was not a new idea, but out of it grew the system of payment by royalties instituted by Boucicault. By doing so he started a vendetta which lasted for years – Jefferson tells how at the first rehearsal of *Rip Van Winkle* Boucicault denounced Webster, who was not absent, as everybody thought, but behind the curtains of a box because he had known what would happen.

With his profits from *The Colleen Bawn* and *The Octoroon*, Boucicault redecorated Astley's and called it the New Westminster Theatre. The ring was boarded over, and filled, after a new fashion borrowed from the opera, not with the pit but with stalls. Between these and the orchestra was a row of shrubs with little fountains. His next project was to be a café for chatter in the intervals, with a Moorish restaurant on the flat roof overlooking the river, to be built on the site of what had been known for years as Astley's Cottage. Among the plays he presented was his *The Relief Of Lucknow*. This had first been acted under the title of *Jessie Brown; or, The Relief Of Lucknow* at

Wallack's, New York, in the spring of 1857, with Agnes Robertson as Jessie, the heroic Highland girl who throws back the mutineers' bomb before it can explode, and listens for the bagpipes. No member of Wallack's company would play the Demon of Cawnpore for fear of public disapproval, but, when Boucicault played it himself in a magnificent Oriental make-up, the gallery was too amazed to throw anything. The play came to Drury Lane on September 15th, 1862, and to the New Westminster on December 22nd the same year to celebrate the author's fortieth birthday. *The Trial Of Effie Deans*, Boucicault's adaptation of *The Heart Of Midlothian*, took its place towards the end of January. When that failed, Boucicault became panic stricken on discovering that his theory was wrong. He left the Surrey side heavily in debt, which took some time to discharge.

So the Astleian Shakespeare exits from the scene with a title bestowed on him in mockery. But, though he was not the Shakespeare of his age, he might reasonably claim to be the Dickens of its stage. The trouble was that Victorian critics were so busy looking for Shakespeares[1] they could recognise merit in nothing that did not imitate him. They preferred pinchbeck and brilliants to silver and (very fiery) opals. That is why we still talk of 'dramatic literature.' By setting up a false standard which requires plays to look well in print, this term has led to a huddle of thought. Plays like *The Colleen Bawn*, which regularly held the stage for over half a century, are ranked below 'poetic dramas' that

[1] The one they found, whose name was Richard Hengist Horne, proves, by the little we know of him now, the futility of their quest.

are not only unactable but unreadable. High time we
realised that the Victorian theatre is not to be judged by
what Tennyson, Browning, Arnold, and Swinburne
tried to do for it, but by the authors who were never
out of 'stock.' High time we discovered the merit in
characters so many great players of Irving's generation
tried when they were technically teething. High time
we gave less thought to Chastelard and more to
Myles-na-Coppaleen. Mid-Victorian pieces that inspire in us the pleasure a collector feels when he examines
workmanship which is genuinely of its own period are
all at least a little Astleian.

Nor is this spirit confined to circuses and plays :
nor to the nineteenth century, despite our long effort
to pretend that it does not exist. Although ignored,
it is an active will-o'-the-wisp. Perhaps, if I may
have the impertinence to pry into your private affairs,
it has played the devil sometimes with your life as it
has with mine.

3

The Female Mazeppa

'Fierce and luxurious Dolores, sleepless and deadly,' that Cleopatra in a crinoline, created the sensation which saved Astley's. Neither of these titles, nor any other bestowed upon her, would fit: barely one in four of the stories told about her were true – least of all those told by herself, for she was a born liar; and none of the prevailing views of her character were justified. In life Adah Isaacs Menken certainly drew Londoners across the river after they had tired of Astley's, with its 'ride, ride, for ever ride' monotony of *Mazeppa*, and in death she keeps the memory of that playhouse and that play green with argument. What else may we believe? She has come down to fame as the friend of Dickens, although, if one thing about her seems more certain than another, it is that she never met him, and as the mistress of Swinburne, although such a relationship seems to have been impossible. She was an actress who could not act, a poet who never wrote poetry, and a nudist who was always, in public, decently clad. We read of her Jewish looks, although she was not Jewish by birth, and find her described as a creole (either an all-black West Indian or a pure French-Louisianian), although her father, Joseph McCord, came from London. There is more certainty in the characters of fiction than in this unearthly creature of fact. And yet the memory of her fascinates us more than the memory of the greatest actresses of her time.

If any of the statements made about her can be true, we may assume that she was born in New Orleans on June 15th, 1835. Then three early influences must be noted: first the 'literary' education provided by a stepfather; next the necessity (through his death) of earning her living at an early age as a dancer; and then, after she had spent a few terms as a teacher of French at a ladies' seminary, her engagement in Franconi's travelling circus,[1] where she learnt how to ride for show. These are the threads of her fate, for the love of letters in her becomes most curiously intertwined with the garish romance of blood-tub theatres as well as with fearlessness towards horseflesh.

Such jumbled experiences brought on a fever of imagination which nothing could satisfy short of frequent marriages and attempted poetry. She took her first husband at seventeen, and there was a divorce. She went to dance at the Opera House, Mexico, and on the return journey through Texas decided that here was the place where she ought to be captured by Red Indians. Accordingly she was – in fiction that long passed for fact. She escaped from becoming the chief's

[1] George Washington Moore of the Nigger Minstrels started life by driving ponies, forty at a time, in Franconi's circus while it was playing New York. That was why he was called 'Pony': his habit of backing horses for a 'pony' (twenty-five pounds) was not the cause of this nickname, but the effect.

squaw by discovering a bond of sisterhood in the breast of Laulerack, his other bride-to-be. The 'white beauty' and the 'red beauty' rode away together, only to fall into an ambush of the Rangers, whose volley sent Laulerack's soul to 'the Happy Hunting Ground far, far away.' That is Menken's story, and, to enforce belief, she inserts one phrase of truth into this final sentence: '*After a march of many miles*, we arrived at Austin, where for three months I was kindly taken care of by General Harney, who was stationed there.' Then she wrote a poem to

>. . . that dark-eyed one,
> Whose bounding heart God folded up.

At twenty-one she married her Jewish singing-master, Alexander Isaac Menken, and adopted the Hebrew faith for life. But though she gave up her religion for his sake, she would not give up cigarettes: so, pending another divorce, she turned actress – specialising in breeches parts. She spent some time as model for a sculptor, and that upset her imaginative balance still further. Yet at twenty-four she threw art to the winds – unless she saw Apollo Belvidere in the form of a prize-fighter – and became the wife of Heenan, the Benicia Boy. That marriage began in the spring of 1859 and ended in the autumn.

Other Americans were being talked about in 1860. Near Vancouver Island, General Harney strove to make war against a British naval force at Harper's Ferry; John Brown had lit the first flame of a civil war; Lincoln was elected President, and Heenan joined a circus in England after his drawn fight with Sayers, now billed by a rival circus. From the June of 1861, two series of events must be noted: in the South bloody battles were being fought, and in the North Menken had found a vehicle to make her famous. It was nothing more remarkable than *Mazeppa*. Nor was it a novelty for a woman to play the name part. The first female Mazeppa, who appeared at the National Theater, New York, in 1859, was Charlotte Crampton. As her purpose was to exhibit 'the most intrepid feats ever performed by a lady on horseback,' she acted it among several such parts as Richard III, the French Spy, and the Wild Rider of the Santee, and there was no sensation. Two months later, at this theatre, Adah Isaacs Menken acted for the first time – not as Mazeppa – in New York; she was reproved for undressing, and praised for her hearty earnestness and dashing style. The next spring (still without a horse) she announced herself – so Professor Odell records in *Annals of the New York Stage* – as Mrs. John C. Heenan, thus proclaiming her marriage to the Benicia Boy who was then in preparation for the Heenan-Sayers fight that almost interrupted the business of the world; she responded to the cheers for 'Mr. and Mrs. Heenan.' On his return to give sparring exhibition bouts in New York, she gave readings from Shakespeare as a 'distinguished actress and authoress,' and next appeared as a dancer, with engagements in the despised 'saloons.' After making trial of the part elsewhere, she performed *Mazeppa* in New York in the summer of 1862, and repeated it on certain nights during a season of six weeks, in a very varied repertoire, which presented her as a Nigger Minstrel, Joan of Arc, Sixteen-String Jack,

Corinthian Tom, an Unprotected Female, Lola Montez, and Richmond on horseback in conflict with Richard III. She was no longer announced as Mrs. Heenan. The Benicia Boy had sworn in a letter to the Press, 'I declare I was never married to her or to anyone else. I was never possessed of any of her means, and never to my knowledge, received or spent a dollar of her money.' There was a divorce, and Menken married again.

She left New York. While civil war continued, while Redskins were revolting in the north-west, while 'Stonewall' Jackson was driving Federals behind the lines of Washington, while Lincoln was changing his call for volunteers into a command for conscripts, the wild horse of Tartary was carriyng the second female Mazeppa right across America from Broadway to the gold-rush townships of California. But there were now third, fourth, fifth, sixth, and several more female Mazeppas who would ride not only up and down scenery, but round the first tier of boxes as well. So Menken decided to go where she would be the only female Mazeppa. On April 22nd, 1864, she sailed from San Francisco in a fast clipper for England. In her luggage, besides a scanty stage costume, were her poems – newspaper cuttings and MS. She added to these a hymn in the clipper's praise:

> How defiantly she flaps her white sails at the sun, who, in envy of her beauty, screens his face behind a passing cloud, yet never losing sight of her.
> The ocean hath decked himself in robes of softest blue, and lifted his spray-flags to greet her.

The crimson sky hath swooped down from her Heaven-Palace, and sitteth with her white feet dabbling in the borders of the sea, while she sendeth sweet promises on the wings of the wind to my fair Ship.

The others, written for American newspapers, were of many kinds. Some were melancholy and some warlike. One, in a style inspired by *Leaves Of Grass* — for Whitman was making a stir in literature to rival hers on the stage — was sadistic:

I wait for the head of my Holofernes!
Ere the last tremble of the conscious death agony shall have shuddered, I will show it to ye with the long black hair clinging to the glazed eyes, and the great mouth opened in search of voice, and the strong throat all hot and reeking with blood, that will thrill me with unspeakable joy as it courses down my bare body and dabbles my cold feet!
My sensuous soul will quake with the burden of so much bliss.
Oh, what wild passionate kisses will I draw up from that bleeding mouth!
I will strangle this pallid throat of mine on the sweet blood!
I will revel in my passion.
At midnight I will feast on it in the darkness.

And such was her versatility that she could also write:

Comrades! At roll-call, when I shall be sought,
Say I fought where I fell, and fell where I fought.

When Menkin sat alone in Westminster Palace Hotel, contemplating the gulf fixed between herself and the literary lions she was hunting, she had a visitor. His frock-coat was ducal and his nod had the condescension of a crowned head. His name, she read on the card, was E. T. Smith – a showman who had publicly presented addresses of vellum to Heenan and Sayers – but it meant nothing to her. He was as little grieved as Lincoln might be at meeting a squaw who was ignorant of presidents.

Edward Tyrrel Smith was undoubtedly the English Barnum, however mute and inglorious now. There never was a showman so full of unrelated ideas: if they had been related there might be a monument to him somewhere. Though an admiral's son, he began life as a red-waistcoated Bow Street runner. Then he became a publican in Red Lion Street, Holborn. When Mrs. Bloomer gave to the world a new garment, he made the barmaids of his tavern wear it. This so attracted custom that he amassed funds enough to finance, among many other things, a bonnet-shop at Brighton, a song-and-supper room in the Strand, a restaurant in the vaults of the Royal Exchange, opera at Her Majesty's, and orgies at Cremorne. He put up for Parliament at Bedford, but was badly beaten by a brewer. He gave a performance, during his ten years' rule over Drury Lane, to provide funds for the establishment of a 'Free Library for the People.' He went in for anything and everything. At the sale of any kind of opera-house, theatre, music-hall, or circus he would make the highest bid, flourish a £1,000 banknote to show means, and trust to luck to raise funds afterwards.

That £1,000 banknote, which he always carried in his pocket, was hired from a moneylender at the rate of £1 a day. His friends all believed it was spurious. One of them at a luncheon held out a genuine £1,000 note. Smith took it, rolled it into a ball, dropped it into a spoonful of soup, and swallowed it.

There was a time when he had been genuinely impressed. This happened when Sayers and Heenan met on that chilly morning in 1860. The fight had moved him to the soul, and he was now ready to plead the cause of the Benicia Boy before the wife with whom the prizefighter wished to be reconciled. However, after he had slapped her on the back as he slapped everybody, no matter how august, it was not Adah Isaacs Menken who listened, but Edward Tyrrel Smith. She unpacked the costume of Mazeppa, and he arranged for her to appear at Astley's. Posters showed frantic horses, pawing the air over frightful precipices while the captives on their backs exposed arms and legs and threatened to expose beauties of form such as Mazeppa himself never possessed. Protests against the American 'naked drama,' were what Smith counted on. Menken was already primed with facts about degrees of nakedness on the stage, and could quote cases not only of Cerito in ballet, and a host of young limbs in burlesque, but also of Mrs. Charles Kean as Ion. 'I have long been a student of sculpture,' the former artist's model declared, 'and my attitudes, selected from the works of Canova, present a classicality which has invariably been recognised by the foremost of American critics.'

In majestically quilted crinoline and sweeping hat, she drove through the town in a landau and pair adorned with sleigh bells – a sight that brought back memories of Ducrow in the coach of Premislas, the Count Palatine. Her short black hair, curled close to the head, her dark eyebrows and dark eyes, had the right touch of 'foreignness' which was necessary to the happiness of playgoers in the sixties. There was firmness in the straight line of her small mouth, and in the carriage of her head. There was a hint of the *retroussé* in her nose, and her cheeks had fullness enough to justify the word plump. She brought with her the spirit of emancipated womanhood. That is to say, she could not, no matter what might be said of her behaviour, be dismissed as another frail beauty of the footlights. She had 'views.' She did not believe that marriage was good for women – 'Somehow, they all sink into nonentities after this epoch of their existence.' Good wives, she said, were rarely clever, and clever women rarely good. What shocked the public still more was what had shocked Menken. She was always smoking.

William Cooke went to see her behind the scenes at Astley's with Victor, his son. Though too young to understand the gossip about her, the boy was deeply impressed. It was the first time he had seen a woman smoking a cigarette. And it was not merely one cigarette. She was smoking the whole time she was not on the stage, and while she was 'acting' a page-boy stood in the wings with cigarettes on a silver tray in readiness for her.

For the first time in the history of *Mazeppa*, no substitute was to be used. In its scramble to the dizziest heights of Astley's practicable mountains, the wild horse should bear Menken. There would be no double, and no dummy of the kind that took the place of Cartlitch or Holloway after they had passed across the first raised platform. As Menken's courage was equal to any task, the new sensation was duly rehearsed. She was borne along zigzagging inclines at a speed of about half a mile an hour, so that the horizon took a long time to reach. The public, Smith decided, must be given plenty of anatomy for its money.

Astley's doors opened on October 3rd, 1864, to admit a vast press of spectators, who could barely restrain their impatience while a curtain-raiser called *The Double-Bedded Room* was being played. So well had Smith done his work that there was an outbreak of applause at Menken's first appearance, though she was completely dressed (as the Tartar captive, disguised as the page of the Polish Castellan). After declaiming each line with a strong foreign accent, she struck a pose 'as if with the view of satisfying an audience of photographers.' But in the scene where Mazeppa marched into the apartments of the Count Palatine to fight him for the love of Olinska, the Castellan's daughter (nothing so immoral as the unfaithful wife of Byron's poem had ever been tolerated at Astley's), Menken dropped her attitudinising and fought with 'wonderful vigour and spirit' until the would-be bridegroom was overcome.

Here the audience held its breath in exquisite anticipation. The Castellan was about to wreak his vengeance by ordering 'the punishment inflicted on rebel slaves.' First Mazeppa must be stripped. This was the great moment of the play. Menken retained, of course, the tight fleshings which had been properly worn by previous Mazeppas in this situation, but instead of the usual dark brown 'half-body' she had loose folds of white linen which descended 'only slightly towards the knee,' and left the upper limb exposed, though not indelicately. Some spectators might murmur, 'Not the sort of thing one would care one's sister to see,' but others had been educated by Smith into thinking, not of their sisters, but of the ladies of ballet or burlesque. Only a very small minority were bold enough to observe that the Mazeppa on Astley's stage was better clothed than those of the hoardings: all watched the binding with many a thong of hero to horse breathlessly, and shuddered as they saw both rush over the raking platforms, followed by the heads of wolves with movable jaws. These were worked by stage-hands who crawled, concealed by the painted canvas parapet, carefully behind the clattering hoofs, in order to represent the stealing, rustling step of that

> long gallop, which can tire
> The hound's deep hate and hunter's fire.

When the top platform of the stage (there were three) had been passed, cardboard figures of diminishing sizes continued the flight in order to represent how

> With glossy skin, and dropping mane,
>   And reeling limbs, and reeking flank,
> The wild steed's sinewy nerves still strain
>   Up the repelling bank.
> We gain the top; a boundless plain
> Spreads through the shadow of the night,
>   And onward, onward, onward seems,
>   Like precipices in our dreams,
> To stretch beyond the sight.

The curtain fell amid cheers, and Menken was twice led forward by Smith. In the next act she posed to represent Mazeppa's gradual awakening, amid a snow-clad landscape, from the recollections of his fearful ride to the comprehension of his present safety among the Tartars of his father, the Abder Khan. To give vent to his rejoicings at once more assuming 'the god-like attitude of freedom and of man,' she armed herself with sword and shield and struck a series of poses 'taken from the most celebrated sculptures of antiquity.' On the abdication of the Abder Khan in Mazeppa's favour, she bestrode the wild horse in masculine fashion, and, after marshalling her troops (Astley's stud of forty horses and company of two hundred performers), she responded to a clamorous recall by waving her acknowledgments from the saddle.

No fresh sensations were to follow. The spectacle of Menken's sudden interruption of the deferred wedding of Olinska and the Count Palatine was merely an echo of the Christmas pantomime, while the onslaught of the Tartars was not calculated to impress a generation whose childhood had been spent at the knees of Ducrow. All the same, Menken had, to borrow the thunder of Smith's rhetoric, 'enchained the Old World' as she had 'astonished and enthralled the New.' Each night the house was packed. During the first month of the run, Dickens was unable to find a seat. He had left his office on one of his strolls to cool 'a boiling head' and was drawn to Astley's. 'Standing room only' was the answer at the box office. He asked for a box. The clerk, recognising him, said there was not one to be had, but he could have a seat in Mr.

BEHIND THE SCENES AT ASTLEY'S
From an illustration by John Tenniel, *Punch*, 1851

Smith's box. Dickens preferred to walk away. Menken heard of it with a pang of disappointment, and wrote a lengthy letter of apology. When he did write to her, it was in the customary style of a hero acknowledging hero-worship. She received two such very brief notes. Printed in facsimile *over one signature* on the dedication page of her book of verse, they deceive all who are eager to be deceived as proof of the friendship she said existed when writing from London to a 'puff paragraph' expert in New York.

She played at Astley's for ten weeks. When *Mazeppa* had to be withdrawn on December 17th for the pantomime of *Harlequin Jack Sprat; or, The Three Blind Mice, Great A, Little A And Bonny B, The Cat's In The Cupboard And She Can't See Me*, she went to Paris. Dumas was easy of approach now that the Gordosa, with her impudent pretensions to have a voice and her retinue of poets and musicians, had left him after one scene even stormier than the rest. Menken was taken to a party in his rooms at the Rue Saint-Honoré. We know she was delighted with his large face and great mop of hair, and not repelled by the darkness of skin which he had inherited from his grandmother, a West Indian negress. So much is proved by two of the photographs they had taken together. In one Dumas is fully dressed. In the other – a second pose at the same sitting, since it reveals the same chair, same book, same crinoline, and same trousers – he has had to take off his frock-coat, waistcoat, and tie so that Menken may place her head close to his heart while composing herself into a state of soulful content. Since the first was not compromising enough, the second had to be

ADAH ISAACS MENKEN
From *La Lune*, Paris, 1867

taken so that she might possess a souvenir of her conquest. Then she sent the negatives to a firm which supplied the public with portraits of celebrities to be sold in the streets. Though his friends were scandalised, Dumas raised no objections to Menken's way of conducting their romance as though it were an advertising campaign. They enjoyed the careless life he had led ever since he 'let fall the pen to take up the frying-pan.' Those were the days when he cooked epicurean dishes for unexpected guests out of any oddments they might bring with them. He was not upset by the refusal of servants to stay in such unruly quarters. Nor was he disturbed when the time came for Menken's departure, for he resumed work with one young woman half on his shoulder and half on his desk, another on the arm of his chair, and a third on the fur rug at his feet – all in the costume of Eve. Menken, back in San Francisco, was with a circus in the spring of 1865.

Early that summer her 'matchless inspired realisation of Byron's sublime ideal' was again beheld at Astley's. It had altered somewhat. Critics the year before had described her as slim. Now they debated whether she padded. One of the supers who lifted her on to the horse gripped her by the leg to supply evidence. Though she boxed his ears, he returned good for evil by testifying that all of her was real. She made a few literary friends, among them John Oxenford, who took her to the first performance of *It's Never Too Late To Mend* at the Princess's. There she met Reade, who admired her heart and her eyes. She next appeared at Astley's as a player of many parts. *The Child Of The Sun* was the piece, and John Brougham, an American, its author. In this she acted Leon, a creole; Zamba, a dumb peon slave; Metoxa, chief of the Comanchas; and Don Leon de Mondex, a Mexican caballero. It opened on October 9th, 1865. On November 20th it had to give place to a revival of *Mazeppa* which lasted until the pantomime season was near. At Christmas she returned to New York. In the summer of 1866 she married James Paul Barclay, an outside broker on Wall Street. Their home in Seventh Avenue was named Bleak House. It proved so for him. After his fortune was spent, he left her, and was found dead in Philadelphia without a cent. She returned to

England to play *Mazeppa* in Liverpool and London, and at the end of the year went to France. From December 30th, 1866, to the spring of 1867, she played *Les Pirates De La Savane* in Paris. Kings and princes were among her admirers.

Back in London in 1867, she held a *salon* at her hotel, where Dante Gabriel Rossetti visited her. She was interested in him, but far more interested to find he was the friend of the author of *Dolores*, which was then firing the imagination of undergraduates and other morally rebellious souls. On reading its invitation to an imaginary lady to 'come down and redeem us from virtue,' she appointed herself Swinburne's Galatea. She asked Rossetti to describe him, and was told to see him herself. She proposed to visit his rooms at 22*a*, Dorest Street, Portman Square, uninvited. Rossetti supposed she would stay. After he had challenged her to with a wager of £10, she set out for Dorset Street at once.

This, I suppose, deserves to rank as the most surprising moment in a very surprising life. If we accept the general opinion that Swinburne's experience of 'lips intertwisted and bitten till the foam had the savour of blood' and 'hair loosened and soiled in mid-orgies with kisses and wine' was as phantasmagoric as these phrases suggest, we may understand his alarm that evening. On opening the door, he found himself confronted by overwhelming masses of velvet and lace that relentlessly advanced upon him. In language of the kind then described as 'Zolaesque' she plainly said she had come to stay until the morning. She did stay. Yet the £10 Rossetti sent her was returned – according to a story that is no more to be disbelieved than most of the others told about her. The anonymous author of *Things I Should Not Tell*, who swore he had the story from Swinburne's own lips (as many did), doubted 'whether Adah was wholly satisfied with her visit when she drove back to the very respectable and highly fashionable hotel – Fenton's in St. James's Street – where she was staying, and whence she was expelled a few days later for unseemly conduct.'

Provincial engagements took her away. On her return in December, he did not hurry to see her. 'Let me know as soon as may be if you see Dolores before I do,' he wrote (on December 9th, 1867) to a friend:

> Tell her with my love that I would not show myself sick and disfigured in her eyes. I was spilt last week out of a hansom and my nose and forehead cut to rags – was seedy for days and hideous.

In the January of 1868 he was worried with 'influenza, lovemaking, rather unwholesome things such as business, money, etc.' When he recovered, he was led to the photographer's. Though not persuaded, like Dumas, to part with his frock-coat, he posed with Menken, gazing into her eyes while holding her hand, in the pose strongly recommended to engaged couples. Because she sat down while he stood, he was able to tower above her by at least three or four inches, and thus any unfortunate suggestion of the female dominating the male was avoided – 'Both come out very well,' was Swinburne's comment. Menken was pleased – she sent the negative to the firm of distributors in Paris, and pictures of herself with Swinburne, like those of herself with Dumas, were sold in the streets. Swinburne heard of it, and there was 'a great row.' He demanded the destruction of copies, printed for private circulation, of *Dolorida*, a sonnet he had written for her.

> Combien de temps, dis, la belle,
> Dis, veux-tu, m'être fidèle ?
> Pour une nuit, pour un jour,
>   Mon amour !
> L'Amour nous flatte et nous touche,
> Du doigt, de l'œil, de la bouche,
> Pour un jour, pour une nuit,
>   Et s'enfuit.

Swinburne was now in his prime, not having reached the middle of his long life, while his Dolores, though about the same age, was nearing the end of hers. Arthur William à Beckett's description of her gives, in the callous way of a Victorian professional humorist, a sad insight into her condition:

> It was about noon when we called on the female representative of 'Mazeppa,' and found her having her breakfast (which consisted, among other luxuries, of a red herring), in a venerable morning robe. She looked rather sallow by daylight, but was most kind and courteous, still extremely taciturn.

'Rather sallow' would be natural in one suffering from a complaint which, undiagnosed almost to her death, was beginning when she first rode the untamed steed before London's amazed stare. And taciturnity would not be unnatural in a lively, passionate woman afflicted with dull, spiritless lovers:

Friends fly from me, only to fill my being with the painful remembrance of their lost love for me – even me ! Once the blessed and chosen !

The next line of that letter may give the complaint a humorous twist by describing herself as 'a royal tigress waiting in her lonely jungle the coming of the king of forests. Brown gaiters not excluded.' But she would have been less than human not to have suffered from the egoism of literary lovers. 'Yours, through all stages of local degradations,' she signed herself, and the phrase seems to have meaning when you think how she played *Mazeppa* in all parts of the world while her strength was failing. She acted in *Black Eyed Susan* and *The French Spy; or, The Siege Of Constantine*, and played for the last time on the stage at Sadler's Wells on May 11th, 1868.

She had been at great pains to have a collection of her poems, with the general title of *Infelicia*, published. She waited with impatience during the slow stages of printing, correcting proofs, and finding fault with the frontispiece :

Perhaps I am a little vain – all women are – but the picture is certainly not beautiful. I have portraits that I think beautiful. I dare say they are not like me, but I posed for them.

Still there were delays and her illness was growing acute. She had to leave for Paris to act in *Les Pirates De Savanne*. At the second rehearsal she was unable to stand. She could not eat, and all she could drink was iced water. After struggling from her bed, she travelled to a village a few miles from Paris, but the effort overcame her. She was brought back, and on August 10th, 1868, at the age of thirty-three, she died. They buried her in Père Lachaise, where Philip and John Astley lay. The next year the Rothschild family had her body removed to Montparnasse and on her tombstone cut the words 'Thou Knowest.'

Her lovers were not kind to her memory. 'These ghosts of mine,' she had written, 'are sad soft-footed things that wear my brain and live on my heart, that is, the fragment I have left to be called heart.' They gave her little in return. 'Poor girl, why was she not her own friend?' was all Dumas could say, thinking of her in the way the world thought of him. Swinburne was ill for some days through 'the great shock' of her death. 'She was most lovable, as a friend as well as a mistress.' he said then. In a year or two, he had so completely recovered from what he called his 'real grief' that, on visits to Oxford, he said that when she wished to speak of poetry in the mornings he told her, 'My darling, a woman with such beautiful legs should not bother about poetry'; in a letter he wrote of 'poor old Menken' and her life's 'farce-tragedy.'

VI

LORD GEORGE SANGER

I

Zoological Pantomimes

LONG before Menken appeared, long before the day of the Cookes, an old showman who travelled from fair to fair with a peep-show brought his sons to Astley's and sat with them in the gallery. John Sanger was a youth and George Sanger a child, but they were already showmen. Instead of falling in love with Louisa Woolford, they envied Ducrow. 'I thought I would give the world to become the proprietor of such a show,' was how the younger, years later, described his thoughts that night. John was born in 1815, and George, the genius of the family, in 1827. They had come to town for the great Hyde Park Fair to celebrate Victoria's coronation.

While he pattered outside the booth of the drunken juggler who hired him, or lisped the 'eye-witness's' patter for 'the authentic representation of the terrible murder at the Red Lion' in his father's show, George Sanger cherished the hope of running Astley's one day. All the hardships of life on the road could not shake his resolve to run a show of his own. In partnership with his brothers, he travelled, through wintry and rough weather, about the countryside with a conjuring booth. Deaths were the heaviest of his many heavy misfortunes. Their mother died. The wife of their clown died. His own son died, and the company had to parade in the snow, leaving his body in the caravan, in order to earn money for the funeral. But George Sanger learnt from misery. While growing up among the hardships of chill caravans, he had watched a genuine giant starve to death while a spurious pig-faced lady (clean-shaven bear) made money. Therefore, he prepared for Stepney Fair a 'Tame Oyster that sits by the fire and smokes his yard of clay,' with the help of an urchin, under the table, who drew the smoke down one tube and blew it up another. Out of the golden egg thus laid, his show was hatched. From the Christmastide of 1853, to the following spring, he retired to Norwich. There, in the grounds of a public-house by the riverside, he and his brothers painted the portraits of themselves and their horses on a show front, in odd hours between teaching their children how to tumble and their Welsh pony how to count in response to the click of finger-nails. Old James Sanger, their father, now retired from the life he had followed ever since he was paid off after Trafalgar, smoked his pipe in a corner of the yard, and offered sound advice about not being too sparing with the crimson. When this was ignored, peep-show murders having no place on the front of a circus which lacked tamer-devouring lions, he hobbled off to inspect his new grandson (John, the son of John, who was to be the head of the circus one day).

Guided by George Sanger, the family now prospered so rapidly that in ten years their name was famous throughout the land. While one brother, William, went off on his own with 'Sanger's Waxworks,' John and George, in partnership, built ten permanent circuses between Plymouth and Aberdeen, in the sixties, and then eyed London, planning to take the Agricultural Hall at Islington in the north, and the famous birthplace of circuses at Lambeth in the south. At this time Astley's had 'Theatre Royal' on the pediment over its portico, and was playing its part in the history of 'legitimate.' Here, on July 29th, 1868, Disraeli's tragedy of *Alarcos* was made the subject of a 'courageous exhibition of incapacity' by Agnes Cameron, an American 'directress,' who was her own leading lady. The play had been written in a fit of Astleian temper thirty years before. After being moved by Lord John Russell's stage-poem, *Don Carlos*, to assure the author,

> When you returned from Spain, the solitary life of travel, and the inspiration of a romantic country, acting upon your ambition, had persuaded you that you were a great poet; your intellect in consequence produced the feeblest tragedy in our language.

Disraeli had followed his example by producing *Alarcos* with this difference: the elder Premier – these have been the only two Prime Ministers to write plays – did not turn critic.

Astley's was particularly unsuitable for this dramatised legend of the Prince of Castille, who stabbed his wife, heard that the Infanta he loved had been struck dead by lightning the same moment, and then killed himself. Audiences accustomed to the equestrian drama expected the entrance of an unrivalled stud when Alarcos was declaiming:

> Yea, as I glanced from off the Citadel,
> This very morn, and at my feet outspread
> Its amphitheatre of solemn towers,
> And groves of golden pinnacles, and marked . . .
> The flash of lances, blaze of banners, rush
> Of hurrying horsemen, and the haughty blast
> Of the soul-stirring trumpet . . .

and that was by no means the only false cue for horses, although none entered or was meant to enter.

There were references to a tourney, and of 'speed for the chase and vigour for the tilt,' besides another –

> . . . this marvellous beast,
> This Pegasus, this courser of the sun –

that mentioned one of Ducrow's favourites by name. In the last scene a noble Moor's soul was described as

> Cowed as the beasts now crouching in their cave,

which reminded the audience that the caves of Astley's were empty. When 'a blue sea of flame' struck the turrets while Alarcos approached, riding through the storm, the audience became restive. What they were watching resembled *Mazeppa* without the wild horse.

So to keep *Alarcos* running it was acted one night a week, and on the other five Tom Taylor's *The Ticket-Of-Leave Man* filled the bill. The great moment in this masterpiece among melodramas, which had run for over four hundred performances in 1863 at the Olympic – the little sister of Astley's – occurred in the tavern scene when Bob Brierly scrawled a message to the merchant whose office was to be robbed, and asked in soliloquy, 'But who'll take it?' The drunken navvy, reading over his shoulder said, 'I will.'

    Bob. You?
    Haw. I. (*Pulls off his rough cap, wig, and whiskers, and speaks in his own voice.*) Hawkshaw, the detective.

After a particularly violent quarrel between two leading gentlemen concerning which should play which of these two parts, the defeated player, who had to play Bob Brierly, took his revenge during the actual performance by responding to 'I will,' not with the 'You?' that is the cue for the other's sensation, but with 'Thanks very much.'

In August, Miss Cameron announced 'the last performance before the re-assembling of Parliament' as though the withdrawal of the play was caused by the author's activities on the other side of the River, and *The Conquest Of Magdala* was billed for Saturday, September 5th, 1868, with auxiliaries consisting of 'the finest stud of horses that can be procured, Detachments of Troops, and other accessories.' It was written by the author of *The Battle Of The Alma*, whom critics accused of simply changing his Russians into Abyssinians. Lord Napier was impersonated by an actor in huge boots, who bore himself well until he dismounted and tried to walk in them. The performance was saved when he stood still to recite 'several leading articles' to an excitable Frenchman, a dour Scotsman, and an eccentric English war correspondent. After Theodore had been slain in single combat by one of his British captives, 'a choked and blinded and deafened audience' awarded the piece unmeasured applause.

'Everything,' wrote Dutton Cook, 'is permitted in an Astley's drama except the privilege of being dull. That pertains to more pretentious establishments, and is not likely to become forfeit from disuse.' The handicap was too heavy. Besides, a blight had settled on the district, both for business and pleasure. Astley's, damp, dismal, and dreary, was called 'the abomination of desolation.' It had been taken over by W. H. C. Nation, who ranked high above all other dramatists, Shakespeare included, not in honours, but in riches.

On inheriting a fortune of about half a million pounds, he took to the writing of plays as a hobby. As no manager would accept them, he leased theatre after theatre in order to stage them himself. Critics found his work incomprehensible. The public stayed away. One audience numbered three, himself included. But he paid handsome salaries to all his players, and still had £300,000 left when he died in 1914. It was in 1866 that he became manager of Astley's. There he presented his National pantomime of *Hush-A-Bye Baby On The Tree Top; or, Harlequin Fortunio, King Frog, Of Frog Island, And The Magic Toys Of Lowther Arcadia!*

Batty died in 1868. 'To Let' notices subdued the spirit of the place while managers, including E. T. Smith once more, came and went, each with a pantomime. How low Astley's had fallen is expressed in Arthur William à Beckett's story of the revival there of *The Battle Of Waterloo* with only one horse. Napoleon rode it in Act I. Wellington rode it in Act II. 'Where did you get that horse?' asked a galleryite. Napoleon rode it in Act III and ended an address to his infantry with, 'But what I am most proud of in ye is that by the prowess of your glorious arms, ye have rescued from the hated thralldom of the blood-thirsty British soldiery, my favourite charger, who has on so many occasions carried me – and ye – to victory !'

All that changed when Batty's widow sold out to the Sangers for £11,000. How royally they took control was described by George Sanger in his lives – *The Life And Adventures Of Lord George Sanger*, and *Seventy Years A Showman* – after a fashion that reveals the solemn way he regarded his vocation as a showman (John had no such fine feeling: he was happy if mistaken for a groom, so modest was his nature):

> About the very time I entered Astley's – namely, the last months of 1871 – a great shadow and anxiety fell upon the Queen and nation in the shape of the serious illness of the Prince of Wales from typhoid fever. After his happy recovery her Majesty, in gratitude to the all-merciful Power, arranged thanksgiving services and festivities, including a grand State progress through London. I was very anxious to take part in that Royal pageant.

What he had in mind was a triumphal progress across London from one of his new strongholds to the other. It was a daring project that no ordinary showman could have carried out; and that he should have succeeded, proves not only how extraordinary were his powers, but also how firm a hold he had already taken over the imagination of the country. Being on friendly terms with the police he was able to arrange that he should 'not be interfered with beyond an order to go back at a moment when retreat would not be possible.' In top hat and frock coat he led his £7,000 parade from the Agricultural Hall to 'drop in behind' the Royal procession; he was stopped, according to plan, and then forced by circumstances to continue. His procession excited tremendous cheering, for its tinsel finery had a great deal more glitter about it than 'the solid grandeur' of the other:

> We had our Britannia, Mrs. George Sanger, with her living lion on the top to typify the nation and its strength. The Queen, too, was impersonated, in her crown and robes, surrounded by representatives of her dominions all in correct costume. At the top of Park Lane there were about a dozen carriages that had fallen out of the Royal procession and as our mimic pageant came along the occupants of these carriages, amongst whom Lord Beaconsfield was conspicuous, rose and acknowledged the endeavour of your humble servant to enhance the circumstances of the great occasion.

To all who worked for him George Sanger was 'a very god of a man.' He must rank with Philip Astley and Andrew Ducrow among the geniuses of the show. His energy, his courage, his authority, and his enterprise were equal to every task he set himself, from sitting up all night with a sick lion, while rubbing its chest with mustard, or securing a maddened elephant, to playing the title rôle in *Mazeppa*, or teaching advertisers their business by his invention of the coloured pictorial poster, all in the few moments he had to spare from his labour in transporting vast arsenals of amusements, no matter what the difficulty, throughout Great Britain and the Continent. The task he undertook that autumn of 1871 was formidable enough in itself. At the beginning of November he determined to pull down the greater part of Astley's, for the purpose of enlarging, modernising, and beautifying it, and installing a ring half before and half behind the curtain, with a stage to be lowered into position directly the scenes in the circle were done.

Three weeks later the workmen called a strike, and by the time it was settled there had been so many doubts and delays that the pantomime had not been written. No author would undertake the task at such short notice. 'There was nothing for it but for me to write my own pantomime,' he decided; he drank 'a strong cup of tea,' and spent the night jotting down situations – notably a set-to with the gloves on between Lady Godiva and Peeping Tom for the sake of poetic justice and 'Women's Rights.' On Boxing Day he presented two prodigious spectacles. At the Agricultural Hall his *War In China* opposed sixty British sailors and as many infantry-of-the-line to hundreds of Chinese in junks, which were wrecked by the broadsides of a British man-o'-war. At the Amphitheatre 'Amy Sheridan, the finest woman upon the British stage at the time,' was the heroine of *Lady Godiva; or, Harlequin St. George And The Dragon And The Seven Champions*, with Marie Henderson (also a celebrated Mazeppa) as St. George, and Mrs. George Sanger (in the last grand scene of 'The Golden Future') as Britannia. Remembering the wish of his boyhood, Sanger looked around the brilliant crowded house that was his own. He had achieved another of his ambitions, 'and my heart went out in thankfulness to the Providence that had been so kind to me, while at the same time there was a dash of sorrow in my cup of joy, inasmuch as my beloved parents had not lived to share it with me.'

What Sanger forgot to mention in his lives was that his pantomime did have an author in the end, for it was announced on the programmes as by W. M. Akhurst, a writer of burlesque, who provided these puns for the Great Macdermott (remembered to-day as the singer of 'We don't want to fight, but by Jingo if we do,' that Astleian music-hall song which brought the country to the brink of war) when he played William the Conqueror in the next Astley's pantomime:

> One of these days it will be ascertained,
> I was the horsiest king that ever reigned;
> *Aus*picious was my birth, and when an urchin,
> I frequently was *horsed* and got a birchin'.
> My first love was a *Mare*-y, her I vexed,
> And jilted, then young *Phillis* was my next;
> I married dear Matilda, whom you know
> Is (s)*aucy* and a (n)*auseous* thing also;
> I'm *os*tentatious, even to my house key,
> I get my music from Prince *Poni*alowski;
> And when I want a drama off I bolt,
> Like a veterin'ry to a *poor sick colt*[1];

[1] Meant as a pun on 'Bourcicault,' as the former lessee of Astley's had originally spelt his name. Other puns in the pantomimes of Astley's included this one on Easter:

> Crusoe. Now yourself bestir,
> I'll remain here *Good Friday.*
> Friday. Yes, don't *ee 'stir.*

And this one on the family name:

And when I die 'twon't be from sword or dart,
But from *oss*ification of the heart;
More I would say, but just now am not able,
My humour like my horse is *in its horse stable* [inexhaustible].

You have heard of W. G. Ross, singer of *Sam Hall* with its ferocious refrain of 'D-n their eyes' which caused an outcry because it expressed so brutally the despair of a murderer about to be hanged ? If so, you know he sang it at the notorious Cyder Cellars in Maiden Lane, which appear in *Pendennis* as the Back Kitchen where the chief singer's demoniac 'Ha ! ha !' causes the very glasses to quiver on the table, as with terror. Ross came to Sanger's in the seventies to undergo Astleian punishment for his sins. He played, in *Cinderella And The Little Glass Slipper; or, Ride A Cock Horse To Banbury Cross, And The Fairy Of Golden Dreams*, the parts of Father Christmas and Baron Stonebroke.

Not that comedians were of any great account at Sanger's. Even horses were retired to the chorus now that the character of its pantomimes became more and more zoological with stranger and still stranger beasts as 'stars.' In *Aladdin*, on the Boxing Day of 1874, the bridal procession included 'a herd of trained elephants 11 in number (a sight never before seen in England), Camels, Dromedaries, Trained Oxen, 50 Horses and Ponies, etc.' Two years later *Gulliver On His Travels;*

Aladdin. It's love will prompt us to go through with it,
But still its (S)anger has as much to do with it.
As well as this one from *Cinderella* concerning the coach :
Oh here's a turn out envious folks to anger –
Splendid ! by George ! Exactly ! by George Sanger.

or, *Harlequin Robinson Crusoe, His Man Friday, And The Wonderful Spirit Of Romance* caused the Lord Chamberlain to protest that 'nothing but solid masonry foundation would be necessary to support such a weight of wild beasts.'

'The biggest thing ever attempted by any manager of theatrical fame' was Sanger's own description of it. One scene presented three hundred girls, two hundred men, two hundred children, thirteen elephants, and nine camels, besides fifty-two horses, arranged upon a gallery which reached the flies, 'completely hiding,' he comments with pride, 'the whole of the scenic artist's work.' Nor was that all. To make up the wonders depicted in the travels of Gulliver, he 'used to drive in from the prompt side ostriches, emus, pelicans, kangaroos, reindeer, hog deer, ascis deer, and other species, Brahma Bulls, the Indian or Water Buffalo, Chamois, Ovdod Mouflons.' To crown the picture, two living lions were led, by collar and chain, into the centre of the group, which 'fairly knocked the public and profession alike, and the financial success was enormous.'

Each summer, when Sanger took his circus tenting, the Amphitheatre was let for a great variety of purposes. At times plays[1] were acted there. Nigger minstrelsy took a turn when the Mohawks occupied it; also a 'Myriorama' offered 'cheap trips to all climes' with Niagara in a series of tableaux and a 'marvellous mechanical effect' to show the march past of the troops

---

[1] As a theatre it showed enough spirit in 1879 to present the fourth or fifth London production of *East Lynne*. If the provinces are included, the number of times Mrs. Henry Wood's novel had been dramatised would be by then hard to number.

after the Egyptian Campaign. Thus it maintained its character, even in its off seasons, as the temple of holiday-makers. As such it had had no equal during the century and a quarter of its existence.

Yet there was nothing in its records to surpass Sanger's zoological pantomimes. For *Harlequin Cinderella And The Little Glass Slipper*, in 1879, the company was increased to eleven hundred persons, one hundred and eighty horses, sixty ponies, eight camels and dromedaries, zebras, the horned horse, Polar bears, four giraffes and 'twelve ponderous performing elephants, also eighteen splendid performing lions that had been playing at the Porte St. Martin Theatre, Paris, during the Exhibition, and those that had been travelling with Mr. George Sanger's Company in Belgium and Germany.' The Monstre lion, the son of Nero, who had been christened Lord Beaconsfield because Lord Beaconsfield had spoken very civilly to Sanger when they met abroad, was led triumphantly in advance of the British troops on their march to Cabul during the incidents of the Afghanistan War and the freeing of the Khyber Pass in the pantomime.

Little Sandy was Sanger's most famous clown. He is remembered by Mr. Charles Hughes, a circus veteran of rare quality, as a versatile genius whose like we have never seen since. Alike as clown, tumbler, rider, pantomimist, and trainer of dogs, geese, goats, pigs, and fowls, he was without a rival. When he acted as ringmaster, some people did not recognise 'the slender, graceful figure in evening dress' of Mr. Alexander Coleman, as the Great Little Sandy, clown. During the pantomime season he appeared daily and nightly at

Hengler's Cirque in Argyll Street, Oxford Circus, as well as at Sanger's. He was known as the favourite clown of Alexandra, Princess of Wales.

There was great disappointment in London when he left, in 1882, to manage a provincial circus for the two Sangers. The reason was that he had no heart for clowning: his wife 'Topsy,' the equestrienne, who was Lord George's daughter, Laurina, was dead. Mr. Hughes told his story in *The World's Fair* five years ago:

> He appeared at Astley's the following Christmas in the ring and on the stage, and early in 1885 I was present when he met with a serious accident in the same building. Entering the ring with one of his high-thrown somersaults, on landing he injured the large tendon of the right leg and just managed to limp out of the ring – the ring where he had scored so many successes and which he never entered again. After a few weeks' treatment in St. Thomas' Hospital, he travelled again and was booked the following Christmas at Covent Garden Theatre, where Mr. William Holland produced a big circus show. But after the first and second week Sandy mysteriously dropped out of the bill.
>
> A year or two later he was with Mr. George Ginnett's Winter Circus at Dalston, and the last time I saw him was in 1898 tenting again with his father-in-law, Lord George Sanger. Between then and the time of his death in 1904 – at the age of 53, I have no more knowledge of his movements. I only know that his light never shone again, as it had done, after he lost his wife.

Though the Mazeppa of Lisa Weber caused a stir in the summer of 1878, Lady Godiva was the ruling favourite of the equestrian pantomimes. She was represented by Maud Forrester in 1883 in Chance Newton's *Giddy Godiva; or, The Girl Who Was Sent To Coventry* and she was described as 'Godiva Golightly, a giddy, gushing gyurl, whose walking weight is 14 st. 2 lb.' This was one of the last spectacles staged under the joint management of the brothers. Because the families of each were growing, they decided to dissolve partnership. George bought John's minor interest in the Agricultural Hall and Astley's. The division of stock they settled by tossing with a shilling for each article as they inspected them in the Amphitheatre's stable yard. The winner of the toss 'took the goods and paid over half their value to the loser, or took half the value and handed over the goods, just which he chose, each tossing in turn.' As sole proprietor, George had to face competition with Covent Garden, which was transformed into a circus for the Christmas seasons of 1884 and 1885. He met this by returning to his favourite subject in *Old Dame Trot; or, Harlequin Godiva And Peeping Tom St. George And The Seven Champions Of Christendom*, of which he never tired.

The tale has been told by Mr. Charles Hughes in *The Sawdust Ring* (for the Winter season of 1936–7) of the way Sanger engaged an actress named Ray Lancaster. After satisfying himself of her credentials and talent, he asked, 'Now, what will you want to play the part of Richard III and let me bill you how I like?'

Terms were soon arranged and, to put it in her own words, she 'left the theatre walking on air' with the assurance of a two-months' engagement. A week or so later, starting off one morning to commence rehearsing, she espied, on her way to the theatre, a large poster announcing that Sanger's Great Christmas Production of Circus and Pantomime of *Cinderella* would be preceded by a special version of Shakespeare's *Richard III*, for which 'the services had been secured, at enormous expense, of the famous American actress, Miss Washington Irving, who would portray the title role.' Miss Lancaster's ambitous hopes went down again as she hastened towards the theatre meaning to 'have it out' with George Sanger for giving her promised part to the American actress. Excitedly she began to give him a piece of her mind but he only smiled and softly said: 'Well, well, don't you like the name of Washington Irving? Wasn't it stipulated that I should bill you how I liked?'

With one or two real buffaloes, a number of unreal Red Indians, some mules, and a rickety stage coach, George Sanger was in the habit of presenting *Scenes From Buffalo Bill*. He gave special prominence to it when Colonel Cody, the real Buffalo Bill, came to England in the Jubilee Year of 1887. During the Wild West season at Earl's Court, the 'Hon. William F. Cody' – he acquired this title by becoming a member of the Nebraska Legislature – received the honour of a royal command. All such performances were now in private, and when Queen Victoria watched Annie

Oakley's marksmanship, the lassooing by cowboys, and the attack on the Deadwood coach, the public was excluded. But the Prince and Princess of Wales and their children, with the King of Denmark, the King of the Belgians, the King of Greece and the King of Saxony – in London for the Jubilee – joined the throng of amusement-seekers. Alexandra, Princess of Wales, was the life and soul of that Crowned Heads' Holiday. 'I do not think there was a funnier sight,' wrote an American journalist, 'than that where the Princess of Wales came forward with the sweep of a schoolgirl and climbed into the Deadwood coach without any assistance.' Prince George, 'a dashing young naval officer,' was upon the back part of the coach, Prince Albert Victor sat inside, puffing cigarette smoke 'alternately into his mother's face and in that of the King of Denmark.' Buffalo Bill's fellow-countrymen watched the Prince and Princess of Wales take their children (including the future King George V) on the switchback railway. While the four kings sat 'as solemn and stiff as so many wooden men,' making no movement except to clutch their hats, the Princess of Wales held up both her hands and gave a real feminine scream of delight as the car plunged up and down. Prince Albert Victor 'went on puffing his eternal cigarettes.'

So many favours were shown to Cody that English showmen were disgruntled. Vesta Tilley expressed their point of view in the otherwise loyal and laudatory Jubilee ballad of *May Queen Victoria Reign*. After several flattering verses, the critical note occurred in:

She's seen the Yankee Buffaloes,
The circus, too, from France,[1]
And may she reign until she gives
The English show a chance.

May Queen Victoria reign
May she with us long remain
Till Irving takes rank with a war-painted Yank,
May good Queen Victoria reign.

Although Colonel Cody secured an injunction to restrain rival *Scences From Buffalo Bill*, Sanger continued the performances until called up for contempt of court. As this tried his temper he entered a tavern, which was contrary to his habits, for a tankard of beer. There he was asked by a farm labourer, aware only that he was talking to a circus man, 'Bain't Sanger a Lord?' Sanger thought highly of the idea. He had telegrams dispatched at once to all printers that the title must precede his name on all posters. On receiving news that he had won the day in the Law Courts, he announced – as though freshly inspired – 'If he's the Honourable William Cody then I'm *Lord* George Sanger from this day out!' That title (his finest advertisement) which the farm labourer suggested created a circus custom. John Sanger became a lord. Heads of rival families became Sir John Henry Cooke and Sir Robert Fossett. Captains were numerous, for some of the grooms adopted this style. To crown all, an acrobat-proprietor, famous for his fall head-downwards at the end of a rope to within a few inches of the ground, proclaimed himself King Ohmy.

[1] The company at Olympia from the Hippodrome, Paris.

WILD WOLVES IN LONDON

From 'A Sketch by an Eye-Witness' in *The Illustrated London News*, 1888

When business was bad, a sensation became necessary to attract attention. Sanger brought twelve wolves, 'all as tame as dogs,' from his zoo at Margate to Astley's, where an old worn-out Hanoverian Cream was killed and left lying by their cage. At the end of that night's performance Sanger let them loose in the stables, and went to the bar. The fireman saw wolves at large and gave the alarm which caused twenty policemen to guard the building, reporters to besiege every door, traffic to be held up, and thousands of people to fill the road. Alpine Charlie, picked for his formidable looks and voice, had been cast for the part of the hero. Although all he had to do was to tell the wolves to 'get in,' the newspapers the next day commended him for his courage in saving the public from being devoured. After being publicly presented with a purse for a hundred guineas, which he privately handed back, he was starred with the wolves in the next pantomime.

With thoughts turning again to Lady Godiva, Sanger went to see Irving in *The Dead Heart* at the Lyceum in 1889, took a fancy to some of the settings painted by Joseph Harker, and asked him to do the scenery for yet another Godiva pantomime. When invited by Harker to inspect the models, he exclaimed, 'What do *I* want with models, I should like to know ? If you don't know your own job, I can't damn well teach you, can I ?' When asked what he would pay, his answer was, 'I like the look o' your mug – charge what you think fit !'

Part of the rehearsals of a Lady Godiva pantomime was to teach the Champions of Christendom to ride. When the seven amply proportioned ladies were mounted, Lord George would cry, 'There, ain't that nice, my beauties? Ain't it easy now, aye?' While they were answering, 'Oh, yes, Mr. Sanger. It's delightful!' he would give a mighty crack of his whip, Harker said, 'and the next moment the horses would be plunging and rearing in all directions, sending the Seven (shrieking) Champions of Christendom sprawling ignominiously in the sawdust.' Another terrific crack of the whip, and Sanger, swearing with equal emphasis, would exhort, or rather command, the ladies to remount and go through the rehearsal again, mingling with his vituperation any number of 'my dears' and 'my pretties.'

At the first rehearsals, before the band attended, an old fiddler played *The Girl I Left Behind Me*, while Sanger instructed the chorus girls how to march, concerning which Mr. Charles Hughes has written in *The Sawdust Ring*:

> Now Sanger was very fortunate in always obtaining for his pantomimes a really pretty and fine looking lot of ballet and chorus girls, but on one occasion a girl with a very pronounced glide or squint in her eye managed to get engaged. She was also rather clumsy in her movements, and it was so easy to see that she was a source of annoyance to Lord George who was superintending the rehearsal. At one side of the stage was placed a length of canvas which would, when the scene was complete, represent a brook or stream of water. In rehearsing a march, each time the troupe of girls passed by the 'brook,' the squint-eyed girl persisted in walking on it. The

old fiddle player was accompanying the march with his favourite *The Girl I Left Behind Me*, which suddenly Sanger began to hum and then to sing the following words:

> The right foot first and then the left,
> And make your footsteps shorter,
> [Raising his voice]
> And can't you see, you cock-eyed cat
> You're walking in the water.

His dragon was a property as terrifying as any of his wild beasts. When it descended from the flies, flapping its wings and breathing forth fire and smoke, it flew too near the mounted champions for their comfort. It swooped down and dragged St. George from his horse when that principal boy, wielding her sword in the left hand, grasped a bar inside the monster's mouth with her right and was hoisted aloft while the curtain fell on a grand conflict in mid-air.

Full-blooded entertainment inspired by an ardent patriotism which interpreted even Cinderella's dreams by the fireside in terms of a military display (with children to represent all the regiments, horse, foot, and artillery, of the British Army), might have been thought safe from persecution. Yet the life of Astley's was now being cut short by bureaucracy whose interference began in 1888 with the Metropolitan Board of Works demand for extensive alterations, costing £6,000. That did not curb Sanger's enterprising spirit, for noting the success of aquatic spectacles at the Nouveau Cirque, Paris, he fitted the arena of his Amphitheatre with a tank for a carnival of real water at Christmas 1890.

But he was still subject to annoyance. A surveyor caused him to be summoned before the magistrate for not putting a spring fastening to a door – one that had had to be bricked up outside by order. Sanger 'came out with flying colours' and obtained his costs:

> At the same time the matter rankled. It was a sign that officialdom was growing in power, and had every desire to become tyrannous. The following year the County Council was inaugurated, and, when it got settled down to business, plied the new broom with more zeal than discretion.

Under these depressing conditions he was still alert in showmanship. In *St. Petersburg On The Ice*, at the Christmas of 1891, he put his company on roller-skates. The next year he turned author again with *The Jockey Club*, an equestrian and water pantomime. That was the last spectacle at Astley's. After it had been re-painted and redecorated throughout, down came the new inspectors:

> To them the name of the old Board of Works was simply 'anathema.' No matter how good anything might be, the fact that it had the sanction of the previous authority was sufficient to damn it in L.C.C. eyes. The consequence was that the whole of the work I had had done, at the cost of so many thousands, was utterly condemned, and I was called upon practically to rebuild the theatre.

All occasions were informing against Astley's. At this same period Sanger was being pressed to sell the site until he could no longer resist the offer. The ground landlord, 'the see of Canterbury, or rather the Ecclesiastical Commissioners,' had been negotiating for four years to acquire the property. Determining to destroy his white elephant, Sanger took their cheque. After twenty-two years' management he gave up the key on March 4th, 1893, and 'surrendered Astley's world-famous amphitheatre to destruction.' Circus people came from far and wide to take a last look at the ring and carry off souvenirs.

Right to the end this strange old place could not escape its fate of exciting mixed emotions. Near at hand great relief was felt at the news of its doom. It had been a very trying neighbour for St. Thomas's Hospital, which lay between it and the River. Although Lord George Sanger had always been open-handed in his gifts to the patients, they had lost many hours of sleep during the winter seasons through the shouting and tumults, the drums and bombardments, the singing and music, the roaring and the neighing of his 'shows, mighty shows.'

2

Battles In Tents

Astley's was dead, but Sanger's still lived. For a time 'Lord' George had agreed to sell his tenting show for £150,000, but he became 'so depressed and disheartened' at the idea of parting with his business that it 'fairly made me ill.' The syndicate delayed payment. Gladly refusing their cheque with this excuse, he 'breathed again and became quite a new man, devoting even more energy to the thing I loved than I had previously done.' In his tents he exhibited the disembodied spirit of Astley's:

> The circus now required some new element, and I bethought me that I would produce a great military performance in the provinces. The Matabele War was recent, but not popular, so I thought I would go back to the Egyptian Campaign, the Fall of Khartoum, and the death of General Gordon.

He had previously staged this subject at his Amphitheatre with three hundred of the Guards nightly, four hundred supers, camels and Arab horses, the fife and drum band of the Grenadiers, and six pipers of the Scots Guards. 'I ran the piece in that large theatre,' he said, 'for two hundred and eighty performances, but the expenses were too high, and I must have lost in all £10,000.' Thinking how attractive the spectacle would be for his travelling circus, especially after the advertisement gained from its run in London, he began by ordering 'ambulance wagons, Martini-Henry rifles, doctors and Red Cross nurses, and all the paraphernalia that is necessary for a street parade.' When required to attend the House of Commons because of the Bill that was to forbid the copying of naval, military, and police uniforms, his evidence obtained for circus performers the privilege to appear as soldiers and sailors of the Queen.

Romance was carried throughout the length and breadth of the land by his company. Every summer he brought magic to children at the seaside, who anxiously watched the hoardings to see whether his tent would arrive before their holidays were over. At length the brightly coloured sheets would be plastered down, square by square, with sweeps of the paste brush, while eager eyes watched for the last slip which bore the date. One morning sand-castles would be left unattended to the waves, and the rail of the promenade would be crowded. In the distance sounded the stirring strains of the brass band as the parade slowly approached along the road by the sea front. First came the solitary ringmaster, in top-hat and curled moustache, on a dancing horse, then a Red Indian riding by the side of a Roman and an Empress (what of or when could not be told, but most emphatically an Empress), then some more notabilities in threes, like a 'fancy-dress ball on horseback' and a clown on the unridable donkey. There

1896

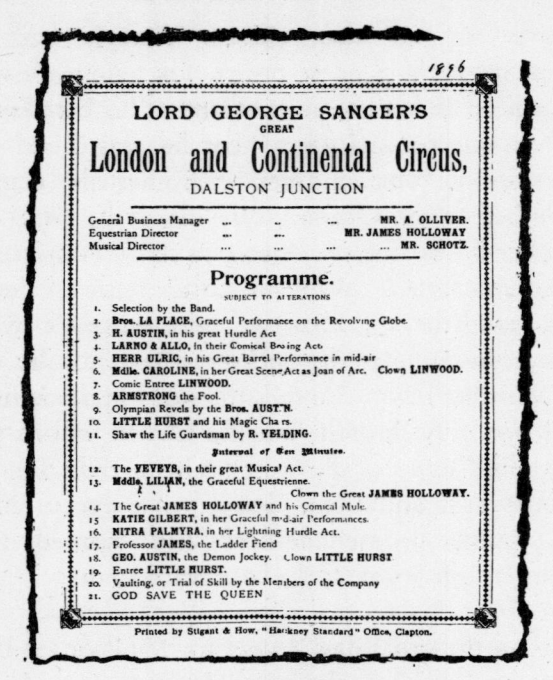

LORD GEORGE SANGER'S
GREAT
London and Continental Circus,
DALSTON JUNCTION

General Business Manager	MR. A. OLLIVER.
Equestrian Director	MR. JAMES HOLLOWAY
Musical Director	MR. SCHOTZ.

Programme.
SUBJECT TO ALTERATIONS

1. Selection by the Band.
2. Bros. LA PLACE, Graceful Performance on the Revolving Globe.
3. H. AUSTIN, in his great Hurdle Act
4. LARNO & ALLO, in their Comical Boxing Act.
5. HERR ULRIC, in his Great Barrel Performance in mid-air
6. Mdlle. CAROLINE, in her Great Scene Act as Joan of Arc.   Clown LINWOOD.
7. Comic Entree LINWOOD.
8. ARMSTRONG the Fool.
9. Olympian Revels by the Bros. AUSTIN.
10. LITTLE HURST and his Magic Chairs.
11. Shaw the Life Guardsman by R. YELDING.

Interval of Ten Minutes.

12. The YEVEYS, in their great Musical Act.
13. Mdlle. LILIAN, the Graceful Equestrienne.
    Clown the Great JAMES HOLLOWAY.
14. The Great JAMES HOLLOWAY and his Comical Mule.
15. KATIE GILBERT, in her Graceful mid-air Performances.
16. NITRA PALMYRA, in her Lightning Hurdle Act.
17. Professor JAMES, the Ladder Fiend
18. GEO. AUSTIN, the Demon Jockey.   Clown LITTLE HURST
19. Entree LITTLE HURST.
20. Vaulting, or Trial of Skill by the Members of the Company
21. GOD SAVE THE QUEEN

Printed by Stigant & How, "Hackney Standard" Office, Clapton.

BILL OF SANGER'S CIRCUS
Reproduced, by kind permission, from *The Sawdust Ring*

were red-and-gold cages with wild beasts prowling up and down inside, elephants with swinging trunks which made us wish we had brought lumps of sugar, and musicians in uniform blowing trombones and bombardons in a curly carriage. The glittering Queen's Tableau, surmounted by Britannia and her lion, was drawn by eight skewbalds; it was followed by the still loftier King's Tableau, topped by a globe which had to be removed when they came to a railway bridge.

The wonder deepened when we saw the title of 'Lord' on the wagons at the rear. We believed a very persistent rumour that Queen Victoria had made George Sanger a peer in return for being allowed to put her head inside the jaws of one of his best lions, for not even our parents knew that he was 'Lord' of his own creation. One summer he did actually confess to his title before the Queen. On July 17th, 1899 – seven years after his brother had been similarly honoured – he was commanded to Windsor Castle with all the men, horses, wild beasts, chariots, and tableaux we had admired whole-heartedly and she was to admire almost as much in her turn. He tells the story in a manner that reveals not only himself, but the Queen whom we see in our mind's eye as she watches his parade ride round the courtyard, and then, doing what every child by every seaside promenade-kerb had wanted to do, ordering it to ride round the courtyard again:

So on the great day I went to Windsor, and in the courtyard of the castle paraded my show, with every adjunct and embellishment I could think of, before the Sovereign I had so often longed to see and have speech with. The Queen watched the spectacle from her carriage, and liked it so well that she had the parade repeated. When it was over Sir Arthur Bigge came to me and said that her Majesty desired that I should be presented to her. Then he led me to the Royal Carriage, and as I bowed low, said 'Your Majesty, this is Mr. Sanger.' Never, if I live to be a thousand years old, could I forget that interview. As I straightened myself from another bow I saw the eyes of my Sovereign upon me, the gaze full of kindness. In a voice singularly high, clear and penetrating the Queen said, 'So you are Mr. Sanger?' 'Yes, your Majesty,' I replied.

Then with a smile and a twinkle in her steadfast eyes, '*Lord* George Sanger, I believe?'

This, with the accent on the 'Lord,' was distinctly embarrassing, but I managed to stammer out, 'Yes, if your Majesty pleases!'

'It is very amusing,' was the Royal lady's answer, 'and I gather you have borne the title very honourably!'

'Thank you, your Majesty,' I said; 'your gracious kindness overwhelms me!'

'Do you know, you seem very young, Mr. Sanger?'

'Yes, your Majesty,' said I, 'but it may surprise you to hear that it was on the day of your Majesty's Coronation, at the fair in Hyde Park, that I put on my first performing dress!'

The Queen expressed her astonishment at this, and then I had to answer a whole fire of questions about my circus and the animals, particularly the elephants, in which her Majesty took a great interest.

In his tent we saw *The Zulu War*, in which the hero, in blood-stained shirt, standing astride the prostrate body of his performing horse, waved his sword and shouted, 'Food and drink have I not tasted for several days, but as a soldier and an Englishman I can at least resolve to sell my life dearly to the last drop of my blood.' Then there was *The Sudan Campaign*, which included gunboats with horses' heads sticking out of the decks, and wheels and hoofs showing below the waves. During the Boer War British victories were won over again two or three times a night in that tent. Round and round the hippodrome track outside the ring 'gentlemen in khaki ordered South' rode after two-horsed, rattling wagons driven by hairy riflemen in slouch hats. What aroused our curiosity was the chivalrous way our troops spared the life of any Boer who stayed behind in the retreat – they had to stop to let off fireworks fixed at the base of the tent-poles. Those dear old-fashioned British victories! Mafeking and Ladysmith could be celebrated by tableaux on carts, with C.I.V.s reclining on sand-bags, by the long barrels of 4·7 Naval guns, at sixpence a night. Realisation of that war was small enough to go comfortably inside a circus – and if more was needed Sanger could rise to the occasion. For instance, when his ground at Bedford was rented by an American company and he had to take a field at the other end of the town, he burned a wicker-work effigy of President Krüger on a 'patriotic bonfire,' gave away torches to all-comers, formed the crowd into a procession and marched them to the box-office of his tent. He invented the three-ring circus, for he enclosed three rings and two platforms in a hippodrome track on the Hoe at Plymouth very early in his career. This was the plan of his circuses at the Agricultural Hall, which included a stag hunt, chariot races, steeplechases and *The Congress Of Monarchs*, which Barnum purchased in 1874 and made his own. At that time 'Howes' Great London Circus and Hippodrome Combined With Sanger's English Menagerie Of Trained Animals' was touring America, and startling the public with a quintette of elephants who performed 'the pyramid.' Barnum bought that show also. Though he also liked to use the word 'London' as an advertisement for his wares in America, the sale of *The Congress Of Monarchs* to America deprived Britain of future claims to dominate the world of showmanship. It was the foundation of Barnum's circus celebrity.

Sanger renounced the magnificence of sawdust. In 1905 he sold his circuses and most of his animals. Some horses and ponies he could not bear to part with; he also kept scenes, machines, and costumes, as though he planned a revival of *Mazeppa*. With a fortune of £30,000 he settled down at Park Farm, East Finchley, among the many trophies, on sideboards, on mantelpieces, in corners, on his fingers and adorning his tie, bestowed by admiring crowned heads. His handsome double-bed bore another relic of his travels – a box, rather like a lidless coffin. Being accustomed for so long to sleeping in a caravan, he could not rest unless there were boards for his elbows to knock against.

For years his life was spent in retirement except for semi-show progresses such as a drive to Margate in his coach drawn by miniature ponies. One Tuesday evening, at the end of November 1911, a labourer on his farm, named Herbert Cooper, entered his kitchen and drew a razor across the throat of a youth sitting there, wounding him, but not fatally, for the collar had stopped the blade from entering deeply. Maddened by some grievance, Cooper snatched a long-handled hatchet and rushed towards the drawing-room. At the door he met the steward and struck him, so that he fell unconscious. What happened next cannot be told with any certainty. Whether the lunatic attacked Sanger, or whether the showman, despite his great age of eighty-four, went to his steward's rescue, is not known. But it was Sanger who received the most terrible blows, and from the wounds on his head he died. On the Thursday morning the murderer's body was found on the railway line near Highgate.

From East Finchley, on a December morning, in pouring rain, Lord George's last procession passed bare-headed crowds to Holborn Viaduct station. He was buried at Margate, and the whole town – blinds drawn, shops closed, and black bows on cabbies' whips – went into mourning. What remained of his circus was sold at Finchley. For the *Mazeppa* equipment, which had cost £500, the auctioneer vainly suggested a bid of £100. According to the report in *The World's Fair* the scenery was sold for twenty-six guineas, six lots of dresses for twenty-five shillings, several other lots for twenty-seven shillings and sixpence, 'and a quantity of helmets and other headgear brought in about threepence each, the total sum being twelve shillings and sixpence.' Such was the end of what had been (apart from *Punch And Judy*) the most frequently acted piece in the world.

. . . .

Children of the English countryside are gathered by hundreds along the benches of the tent. They have been brought by train, tram, governess' cart, wagon, and foot from miles around. Though the old parade of red-and-gold carriages has been abolished (to save labour), and though the posters have lost all colour and untruthfulness, the arrival of Sanger's still causes a flutter of hearts. They have seen the show before, as you will soon realise. While the Plumed Lady is being helped out of her cloak, as she kicks one foot in the air and spreads forth her hands in salutation before climbing the rope ladder, there is not a sound. But when the canvas flap lifts again to show the rain-drenched trees by the lock outside, a stage whisper runs electrically round the benches: 'Here he comes.' He is Pimpo. In case this is your first circus, the name is printed for you in big letters right across the back of his black coat, whose tails dust his heels. He has a large white collar, and large white spats on his tiny feet. His little figure is crowned with a large top hat; under this is a large mop of hair, nearly as red as his tie. He joins the others on the tightrope as bold as brass. But when his turn comes to step on it he is frightened to death. His knee shakes and his balancing-pole trembles. He slips. He falls – but only on the place meant for falls. He gets up and rides a bicycle on the wire. Whether he blunders or whether he achieves, it is all the same. Sounds of pleasure continue like the chirruping of the cicala in Calabria.

That Pimpo is a wire-walker is only the beginning of the story. When the big skewbalds gallop around the ring, he flounders on their bare backs for a while and is sent flying into the sawdust. Then he takes his coat off to it, and braces himself for a leap in his lacerated shirt-sleeves: three steps and a bound take him, with feet firmly planted, on to the croup. When the grooms have finished tugging ropes and planting pegs, he goes hand over hand up the trapeze, where, after being restrained from certain death, he is seen in full flight. There is yet much to be told of his versatility. He has a preposterous pupil, named Bee Bee – whose walk betrays him at once as the wild beast of the lion-taming exhibition a little while before. Pimpo begins to show him 'a few tricks.' They fall over chairs and tables, and decapitate an assistant, who runs away leaving his head behind him. They give us all the fun of humpsti-bumpsti (as these mishaps over and under furniture are called), and then they stand on a double swing. While Pimpo loops the loop one way, Bee Bee circles right round and under and above him, in the opposite direction. The chirruping on the benches becomes deafening.

Redskin Riders of the Prairie are entering the arena before Pimpo – left behind by himself, as we used to be in childhood's nightmares – has finished putting on his coat. Seeing a tomahawk brandished, he crawls out of the sawdust and hides behind the ring fence, where he bobs up in terror, exposing his crimson face with its dazzling white lips; and even when his head is hidden another part of him is offering a splendid target for the Redskin arrows. Nothing worse happens than an argument, which he wins. After floods of Redskin eloquence have been loosed upon him, he answers, 'What did you say?' or, 'Say it again.'

The finale is *Dick Turpin's Ride To York*. As soon as the entrance for performers has been transformed into the picture of an inn in the olden days, various characters troop out of its doors. They seem to be explaining facts concerning Turpin's history, but barely a word can be heard because of the audience's din. One thing is clear. The agitated person in a black tricorn and red coat, who holds a staff with what appears to be a coco-nut on the top as the symbol of

LORD GEORGE SANGER
Reproduced, by kind permission, from *The Sawdust Ring*

DICK TURPIN IN SANGER'S TENT

authority, is offering a reward for Turpin's capture, dead or alive. Just behind him, in a schoolboy's cap and a frilled white pinafore, is Pimpo. At frequent intervals he gives the benefit of his advice to 'Daddy.' But how could any actor make himself heard in the midst of so much enthusiasm? Crowds that surge backwards and forwards in films never show as much excitement as the crowds on Sanger's benches, while this drama is being performed. Directly the attendants are called upon to take part in the play, several hundreds of children boldly advance from the seats and flock to the ringside. They are driven back slowly and return quickly. This is not the least impressive part of the spectacle. But Turpin himself is now sitting Black Bess as still as a statue in the midst of the gesticulating crowd from the inn. Tom King is arrested, and Turpin fires the shot which enters his breast. The way to York is through Exit R. round behind the scenes to Entrance L. While pursuers and pursued are out of sight, the Doncaster toll-gate is placed across their path, and night falls.

Turpin shouts for the gates to be opened, argues with a bearded face under a night-cap and lantern raised aloft at the window, and then, bandying no more words, puts Black Bess to her famous jump. His pursuers are held up until the sleeper again wakes and comes to collect his tolls. They pass through, and the turnpike-keeper goes back to his bed. But Pimpo, executing all the motions of a man riding post-haste, though his hack is slower than any plumed horse before a hearse, has been left behind.

'Who are you?' asked the keeper.

'I'm one of those men who have just gone through,' says Pimpo.

He has no money, but gives up a ring instead. The keeper takes it.

'I know it's gold,' says Pimpo, as he passes on, 'because Daddy gave a penny for it at the fair.'

The York coach, a real four-in-hand, is seen in broad daylight as canvas flaps are lifted for its entrance. Turpin holds it up, and his fellow strips the passengers of their jewels and gold. The guard levels his pistol and is shot dead.

There is one more scene, and when a carpet is laid over the sawdust we know what that will be. Black Bess staggers in. She cannot respond to the last appeal of her master. She drops on the carpet. After his farewell speech, she raises her head to be kissed, and dies. Attendants bring in a stretcher. The body is raised shoulder high, with Turpin standing beside it. All those unruly children are now back at the ringside, shouting with excitement. But there is no obstructing the view, for highwayman and prostrate horse are raised high above their heads at the last exit. Then we have to go too.

. . . .

Half-way through a war too vast to be dramatised for the circus, Ducrow's family vault was opened once more at the funeral of Mrs. Henry Wilson, the daughter Louisa Woolford carried out of the fire seventy-five years before. There was no Astley's left, no trace of Astley's, and no successor to Astley's, and although the Surrey Theatre still marked the site of the Royal Circus it was fated to make way for hospital extensions. But there is still that green plot on the site of Astley's 'Ride.' In Sanger's time it was a long passage with the winter quarters of the menagerie on either side. In *Studio And Stage*, Joseph Harker describes his first walk down it:

> To say that I was surprised at the casual way in which the animals were housed is to express my feelings but mildly. Most of them seemed to be free to roam wherever they liked, seeking, so it appeared, to me, whom they might devour. Dodging gingerly here and there, I at last succeeded in reaching the stage, where, in the course of groping about in the half-light, my hand suddenly touched something soft and warm, causing me to recoil with a start. But it was nothing, I take it, to be alarmed about – I had merely caressed a rather lethargic lion.
>
> Life behind the scenes at Astley's was full of little surprises of that sort. One day a baboon broke loose and charged in my direction, its objective being a doorway behind me. Of course I leapt apprehensively, and got jeered at for doing so.
>
> 'Wot, afride of *'im*?' bawled a cockney keeper, one of those who were trying to round up the animal, 'Meek as a bloomin' lamb 'e is.' I couldn't help noticing, in spite of his assurance, that each man was armed with an iron bar – a fact which seemed to me to shed suspicion on the baboon's lamb-like qualities.

Alma-Tadema visited Joseph Harker in the scene-painting room of Astley's. He stayed so long that they had to walk along The Ride after dark. As Alma-Tadema stepped over the neck of a camel, 'it decided to be up and doing.' To Harker it seemed that the whole of the animal kingdom had been let loose:

> Elephants, camels, a bear or two, several monkeys, and goodness knows how many horses, apparently had the run of the place. At one point I stood for a moment to light my pipe in the shelter of what I could have sworn was a wall, and only when it swayed gently towards me did I realise that I was leaning against an outsize in elephants.

Then a giraffe 'swooped down from nowhere and breathed hotly in our faces.' When they reached the outer gates Alma-Tadema said, 'This is the first time in my life I have had a nightmare *before* supper.'

Little by little the last links with the age of Astley's have been removed from 'the Surrey side,' where the theatre, the music-hall, and the circus all had their birth. In Roupell Street, one summer day in 1928, I watched the breaking up of the Hatch House, the tavern which marked the south-eastern corner of Halfpenny Hatch, where Astley first performed, and a friendly youth showed me the spot he had known, while at school, as 'up the Hatch' – a quiet spot for a fight. I walked by tiny cottages, since destroyed in the slum clearance, which were there in Philip Astley's day, and found in Green Walk (called Collingwood Street since Lord Collingwood's return from Trafalgar), the wooden houses of fishermen who in a remote past had cast their nets in London River. In changing London few spots have changed more of late than this old playground of song, dance, melodrama, acrobatics, and horsemanship. That may leave no excuse for sentimental lament and yet justify, since the history of what people do in their leisure hours is not without importance, the fixing of a tablet by the old entrance to The Ride, commemorating these interlocked centenaries:

> The Birth of Philip Astley, 1742.
> The Birth of Andrew Ducrow, 1793.
> The Death of Andrew Ducrow, 1842.
> The Final Destruction of Astley's, 1893.

The site of Astley's bears a dull burden of bricks and mortar now, but at midnight, while you think how Kit hit a man on the head with his handkerchief of apples for 'scrowdging' his parent with unnecessary violence, and how the hoofs of Ducrow's peerless stud clattered away from the fire, you may imagine that the darkness beyond the gate is shadowed with strange shapes which are being explained by a bearded wraith in top hat and frock-coat to a portly ghost in tricorn and periwig.

VII

EPILOGUE IN PARIS

Heroines Of The Haute École

[*Circus enthusiasts may wish to read what happened in the rings of Paris after 1870, although that lies outside the scope of this book. Many years ago I wrote a comprehensive history of the show. Out of the typescript, like the djin out of the brass bottle, the spirit of Astley's gradually rose in so tenacious a form that I was hag-ridden by it, destroyed my work, and wrote this book instead. The following chapter, a relic of the original work, has survived because it contains information not easily found elsewhere.*]

IN Paris the vogue of the circus was aristocratic. Throughout the politically troubled period from the forties to the eighties, when the excitable public was fed on equestrian dramas, people of fashion took great delight in displays of horsemanship. The *écuyère* of the ring was fêted in the summer as religiously as *diva* or *ballerina* in the winter, and the stables of the Cirque d'Été, in the Champs-Élysées, became as fashionable as the *coulisses* of the opera. Society women, as well as gilded youth, crowded round the stars of the saddle.

Ever since the Anglomania which preceded the French Revolution, horsemanship had been growing in the polite world's esteem. In the ring, Baucher, who had revolutionised its method, displayed *airs* unmastered by the picked riders of cavalry schools. Under his tuition, women matched their grace with their horses' strength in feats of skill which gave the zest of danger to the *haute école*. Nowadays, performances so labelled are often watched with a barely disguised yawn. While Baucher's pupils were its exponents spectators held their breath. Its heroines were tragediennes in real life.

Baucher rode without using the bridle-hand while teaching English thoroughbreds to execute quadrilles 'and steps calculated to arouse the envy even of Vestris.' Those were days of disbelief in equine intelligence. Formerly, riders had praised the nobility and sagacity of their beasts. Now, with ever-increasing vehemence (which has continued to the present day), the horse was dubbed brainless. According to Baucher's system, nothing was expected of the mount – not will, intelligence, or memory. It was nothing but a machine obedient to the slightest touch, so trained as to make the least resistance impossible. Partisan was said to have been mastered at once. In order to make him gallop with his hind legs, beat time with his forelegs, turn upon one leg or another, or move legs diagonally opposite, Baucher merely had to shift in the saddle. According to where his master made his weight felt, Partisan knew what he had to do.

The career of Baucher came to a terrible end in the March of 1855. While he was about to mount in the ring of the Cirque Napoléon, there was an ominous sound of breakage above. The horse bounded violently aside and was saved. Baucher stopped to look up, and saw the immense chandelier in the centre of the roof, directly above his head, come crashing down – a mass of girandoles, gas-piping, iron hoops, and candelabra. He was found, lying face downwards, his head clear of the wreckage, but his body so twisted that one foot was by his head. He was conscious, and asked calmly to be released when the first to arrive stood horror-struck. The annals of the circus contained no further mention of his name.

Trick-riding was despised on the Champs-Élysées. It was thought that the *ballerina* of the *panneau* (the large padded saddle) played to the gallery. The horsewoman in top hat and long flowing black skirts, who sat erect, collared, and corseted, in the side-saddle, was the only idol. There was first Caroline Loyo, who made her début at the Cirque Olympique in 1833, before completing her *éducation équestre* under Baucher. Alone among those stars of the red whip and golden spurs, she never made a false movement. At sixteen, with her black eyes and black Rutler as her only fortune, she crossed the Channel, where society flocked to see her as they flocked to see Taglioni. One rainy day, when her carriage did not arrive, she was conducted 'à la voiture de lord L.... par le duc de B... un des plus grands seigneurs du Royaume, pendant qu The Earl C... la couvrait de son manteau pour la protéger de la pluie.' The great days of the Cirque d'Été were when Baucher rode one day and Caroline Loyo the next, while Auriol, the clown, performed the *saut perilleux à cheval*.

When she went to England, her place was taken by Paul Cuzent's daughter, Pauline, whose name became legendary. She was lame, but in the saddle had unfailing grace. Almost from her birth in 1815 she had travelled with her father's circus. After Paul Cuzent's death from cold, while attempting to gallop from Pavlovsk to St. Petersburg to join a circus, the family returned to Paris. Pauline, *toute gamine*, found employment at the Théâtre Seraphine, where she played the *cornet à pistons*. As an actress she had some success at the Palais Royal, but every day she went to the Cirque Olympique, to watch her brothers and sisters rehearse, until Baucher offered to make her a horsewoman. When the Cirque d'Été was first opened, she rode Buridan, a great Yorkshire coach-horse, not born for the saddle yet trained by Baucher to execute *piaffe*, *passage*, and *travail au galop*, perfectly. Lejars, her sister, was less noted for her riding than for floating, in short skirts, round the ring through a series of garlands (floral hoops). She was admired at Astley's.

Pauline Cuzent bought Partisan and Buridan from Baucher, as well as a jumping horse named after Auriol, and went to Russia. With her brother, Paul, a famous vaulter, and Lejars, she performed regularly in the State circus, before Nicholas I. Her health gave way, and she had to return to Paris, where she died in 1855. Lejars married, and lived to a ripe old age.

After the Franco-Prussian War both the chief circuses of Paris were directed by Victor Franconi, although he had, because he was getting on in years, given up his place in the ring to Claude Léopold Loyal. Every May Day, when the season had ended at the Cirque d'Hiver, their cavalry paraded on the Boulevard des Filles du Calvaire, rode through Paris to the Champs-Élysées, and formed into line outside the Cirque d'Été before dense crowds. Each performance, from the *première* which took place the next night, was attended by enthusiasts dressed *de rigueur*. Each Saturday night was an event of social consequence with evening clothes 'essential' and top hats worn the whole time (there was no cloak-room as yet, for the habit of leaving hats and canes with an official at the door started when English visitors became frequent). These *soirées exceptionnelles* were ruled by custom. Unmarried women of good family could not attend, for the demi-monde and society met here though nowhere else.

There were two codes of behaviour, so Yvon Novy wrote in *Comœdia* some years ago. While one smart set watched the performance from end to end, the other held a *salon* in the stables, where the ground, protected by a barrier of plaited straw, was ornamented with designs in white sand. No acquaintance might be made without a formal introduction, and no man might offer to help an *écuyère* into the saddle – so Victor Franconi's son, Charles, ordered – without first kissing her hand. There were also those who cleared the way by forming escorts to conduct the riders into the ring. Loyal, who had other things to think of, left these in charge of Chadwick, the clown, whose only words, always uttered in the same tone, were '*Prenez garde!*' after which it was advisable to move quickly. There was discipline enough to ensure a perfect performance, but when Oceana[1] walked the slack-wire the ring was

[1] A granddaughter of Thomas Taplin Cooke was christened Oceana because born in mid-Atlantic during his company's voyage to New York. Renz, the German showman, had a grandchild of the same name who became Baroness Oceana Allweyer.

invaded until there was barely room enough for the wire to swing. If the box of resin were not there when her shoes needed treatment, there would be a race to fetch it for her. Victor Franconi chose the Saturday before the Grand Prix for a *soirée* with the programme performed entirely by women. Except Loyal, the ring-master, no male performer might set foot on the fastidiously raked sand (this was before Paris rings were carpeted). Chadwick, who was generally called for, showed his contempt for feminine supremacy.

Another performance was taking place outside. This was the day of the beautiful 'turn out,' valuable horses, ostentatious liveries, and emblazoned carriages. Coachmen found cause for endless dispute in all this rivalry. The curve to be described before arriving at the peristyle of the cirque was considered a trial of skill, and each performance was criticised aloud. In between setting down and taking up, coachmen gave prolonged demonstrations of horsemanship. Some solitary disputants stayed behind until a long time after the last lantern of the last *coupé* had disappeared in the distance, and after the last horsewoman, leaving by a small side door, had gone home afoot.

These circus nights and days were chronicled in the *Soirées Parisiennes* of Arnold Mortier. In the May of 1881 he wrote that the *Samedis du Cirque* with their peculiar elegance, 'where all the world mingles, where all languages are spoken, where for an hour the most blasé public in the world swoons over a clown's antics and holds its breath in suspense over a horse's hoofs,' merited their immense vogue. Émilie Loisset was the Patti of the *haute école*. Her court, like those of *prime donne*, grew each week in dignity and extent until it crowded the stables. She was more skilful and fascinating than her aunt, Louise Loisset, who 'turned somebody's head every time her horse went round the ring.'

Émilie Loisset was always alone – in London, Vienna, St. Petersburg, Paris – though flowers enough had been flung at her feet 'to cover the Champ de Mars.' Once she came back to Paris with five horses that had been presented to her in the way that 'jewels in packets of bonbons' were sent to stars of *opérette*. But whoever gave them had not won her friendship or regard. Every day at the same hour she came alone to the circus. When she claimed the ring, it was hers. There she rode her five horses in turn, practising for four or five hours. After every rehearsal and every performance, she walked home alone to her little flat in the Rue du Cirque. Mortier said:

> I would advise no one to follow her, nor to try to break the ice during this short journey, with any conversation whatsoever; Mademoiselle Loisset does not carry a revolver in her girdle, nor a poniard in her garter, but she has a bodyguard ready to make a mouthful of anyone too daring. Turc, a dog as large as a Newfoundland, white apart from a black spot over one eye, has terrible fangs: he comes to the circus every evening with his mistress, waits in her dressing-room, escorts her home, and sleeps at the foot of her bed. This is a dog's life to be envied.

That she should have no interests outside horsemanship was not surprising, for she belonged, through her mother, to the family of Loissets who had been celebrated among riders since 1830. She was born in Paris in 1856. Her father was a glass-manufacturer named Roux of the Rue Royale. Her uncle, François Loisset, the husband of Caroline Loyo, was the most skilful trainer of liberty horses. His nieces, Clotilde and Émilie, appeared in their early teens, as trick-riders on the *panneau* in his circus. When Émilie severely injured her knee through a fall, she mastered the *haute école* instead.

The death of their uncle caused the Cirque Loisset to disband. In 1878, they obtained engagements at the Cirque d'Été, where Clotilde remained only a little while, for at the end of the season she was married to Prince Jean XXII, who ruled one of the twin principalities of Reuss, and afterwards she became Baronne de Reichenfeld. That had an inordinate effect upon Émilie Loisset. The handle of her *cravache* was inscribed, 'Princess ne daigne, Reine ne puis, Loisset suis,' which explains her aloof, solitary life. And her secret determination seemed justified. Without being remarkably pretty, she looked ravishing. On Mahomet, a fiery sorrel, she would suddenly land in the centre of the ring by forcing it to a great leap from the haunches. When 'sitting on his hams,' he was made to execute five or six bounds, 'high and precipitate,' before she left the ring, putting him through still more spirited paces. Twelve years later Baron de Vaux wrote:

> I see her yet with her pretty little pale face and her large childlike eyes, staking her life to win from the public what she loved above all things, the shouts of 'bravo' and 'bis.'

'Little Loisset,' though now twenty-six, looked barely nineteen. She was loved for her kindliness despite her strict reserve – allure had formed part of her training. At last Turc was ordered not to molest one visitor, for she had become engaged to the Prince of Hazfeldt.

After a season in Berlin, she returned joyfully to the Cirque d'Hiver to rehearse for her last engagement at the Cirque d'Été, where she had decided to make her début on her Irish *cheval sauter*, Pour-Toujours. While in Berlin she had been injured through his fault. In leaping a table bearing candelabra, he missed his footing at the take-off, and the fall dislocated her shoulder. Now when set to the table he refused the jump. She struck him on the flank with her *cravache*. He turned about and rushed for the stables, stopped short before the closed doors, and fell backwards as his hind legs slid under him, with his rider underneath. Charles Franconi helped her from the saddle, thinking she was unhurt. 'I'm bruised. I think I'm dying,' she said. The prong of the saddle had been thrust against her. After two days of suffering, Loisset died.

No one thought of Turc until, a month later, he arrived at the Cirque d'Été, laid himself down in his usual place in the stables, and stayed until the last rider had left. The next day he came again, ears down and whimpering. They tried to feed him. The third day he disappeared.[1]

As Loisset represented the sublime of the circus in

---

[1] Baron de Vaux, though he has taken the story, almost word for word, from the contemporary source quoted here, tags it on to the tragedy of the Comtesse Fanny Ghika, a circus rider who died when her leg was amputated after an accident in the ring.

those days, so Billy Hayden represented the ridiculous. Hugues Le Roux, author of *Les Jeux Du Cirque*, thought he would have as important a place in the history of the ring as Deburau had in the history of the theatre. Hayden was born in Birmingham. In childhood he was lifted on to his father's shoulders to watch street performers of the perch act, a regular part of town life in those days, and from that moment was fated to be in shows. As an apprentice of nigger minstrels, he travelled round the world with a black face, but, while in Germany, he whitened his face like Pierrot. It was a great success. His comical grimaces, obscured by burnt cork, showed through the powder. Nearly all his jokes, Le Roux considered, were borrowed from the minstrels. But the conversations of chairman and corner-man are merely one form of the scenes between knave and butt which occur in all the world's comedies of all time, and Billy Hayden's jests remind you more of John Ducrow with Widdicomb at Astley's than of the conundrums in the halls of Moore and Burgess.

In 1881 Billy Hayden became the clown at Franconi's. All Paris knew his astonishing contortions, his fantasy and fun, for his tricks were the joy of celebrities and children alike. His style of humour may be gathered from his story of having been a pretty young lady until an old woman 'took me, the pretty little girl, out of my perambulator, and put in my place her ugly little boy': ever since then he had been 'an ugly little boy.' Here he took out a large coloured handkerchief and burst into tears. When Paris knew this by heart, he made a new joke of it by searching vainly for sympathetic ears. After being rebuffed by Loyal, by all the horsemen, by the girl who leaped through the balloons, by the grooms, and by the rest of the company, he would anxiously scan the faces along the second tier. As soon as he caught sight of an old woman, he climbed across the benches, sat himself familiarly by her side, opened his mouth wide to begin his tale – and then, trembling with excitement, cried, 'Why, *this* is the very woman.' She was not an accomplice. Billy knew instinctively which one would take offence and which would be flattered by being singled out for attention. He was generally right – although one evening an old dowager did strike him over the head with a heavy umbrella.

If you walked in the Champs-Élysées in the mornings, said Mortier, you might have met a young man carefully shaved and correctly dressed, with one hand behind his back and in the other an umbrella. Seeing him march by, grave and thoughtful, you would have taken him to be an inventor on his way to the Palace of Industry. That was Billy Hayden. From time to time he would stop outside some half-built house before the bills on the hoardings. These he read as eagerly as a girl with a newspaper serial, in the belief that advertisements, notices, and appeals to the public revealed, more than any book could, the finesse of the French language. His studies over, he went to the circus, where he was the first to arrive. Not liking to rehearse before witnesses, he searched the orchestra carefully; he knew the conductor was 'antipathetic' because the music constantly cut short his best effects. When certain no one was there, he began to shout (in English) while dancing, tumbling, falling, delivering blows upon the empty air and getting kicked by imaginary feet. After an hour or two of this, he sauntered once more across the Paris he loved. In America he had been Barnum's clown at a salary, so the programmes said, of six hundred dollars a performance, and wherever Barnum went, Billy received offers of marriage. When he left, it was thought that he had retired to build a palace in the Champs-Élysées.

In the summer of 1883 Billy Hayden sprang a new surprise upon the Cirque d'Hiver – a little pig, all black, with mischievous eyes and curly tail, who jumped over barriers and through balloons or circles of fire, like a poodle. An engagement that summer had taken Billy Hayden to Spain. While staying at a farm in the Pyrenees he had assisted at the birth of a large family of pigs and lost his heart to a little black one. He reared it in his room at hotels, feeding it on milk at first, then on carrots, acorns, and sugar. 'He adores me,' Billy Hayden would say. 'He will never supply me with a slice of pork.' It was docile, amiable, and very precocious; three lessons of two hours, each day for six weeks, were enough for its education. In the ring it gambolled joyfully at the heels of his master, who fled in terror over the fence and into the stalls, with the pig, unafraid of the shouts of laughter, always in pursuit. Thus the mourners for Loisset were consoled.

INDEX

À BECKET, ARTHUR WILLIAM, 243, 254
Addison, Joseph, 27n
Adelaide (Queen), 128, 131
Akhurst, W. M., 258
Albert (Prince), 149, 197-9
Alexandra (Queen), 265
Alma-Tadema, Sir Lawrence, 285-6
Amherst, J. H., 92, 101, 127
Anderson, J. H., *Wizard of the North*, 153-4
Angelo, Domenico, 20
Angelo, Henry, 21, 37
Astley, Edward, 19, 34, 43, 50
Astley, Hannah Waldo, 73-86, 101
Astley, John, 25, 35-84, 97, 144, 164, 166, 174, 187, 245
Astley, Mrs. P., 23-64, 97, 164
Astley, Philip, x, xi, 19-87, 106, 164, 168, 174, 187, 245, 286-7
Auriol, Jean-Baptiste, 173, 175

BARHAM, R. H. *See Ingoldsby, Thomas*
Barnum, Phineas, 16, 198, 279
Barry, Thomas, 195, 199-201
Bates, Jacob, 12
Batty, William, 122, 192, 194-5, 201, 207, 219, 221, 254-5
Baucher, F., 292-4
Beaconsfield (Lord). *See Disraeli, Benjamin*.
Bennett, Arnold, 11n
Bon Gaultier (Sir Theodore Martin and W. E. Aytoun), xi, 8, 105-7

Boucicault, Dion, xi, 221-4
Braham, Augustus, 217
Browne, Hablot, 158
Brunswick, Dukes of, 22 (Charles William Ferdinand); 104 (Frederick William)
Buffalo Bill, 264-6
Bulloch, Dr. J. M., vii
Bunn, Alfred, 127-9, 145
Burns, Robert, 207
Byron (Lord), 8, 117-19, 122-3, 234-5, 240

CAIN, GEORGES, 176-7, 186
Carlyle, Thomas, 27n, 163
Carter, lion-tamer, 146-7
Cartlitch, John, 120-2, 125, 234
Castlereagh (Lord), 105
Catherine the Great, 50
Chadwick, clown, 295-6
Charles X, 163, 175
Charlotte (Queen), 67
Cibber, Colley, 215
Claudian, 27n
Cochran, Charles B., vii
Cody, William F. *See Buffalo Bill*
Coleman, Alexander. *See Little Sandy*.
Coleridge, Samuel Taylor, 61n
Colman, George, the Younger, 82
Colpi, acrobat, 26
Cook, Dutton, 254
Cooke, James, 209
Cooke, Sir John Henry, 266
Cooke, Thomas, 207

INDEX

Cooke, Thomas Taplin, 142, 208
Cooke, Victor Claud, 233
Cooke, William, 208–21, 233
Crampton, Charlotte, 228
Craven, Earls of, 68 (William); 68, 75
Croly, George, 101
Cross, J. C., 77
Cuzent, Paul, 293–4
Cuzent, Pauline, 293–4

DAVIS, WILLIAM, 64–87
Decastro, John, 45, 164
Delpini, clown, 75 (and plate)
Dibdin, Charles, 40, 44–9
Dibdin, Charles, the Younger, 55*n*
Dibdin, Thomas, 46–7, 55*n*
Dickens, Charles, xi, 8, 9, 27*n*, 55, 103, 109, 114, 116, 123–5, 140, 150, 157–9, 187, 191, 218–19, 223, 225, 236, 238, 240
Disraeli, Benjamin, 8, 133, 159, 251–3, 256, 261
Doyle, Richard, xi, 104, 113
Ducrow, Andrew, x, 8, 87–157, 216, 233, 252, 284, 287
Ducrow, John, 114–16, 300
Ducrow, Peter, *Flemish Hercules*, 93–7
Ducrow, Peter Andrew, 156, 159–60
Dumas, Alexandre, *père*, 238–9, 242–3, 245

EDWARD VII, 197, 255, 265
Egan, Pierce (author of *Life in London*), 86, 109, 157, 229
Eliott, George, Lord Heathfield, 20–1, 29, 32, 44
Elizabeth, Princess Palatine and Queen of Bohemia, 68
Ella, Mlle., 201

Elliston, Robert William, 70–1, 101–2
Enthoven, Mrs. Gabrielle, vii

FITZBALL, EDWARD, 191–2, 202–6,
Forrester, Maud, 263
Fossett, 'Sir' Robert, 266
Franconi, Adolphe, 182
Franconi, Antoine, 163–74
Franconi, Charles, 294
Franconi, Henri, 169–72
Franconi, Laurent, 169–72, 226
Franconi, Victor, 183, 294, 296
Frederick the Great, 21
Freeman, James. *See Pimpo*

GARIBALDI, GIUSEPPE, 220
Garrick, David, 12, 34, 217
George II, 22
George III, 13, 29, 33, 55, 62
George V, 265
Gilbert, Sir W. S., 195
Ginnett (family of), 135, 262
Goethe, Johann Wolfgang, 27*n*
Gomersal, Edward Alexander, xi, 104–7, 147–8, 184, 215
Gordon, General, 273
Grimaldi, Giuseppe, 45, 46
Grimaldi, Joseph, 45, 55*n*, 114*n*, 125

HARKER, JOSPEH, 268–9, 285–6
Hauser, Kaspar, 147
Hayden, Billy, 300–2
Haydon, Benjamin Robert, 198–9
Heenan, John C., 227–8, 230, 232
Heine, Heinrich, 179–82
Henderson, Marie, 257
Hengler, Charles, 262
Hengler (Signor), 44, 79
Hill, Rev. Rowland, 41

Holloway, James, 215, 234
Holloway, James, the Younger, 275

INDEX

Horne, Richard Hengist, 223*n*
Hughes, Charles (of to-day), 261–4, 269–70
Hughes, Charles (died 1797), 30–51
Hugo, Victor, 177

Ingoldsby, Thomas, 8, 108–9, 126
Irving, Sir Henry, 224, 266, 268
Isaacs, Rebecca, 217

JEFFERSON, JOSEPH, 121, 222
Johnson, Samuel, 34
Johnson, trick-rider, 12

KEAN, EDMUND, 71
Keats, John, 77, 80
Kemble, John Philip, 63, 121, 129

LAMB, CHARLES, 10
Lancaster, Ray, 263–4
Landseer, Sir Edwin Henry, 144
Le Roux, Hugues, 300
Lejars (Mme.), 294
Leopold II, Emperor of Germany, 33, 40
Lewis, Matthew Gregory, 80*n*, 81
Little Sandy (Alexander Coleman), 4, 5, 261–2
Lloyd, James, 199
Loisset, Clotilde, 298
Loisset, Émilie, 296–9
Loisset, François, 298
Louis XV, 30, 33, 56
Louis XVI, 53, 163, 167
Louis Philippe, 163, 177–8, 183–4
Lowe, Sir Hudson, 176, 187
Loyal, Claud Leopold, 294
Loyo, Caroline, 293, 298
Lutz, Meyer, 217

MACDERMOTT, G. H., 258
Marie Antoinette, 53, 163–4, 168

Meadmore, W. S., vii, 56 (plate), 116 (plate)
Menken, Adah Isaacs, xi, 8, 225–45
Menschikoff, Prince Alexander Sergyevitch, 211–12
Milner, H. M., 117
Moore, George Washington, 226*n*, 300
Mortier, Arnold, 296, 301
Murray, D. L., iii, vii, ix–xi, 113, 203–4, 206

NAPOLEON I, 64, 65, 83, 92, 93, 104–6, 120, 130, 169–70, 175–87, 201, 205, 254
Napoleon III, 163, 175, 180, 184–7, 205
Nation, W. H. C., 254
Newton, Henry Chance, 262
Nicolet, manager, 56, 58
North, Christopher (John Wilson), 8, 135–7
Novy, Yvon, 295

OAKLEY, ANNIE, 264–5
Oceana, 295
Ohmy, 'King,' 266

PALMER, JOHN, 49, 61*n*
Parker, John, vii
Pimpo (James Freeman), 281–4
Pollock, Benjamin, vii, 92–3 (plates)
Pradier, Jacques, 183
Price, trick-rider, 12–15

RAREY, J. S., 218
Reade, Charles, 240
Robertson, T. W., 211
Ross, W. G., 259
Rossetti, Dante Gabrielle, 241
Russell, Lord John, 251

SAMPSON, trick-rider, 13–15
Sanders, funambulist, 56
Sanger, James, 249–50, 258
Sanger, Laurina, 262
Sanger, 'Lord' George, xi, 6, 9, 198, 249–51, 255–80, 282 (plate), 287
Sanger, 'Lord' John, 249–51, 255, 263
Sanger, Mrs. George, 198, 256–7
Saunders, Abraham, 71–2, 74
Saunders, equestrienne, 94
Sayers, Tom, 227–8, 230, 232
Scott, Sir Walter, 204
Shakespeare, William, 12, 34, 98, 214–17, 228, 263–4
Sheridan, Amy, 257
Slater, George, vii
Smith, Albert, 200
Smith, Edward Tyrrel, xi, 231–2, 236, 238, 254
Smith, Horatio and James (authors of *Rejected Addresses*), 65n
Smollet, Tobias George, 11, 83
Stickney, Robert, 115, 126, 156, 204
Stott, Ray, vii
Surtees, Robert Smith, 8
Swinburne, Algernon Charles, 224–5, 241–5

TAYLOR, TOM, 220, 252–3
Tenniel, Sir John, 202–3, 237
Thackeray, William Makepeace, xi, 8, 9, 104, 113, 121, 150, 157, 178–80, 259
Thurlow (Lord), 44
Tilley, Vesta, 265

Tom Thumb, 198–9
Tourniaire, Jacques, 172–3
Tussaud, Madame, 59
Twist, W. H., 195–6

USHER, DICKY, 192–4

VAN AMBURGH, 144–7
Vaux, Baron de, 298, 299n.
Victoria (Queen), 9, 126, 131, 145–6, 149, 196–9, 202, 219, 255–6, 264–6, 276–7
Voltaire, 123

WALLETT, W. F., 146, 199, 200, 201
Walpole, Horace, 53–4
Weber, Lisa, 263
Webster, Ben, 222
Wellington, Duke of, 83, 93, 104, 144, 254
Whitman, Walt, 230
Widdicomb, Harry, 109
Widdicomb, John Esdaile, xi, 107–12, 126, 130, 141, 156, 199, 200, 204, 211–13, 300
Wildman, Daniel, 15
Wilkie, Sir David, 145
William IV, 129–32
Wood, Mrs. Henry, 260n
Woolford, Louisa, xi, 103–60, 284
Wordsworth, William, 65
Wybrow, Mrs., 74 (plate), 75

YORK AND ALBANY, DUKES OF, 13 (Edward Augustus); 62, 66, 67, 149 (Frederick)